The
Distributed
MIND

*Achieving
High Performance
Through the
Collective Intelligence of
Knowledge Work Teams*

Kimball Fisher
and
Mareen Duncan Fisher

AMACOM
American Management Association

New York • Atlanta • Boston • Chicago • Kansas City • San Francisco • Washington, D.C.
Brussels • Mexico City • Tokyo • Toronto

This book is available at a special
discount when ordered in bulk quantities.
For information, contact Special Sales Department,
AMACOM, a division of American Management Association,
1601 Broadway, New York, NY 10019.

This publication is designed to provide accurate and authoritative
information in regard to the subject matter covered. It is sold with the
understanding that the publisher is not engaged in rendering legal,
accounting, or other professional service. If legal advice or other expert
assistance is required, the services of a competent professional person
should be sought.

Library of Congress Cataloging-in-Publication Data

Fisher, Kimball.
    The distributed mind : achieving high performance through the
collective intelligence of knowledge work teams / Kimball Fisher and
Mareen Duncan Fisher.
        p.   cm.
    Includes bibliographical references and index.
    ISBN 0-8144-0367-0 (hc)
    1. Teams in the workplace.   2. Professional employees.
I. Fisher, Mareen Duncan.   II. Title.
HD66.F557   1997
658.4'036—dc21   97-24512
                                              CIP

© 1998 The Fisher Group, Inc.
All rights reserved.
Printed in the United States of America.

This publication may not be reproduced,
stored in a retrieval system,
or transmitted in whole or in part,
in any form or by any means, electronic,
mechanical, photocopying, recording, or otherwise,
without the prior written permission of AMACOM,
a division of American Management Association,
1601 Broadway, New York, NY 10019.

Printing number

10   9   8   7   6   5   4   3   2   1

To the first and finest knowledge workers we ever knew:

Chad Kimball Fisher
Pharmacist, Architect, Inventor, Salesperson, Church Leader, Stained Glass Artist, Antique Automobile Restorer, and Father

Patricia Anne Axelsen Fisher
Caregiver, Historian, Theatrical Producer, Community Activist, Florist, Amateur Small Animal Veterinarian, and Mother

Phyllis Richmond Duncan
Church Leader, Legal Secretary, Paralegal, Volunteer, Athlete, Chauffeur, Chef, and Mother

LaMar Corless Duncan
Attorney, Public Servant, Musician, Mormon Tabernacle Choir Member, Advocate for the Underprivileged, and Father

Contents

Preface

When we started up a small knowledge-work-team-based company together a few years ago, we began an adventure that eventually led to writing this book. The adventure has been both exciting and frustrating. We quickly realized that creating effective knowledge work teams was much more difficult than we had originally thought. At the time, we had a variety of unanswered questions: How do you coordinate multiple specialists into a single cohesive unit? How do you work with rapidly changing teams whose membership expands or contracts with every project? How do you work on several teams at the same time? How do you make teams with members from different companies effective? How do you work with people who are on the team only temporarily? How can you coordinate activities when half the team is gone virtually all the time? How do you create an effective team when you are working with people based thousands of miles away from one another? What self-regulating processes can you use to ensure that you don't need to rely on hierarchical controls? Working with creative, strong-willed, independent people was a mixed blessing—we had our share of both successes and challenges.

We decided that we wanted to begin a process that would help us to better understand the unique characteristics of knowledge work teams—a process aided by a gradual shift in our consulting practice from working almost exclusively in factories to working with a variety of service-based companies, corporate headquarters staff groups, and engineering teams. So we embarked on a mission to interview as many knowledge workers as we could. Enlisting the help of our colleague Lucas Birdeau, we began to contact and interview first our friends, and then others who were kind enough to share with us what they had learned.

It has taken us about three years to collect these stories and techniques. With the publication of this book, we are finally able to bring you information about the challenges and responses of some very remarkable men and women who represent what we believe are the frontiers of the modern workplace.

These are important stories because in the information age, knowledge workers will clearly replace manual laborers as the dominant workforce in developed economies. And knowledge work teams, the prevalent work structure that knowledge workers are using to organize themselves, may well replace the traditional factory as the essential unit of our economies in much the same way that factories replaced the family farm during the industrial revolution. All of us will be knowledge workers in the future. Almost everyone is one already.

As with all things worth doing, the engineers, health-care providers, corporate staff professionals, consultants, managers, professors, and numerous others we interviewed assured us that creating an effective workplace for knowledge work teams is extremely difficult. We still have much to learn about how new technologies and lifestyle changes will affect the knowledge workplace. Some even question whether there will be a physical workplace at all—imagining instead a virtual work location that exists primarily in cyberspace. Regardless of the specific nature of these changes, however, whatever happens to knowledge work will have a tremendous impact on how we all will work and live in the new millennium.

The bulk of this book comes from our interviews, and to avoid making the reading of this material unnecessarily tedious, we have decided to footnote only quotations from previously published sources. We have also tried to write the book in a style that we hope will make it interesting and easier to read than many business books. We have included lots of stories and examples, as a popular magazine article might. You, of course, will be the judge of whether or not we are able to retain your interest. But what we have attempted to do here is to distill a great deal of information into a concise work that will be practical and memorable enough for you to benefit from reading it.

We wish you luck in your efforts to create effective knowledge work teams. We practice what we preach, and consequently we have used many of the methods in this book in our own knowledge work teams at The Fisher Group, Inc. They have helped us, and we hope they will help you too.

K.F.
M.D.F.

Acknowledgments

We sincerely appreciate the help of our agent, Michael Snell, and our editor, Adrienne Hickey, for the extensive assistance they provided us in turning our book into a readable work. Without their patient guidance, we would have had a very different product. Thanks also to Barbara Horowitz of AMACOM for her fine editing.

We wish to extend our heartfelt appreciation to the many people who allowed us to learn from their experiences as knowledge workers. We are especially grateful to Phil Barber of Bellevue Public Schools, Peter Bartlett of Hewlett-Packard, Mike Beyerlein of the University of North Texas, John Seely Brown of Xerox, Richard S. Boyer of Primary Children's Medical Center, Virginia Butler of Rocky Mountain HMO, Dave Csokasy of Delco Electronics, Jack W. Cochran of Shenandoah Life Insurance Company, Wendy Coetze of Vista University, Bob Condella of Corning, Steve Cunanan of Owens Corning, Gibb Dyer of Brigham Young University, Larry Eacott of Amdahl, Bruce Ellis, formerly of AT&T, Tony Gaddis of Hewlett-Packard, LouAnn Gauna of Rocky Mountain HMO, Eileen Gil of Holyoke Mutual Insurance, Jim Graham of Amdahl, Kelly-Ann Hoare of Old Mutual Insurance, Maureen Husak, formerly of Dr. Jon-Marc Weston's office, Amy Katz of the Association for Quality & Participation (AQP), Jan Klein of MIT, Diana Knoles of DAT Services, Karen Kolodziejski of Starr Consulting, David Long of Life Flight Network, J. Loux of the Port of Seattle, Dennis McNulty of Hewlett-Packard, John Meyers, formerly of Rocky Mountain HMO, Mike Morrison of Toyota, Steve Olson of DAT Services,

Jim Parkman of Eastman Kodak, Lee Perry of Brigham Young University, Harold Pinto of Jacobsen Textron, Marge Powell of Blue Cross/Blue Shield of Florida, Dave Pritchard of Microsoft, Mark Reis of the Port of Seattle, John Sivie, formerly of Rocketdyne, Gloria Thatcher of Weyerhaeuser, Larry Travis, formerly of New Brunswick Telephone, Lewis Tuttle of Weyerhaeuser, Nancy Tyler of New Brunswick Telephone, Mike Webber of Rocky Mountain HMO, Stu Winby of Hewlett-Packard, Morley Winograd of AT&T, Bob Wroblewski of Weyerhaeuser, and various representatives of Aid Association for Lutherans (AAL), The Institute for the Study of Distributed Work, and the Mayo Clinic. Pam Posey and Bill Dyer offered especially helpful critique and support. Bill passed away just two weeks after giving us his final feedback. He will be sorely missed by everyone who has studied teams.

We also appreciate those who have allowed us to use copyrighted resources in this book. Special thanks to The Fisher Group, Inc. for allowing numerous models and training tips. Parts of three chapters have been adapted for knowledge work application from our previously published works. Segments of Chapter 3, for example, were modified from selected portions of a chapter entitled "Diagnostic Issues for Work Teams" by Kimball Fisher in *Diagnosis for Organizational Change: Methods and Models* by Ann Howard and Associates (Society for Industrial and Organizational Psychology, The Professional Practice Series, The Guilford Press, New York, 1994, used by permission). Parts of Chapter 10, including some figures, were adapted from Chapter 13, "The Role of the Team Leader," in *Leading Self Directed Work Teams: A Guide to Developing New Team Leadership Skills,* by Kimball Fisher (McGraw-Hill, New York, 1993, used by permission). Selections in these chapters as noted by footnotes are reprinted from K. Fisher, "Managing in the High Commitment Workplace," *Organizational Dynamics,* Winter 1989. Reprinted by permission of the publisher, from ORGANIZATIONAL DYNAMICS WINTER 1989 © 1989. American Management Association, New York. All rights reserved. And much of Chapter 11 is condensed from two sources, including *Team Tools,* a Fisher Group training program © 1989–1997 by The Fisher Group, Inc., and Belgard•Fisher•Rayner, Inc. Selected ideas and charts from that chapter also appear in *Tips for Teams: A Ready Reference for Solving Common Team Problems,* by Kimball Fisher, Steven Rayner, William Belgard, and the BFR Team (Mc-Graw-Hill, Inc., New York, 1995, used by permission).

We wish to give a special note of gratitude to our colleagues Stephanie Ford and Lucas Birdeau. Without them tending the home fires, we would never have completed what was rapidly turning into an eternal project. Luke, in particular, did an enormous amount of book work and is largely responsible for much of the content of the stories in *The Distributed Mind.* Without his interviews, research, writing, and editing work, this would be a less useful book. Thanks, Luke. We're really glad you're on our knowledge team.

The
Distributed
MIND

Introduction: The Distributed Mind— Smart People and Smart Organizations

''Even though I am not religious, the amazement and wonder I have about the human mind is closer to religious awe than dispassionate analysis.''[1]

—Bill Gates, Cofounder of Microsoft

Stu Winby is the leader of an elite team of consultants who quietly work inside Hewlett-Packard. His group helps HP organizations across the globe transform themselves into more effective and flexible operations. The consultants don't produce printers or computers, they produce knowledge—special knowledge about how people and organizations work most effectively. They are knowledge workers—people who work with their brains more than with their hands or backs.

Tina Soike is a knowledge worker too. She works for the Port of Seattle, a public organization that manages the SeaTac airport and the marine port facilities in Seattle. A civil engineer, she is working on the design and management of major construction projects. In addition to her project management and engineering responsibilities, she serves as a member of another knowledge team that has been commissioned to analyze and improve the capital management system for the port. The improvement ideas she and her colleagues on the team have generated have already saved Washington taxpayers hundreds of thousands of dollars.

Bill Ferone is the vice president and general manager of customer service at Amdahl Corporation, a company that provides integrated computing solutions for very computer-intensive work environments. He leads a knowledge team of vice presidents charged with providing benchmark-level customer service. Their combined understanding of customer requirements and corporate leadership has helped to make these businesses the most profitable and responsive in the company.

This is the age of knowledge work. It is the age of the smart worker. The operations that learn the secret of tapping into this knowledge will always outperform those that do not. Those that master the *collective intelligence* of knowledge work teams will be the architects of the future.

As individuals, knowledge workers are smart people. But their individual effectiveness is amplified when they are also part of a smart organization. As an effective knowledge team, they can often create a sort of synergy where the outcome of the whole is greater than the sum of its individual parts. These smart teams appear as though all team members are of a common mind that shares information and ideas seamlessly across the membership—a distributed mind.

The Purpose of This Book

This book is about knowledge work and knowledge work teams. Knowledge work requires a special set of skills related to an area of expertise, such as those of an engineer, a salesperson, a consultant, a manager, or a health-care professional. But it requires much more than technical competence to be successful as a knowledge worker.

Savvy knowledge workers understand that these additional skills include the ability to acquire and transfer knowledge effectively. Knowledge is the stock in trade of knowledge workers—it is both the process and the product of their work. In an age of complexity unforeseen by people of the industrial age, they frequently need to meld their expertise with the knowledge of other experts on work teams. Patients who are admitted to the world famous Mayo Clinic, for example, are often treated by a team of specialists who meet frequently to coordinate their work. This reduces expensive diagnostic redundancies and allows the specialists to provide the patient with the finest integrated solutions to their often-complicated problems. Graduate business schools could not prepare M.B.A.s properly without teams of professors who coordinate their specialized areas of expertise in finance, operations, organizational behavior, marketing, and so forth into a cohesive curriculum. Locating an oil field requires expertise from a variety of technical fields such as geology and geophysics, but it also requires expertise in real estate, law, and drilling technologies. All of these skills are seldom, if ever, present in any one individual. Consider future examples from some of the companies mentioned in the beginning of this Introduction. On a Port of Seattle capital management team put together to develop a new airport runway, there are project and civil engineers from a variety of specialties, lawyers, accountants, public officials, human resource specialists, and outside technical consultants. All must work together effectively and seamlessly to get the job done well.

Hewlett-Packard (HP) new product design teams are often composed of hardware, firmware, software, marketing, financial, and manufacturing experts who not only are located all over the world but come from both inside and outside of the company. The specialized knowledge of each person is essential to the successful completion of the project. But each person has to work effectively with other knowledge workers as well. If the software doesn't mesh well with hardware requirements, or if products are technologically superb but too expensive to manufacture, even extraordinary individual effort won't help much. This kind of problem can lead to expensive scenarios: product introduction slowdowns, scuttled projects, or—worst of all—a flawed product that alienates customers and damages the company's image. These are the challenges (and the opportunties) of knowledge work.

The purpose of this book is to address these types of challenges. We will review knowledge work as well as knowledge work teams, the organizations that are already starting to replace the business corporations that have ruled the planet since the turn of the century. We will also discuss how to successfully create and sustain virtual knowledge work teams—those teams without the obvious advantages associated with being colocated in a single place, time zone, company, or culture.

We have interviewed hundreds of knowledge workers so that we can bring their success stories to you. We have tried to place these stories throughout the book to make it more interesting and to show practical application of the ideas we are introducing.

The book starts with a discussion of knowledge work and knowledge workers and then proceeds to chapters describing how knowledge workers work together in teams. We will show how these knowledge teams differ from the sorts of teams most corporations have used in the past. In so doing, we will also suggest that much of our current thinking about work is bankrupt. It is time to unlearn much of what we know about work and work teams.

How This Book Is Organized

In Chapter 1 we define knowledge work and highlight some of its challenges by looking at the Life Flight Network, a helicopter ambulance rescue service operating out of Portland, Oregon. Multiple case examples in this chapter will demonstrate how knowledge work differs from physical work and illustrate five defining characteristics.

Chapter 2 dispels the myth that knowledge work is limited to the office, hospital, or university. It is true that the shift to knowledge work is becoming obvious in the dramatic rise of service jobs (most of which are knowledge work) and the related decline of manufacturing ones (which have traditionally been physical work). But even within manufacturing organizations—long the bastions of manual labor—most people are shifting toward knowledge work as technologies and worker responsibilities become more sophisticated.

Chapter 3 shows how teams differ from groups and introduces the three characteristics required for contemporary teams: clear purpose, shared understanding of the purpose, and commitment paradigm culture. We illustrate how these teams differ from the traditional organizations of the past by looking at knowledge work teams such as the Boeing 777 product development team. Using examples from several companies, we discuss self-directed work team concepts and identify the four most common types of teams.

In Chapter 4 we illustrate the differences between physical and knowledge work teams by looking at the Hewlett-Packard SAS team, the Corning Admin team, and the New Brunswick Telecom Service team, identifying several characteristics that distinguish knowledge work teams from other teams. In particular, we highlight the differences in the way multiskilling is used. We introduce what we call "vertical" (for knowledge teams) and "horizontal" (for physical work teams) multiskilling.

Chapter 5 describes the processes many organizations are using to redesign traditional functionally based or silo-type operations into knowledge work teams. It then illustrates a popular organization type we call the learning lattice by analyzing a Port of Seattle and a Hewlett-Packard operation in more detail.

In Chapter 6 we introduce an organic metaphor to better understand knowledge teams. Examining an Amdahl customer service team, we show how the metaphor offers a different perspective on the most fundamental elements of traditional team theory. We suggest, for example, that knowledge-based organisms don't need to be reengineered, they need to evolve. They require constant feeding and nurturing—not controlling policies and procedures; information—not budgets, performance appraisals, or staff meetings.

In Chapter 7 we discuss the most difficult, but increasingly common, type of knowledge team: the virtual knowledge team (VKT). We look at these teams in Delco Electronics, HP, and a consulting company. Unlike regular knowledge teams with constant membership, VKTs are part-time, short-term teams with shifting membership from multiple locations. We consider the importance of several techniques designed by companies like Hewlett-Packard to make VKTs more effective.

Chapter 8 addresses a critical challenge for knowledge work: fostering innovation and creativity. We introduce some classic personal and organizational creativity-enhancing techniques from Thomas Edison's Menlo Park experience. We also show that the stereotypical picture of a "mad scientist" creating alone in a hidden lab is not always an accurate portrayal of the creative process. We discuss the importance of public learning techniques that generate genuine innovation.

In Chapter 9 we describe important keys to mastering the challenges of information acquisition and transfer. Just as the human circulatory system employs a myriad of pathways to provide the body with blood, so knowledge workers need to create numerous ways to channel information through their work system. But just as too much blood draining unchecked inside the body can be life-threatening, so too can too much information flowing through the system. We discuss how to avoid the threat of unhelpful or unnecessary information clogging the system.

Chapter 10 introduces helpful concepts for leading knowledge work teams as a team leader. We also examine how knowledge workers must ultimately practice self-leadership. The chapter discusses the leader's role as boundary manager, and we illustrate seven important leadership competencies.

Chapter 11 describes wellness practices for knowledge workers and knowledge work teams. We discuss the value and techniques of planned team improvement activities. The emphasis in this chapter is on how to prevent team illness through team wellness approaches such as creating operating guidelines, distributing work assignments fairly, and engaging in regular work-related team-building activities.

In Chapter 12 we explore how technology aids knowledge work. We look at a Xerox service team to understand the importance of technology. Using a cyborg as a metaphor for a technically enhanced organization, this chapter will discuss how cyborganizations are living organisms supported by technology.

We discuss technologies that facilitate the work of knowledge teams, including groupware, interactive communication devices, and joint decision-making and problem-solving aids.

In the last chapter we look to the future. What are the implications of knowledge work for corporations? How are knowledge teams seeking to ready themselves for the twenty-first century? To answer these questions we will discuss six key work trends: automation of physical work, elimination of traditional jobs, empowerment, knowledge team predominance, workplace flexibility, and the increase of virtual knowledge teams.

Summary

For the first time in human history, our contributions in the workplace come more from our minds than from our muscles. The ability to use and create knowledge may now be the single greatest asset in the workplace—an asset that allows people to do something really significant. This age is fraught with both challenges and opportunities. Not the least of these challenges is how to work effectively in the postindustrial era. Smart people and smart organizations will help us meet this challenge.

We have entered the age of the distributed mind.

Note

1. Walter Isaacson, "In Search of the Real Bill Gates," *Time*, January 13, 1997, 57. Used by permission.

1

Knowledge Work: Understanding Mental Labor

"Their raw materials are of the tangible kind while ours are of the mind."[1]

—Michael Eisner, CEO and Chairman of The Walt Disney Company

"In some areas—and especially in society and its structure—basic shifts have already happened. That the new society will be both a non-socialist and a post capitalist society is practically certain. And it is certain also that its primary resource will be knowledge. This also means that it will have to be a society of organizations. . . . The leading social groups of the knowledge society will be 'knowledge workers.'"[2]

—Peter Drucker, Author and Consultant

It is 4:00 P.M. on a blustery March afternoon. The Life Flight Network (LFN) helicopter is landing at the site of a very serious auto–pedestrian accident. The landing tests the skills of experienced pilot Marti Conroy, who must snake dangerously close to life-threatening power lines in order to get into the loading zone police and fire squads have set up.

A nine-year-old girl named Melissa is critically injured. She has multiple broken bones, is losing too much blood internally, and her own life support systems are rapidly shutting down. A specially trained flight nurse fears the child won't survive the process required to transport her to safety.

Her only chance is to reach an operating room within twenty minutes. From inside the helicopter, Conroy watches what he later describes as a "finely rehearsed dance" of LFN personnel working in concert to save Melissa's life. They anticipate one another's movements. There is no superfluous behavior, no discordant steps. Every motion complements another. Their activities are so intricately synchronized that everybody appears to share a single mind—a mind distributed across several bodies.

In less than four minutes, the stretcher carrying the fragile load is in the helicopter and airborne, headed for one of Portland's trauma centers. It is met at the door of the hospital and escorted immediately into a room prepared for emergency surgery. Melissa fights for life like a champion boxer. She makes it through the first critical operation and just barely survives the night.

Within a few weeks she makes a miraculous recovery. In an emotional report of her story on a locally televised news program, it becomes clear that LFN saved her life. An ambulance would have taken at least ten more minutes to deliver her to the hospital—and that would have been about eight minutes too long.

Founded in 1978, the Portland Life Flight Network uses not only current medical and flight technology but leading-edge human and management technology as well. It is a very effective knowledge work team. Maneuvering the stretcher through tight situations often requires great athletic strength and agility. But it is the mental work of operating the helicopter (e.g., making calculations and decisions regarding weather, the route to take, where to land, the weight of the load, etc.) and making medical determinations about patient treatment that makes up most of the team members' jobs. That makes them knowledge workers. Working together toward common goals makes them a knowledge work team.

Salespeople at AT&T, engineers at Procter & Gamble, accountants at KPMG Peat Marwick, realtors at Century 21, doctors at the Mayo Clinic, information technology specialists at GM, loan officers at the World Bank, and professors at Harvard University are knowledge workers too. So are independent consultants, architects, journalists, lawyers, insurance agents, analysts, scientists, technicians, nurses, government administrators, managers, and a host of others as well. There are more knowledge workers employed today than at any other time in human history. You might say that this is the age of knowledge work.

In this chapter we will try to better understand knowledge work by comparing five characteristics that differ for physical and knowledge work. We will then introduce several challenges associated with knowledge work that will be covered throughout this book.

What Is Knowledge Work?

The term *knowledge work* was first coined by Dr. Peter Drucker in about 1960, when he defined it as *any work that requires mental power rather than physical power*.[3] Dr. Cal Pava, who did seminal work on the topic, added that deliberations between knowledge workers was an important activity for observing their work.[4] A more comprehensive definition comes from the papers of Dr. Richard McDermott, who has studied and written about knowledge work for the past several years. According to McDermott, "Knowledge work involves analyzing information and applying specialized expertise to solve problems, generate ideas, teach others, or create new products and services."[5] Knowledge work is hard to define in more detail than this because knowledge is invisible—it is hidden away in the head of the knowledge worker.

We believe that the easiest way to explain knowledge work, however, is by contrasting it to physical work. Even if we cannot yet fully understand the invisible "black box" of knowledge work, we can at least see how it compares with other work. Consider five key work characteristics, summarized in Figure 1-1. Important differences become clear when we compare the core task, critical skills, work process, work outcome, and type of knowledge employed in physical and knowledge work. Although some of these differences are more a matter of degree than of clear distinction, we believe they are instructive.

Core Task

By "core task" we mean the primary tasks required to do the work. While most work requires multiple tasks, it is the *core* task that differentiates mental from physical labor. The core task of knowledge work, for example, is normally *thinking*, while the core task of physical work is normally *doing*.

When Bill Gates was in the sixth grade, his mother once asked him why he didn't respond to her call for him to come to dinner. Other boys his age might have been distracted by physical work, such as building a model airplane, but not Bill—at least, not this time.

> "What are you doing?" she once demanded over the intercom.
> "I'm thinking," he shouted back.
> "You're thinking?"
> "Yes, Mom, I'm thinking," he said fiercely. "Have you ever tried thinking?"[6]

His youthful rebellion later subsided, but his ability to hit home with a well-targeted intellectual insult has not. He is well

Figure 1-1. Comparing knowledge work with physical work.

Job Characteristics	Knowledge Work	Physical Work
Core task	Thinking	Doing
Critical skills	Mental	Physical
Work process	Usually nonlinear	Usually linear
Work outcome	Information	Product
Knowledge used	Created	Applied

known for his probing questions and acerbic comments during project reviews—one of Gates's favorite observations is, "That is the stupidest thing I ever heard." Since Gates engages only those he respects in such intellectual duels, Microsoft employees collect these comments like badges of honor.

Whether you appreciate his style or not, Gates is undoubtedly a knowledge worker. And if you use money, fame, and power as the yardstick for measuring success, he may be the most successful knowledge worker of our time. One thing that makes him a knowledge worker is thinking—something he has aggressively pursued since his early youth.

Thinking typically includes activities like problem solving, idea generation, or analyzing, which all occur in the mind. Doing, on the other hand, includes activities like producing, assembling, building, or drafting, which end up in something tangible like a widget, a mowed lawn, or a drawing. Doing is done by our bodies or technological extensions of them—it requires physical labor. Thus, interestingly, robotic work (at least at the current level of technology development) is a form of physical labor.

Critical Skills

In his best-selling book *A Brief History of Time,* the British theoretical physicist Stephen Hawking gives a moving example of the second distinction between physical and knowledge work when he describes his personal struggles with ALS, a motor neuron disease that has gradually stripped away his abilities to walk and speak. Hawking is the Lucasian Professor of Mathematics at Cambridge University, the same position that was once held by Sir Isaac Newton and later by P. A. M. Dirac. His many achievements include work associated with black holes, and he is arguably the Albert Einstein of our day (some would say that Einstein was the Hawking of his day). Confined to a wheelchair and limited to a voice that is generated with a special computerized voice synthesizer—a voice that he notes in only slightly veiled gratitude has an American rather than an English accent—he observes: "I was again fortunate in that I chose theoretical physics, because that is all in the mind. So my disability has not been a serious handicap."[7] Had Hawking's chosen profession been physical work, he would not have been as lucky.

As Hawking's story illustrates, the second distinction between physical and mental labor is the key skills required to perform the work. Physical work requires physical skills, and people without those skills have a disadvantage. The same is true, of course, of knowledge work and mental skills. Thus, technical training for physical work normally includes the development of physical skill in things like proper tool usage, hand/eye coordination, and production techniques, while technical training for mental work would include mental skill development in areas such as key theory understanding, critical thinking, or effective analysis and troubleshooting techniques. Specific expertise is required to make one a successful knowledge worker. While thinking alone may qualify a person as a knowledge worker, only skilled thinking like that displayed by Hawking and Gates makes an effective one.

Work Process

In addition to these rather obvious distinctions between knowledge work and physical work, the third characteristic we want to discuss is the difference in the work process itself. What do we mean by work process? If the core task is the *what* of the work, the work process is the *how*. More specifically, to determine whether work is physical or knowledge work, we look at whether the work process is primarily linear or nonlinear in nature. This characteristic is more a matter of degree than of absolute distinction because in our experience, not all knowledge work is nonlinear, and not all physical work is linear. Let us explain.

Physical work normally entails a series of linear activities in which one step builds on another (see Figure 1-2). At the Procter & Gamble plants where we worked, for example, each product had its own detailed formula, which gave minute-to-minute instructions for when to add which ingredients, how long to stir them together, what temperatures to heat them up

Figure 1-2. A simple linear work process.

to, and how long to cool them. These all had to be done in a particular order, just as you must mix up cake batter before baking it. Although these work processes were sometimes very complicated, they were still sequential in nature, as illustrated by the fact that they can be described by using some sort of work flow diagram.

In most knowledge work, however, the work process is often messy and unpredictable (see Figure 1-3). It doesn't fit well with linear analytical tools like work flow diagrams and time and motion studies. Each problem solved or new idea created may follow a very different developmental path. Penicillin, for example, was discovered not because of the hundreds of experiments designed to facilitate its development, but because Fleming decided to test mold spores that had germinated on an open culture dish left on the lab bench when he went away on vacation. In searching for a way to create a technology for transmitting and decoding a television signal, one of our relatives, Idaho farm boy Philo T. Farnsworth, says he was inspired with the idea of breaking the signals into multiple lines of video data and

Figure 1-3. A nonlinear work process.

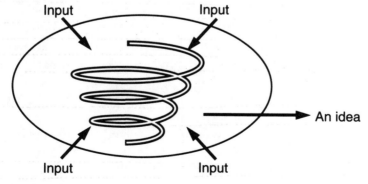

quickly replicating them on the back of a tube in the same way that a farmer plows row after row of furrows for planting. It just popped into his head one day when he was out in the fields near his home, rather than resulting from some sort of systematic linear inventing process.

Consider another example: While we were employees at Tektronix, a company that produces high-tech test and measurement products such as oscilloscopes and logic analyzers, one of us was given a project to help reduce product development time. As one software engineer patiently explained when he was asked to identify the parts of the work process that might be shortened, "I don't know how long it takes to come up with a new design idea. Sometimes it takes a few months, sometimes a few seconds, sometimes it won't come at all. We can do some things to speed up the process of writing code by getting some more sophisticated equipment, but I don't know how to speed up creativity. I can't explain the process. I don't know how I generate new product ideas."

Linear Knowledge Work

Not all knowledge work is nonlinear. Here is where it gets a little more complicated. Certain activities, such as analyzing forms or providing specific types of customer service, may be linear, sequential activities even though they are mental rather than physical labor. This is shown in Figure 1-4.

Let us explain the figure. You can visualize work type and work process linearity as two axes that form a matrix with four quadrants: linear knowledge (LK) work (what we call processing), nonlinear knowledge (NLK) work (what we call creating), linear physical (LP) work (what we call assembling), and nonlinear physical (NLP) work (what we call repairing). Examples of LK or processing work are processing certain types of insurance forms and benefits administration. This work is mental rather than physical labor, but the work processes are linear. NLK or creating work might be things like writing lines of software code or preparing questions to ask a witness in court. LP or assembling work could include types of routine production line work or textile sewing. NLP or repairing work may include certain

Figure 1-4. Work type and work process linearity.

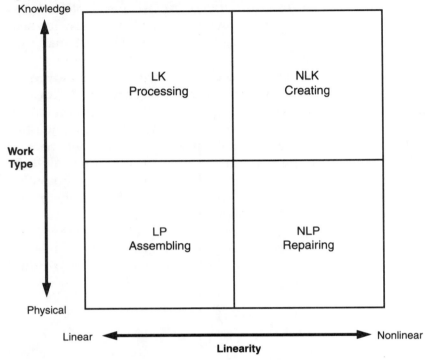

maintenance work or equipment repair that requires physical labor that isn't sequential.

While there clearly are examples of nonlinear physical work and of linear knowledge work, the majority of knowledge work as we are defining it is nonlinear. For the purpose of our discussions about how to distinguish knowledge work from physical labor, suffice it to say that knowledge work is more nonlinear than linear, whereas physical work is more linear than nonlinear.

Work Outcome

The fourth defining characteristic is work outcome. The outcome of knowledge work is usually information of some sort—a

solved problem, a new product idea, or a strategy. Researchers Ronald Purser and Alfonso Montuori note that this information has a special characteristic: It reduces uncertainty. "The product of knowledge work has been viewed as reducing the uncertainty from the environment, reducing the uncertainty stemming from the nature of the work, and reducing the uncertainty associated with customer requirements and product outcomes."[8] In other words, this information answers questions, it clarifies the unknown, it provides a sense of direction. That is why knowledge work is so valuable—it produces knowledge.

Knowledge Type: Applied vs. Created Knowledge

The final important differentiating characteristic of knowledge work is the type of knowledge used for its execution. All work, of course, requires knowledge. It would be ridiculous to assume that performing physical work doesn't require knowledge. But the type of knowledge used is different.

The distinguishing characteristic of knowledge work is that it more often uses what we call created knowledge than applied or elementary knowledge. Let us explain. Knowledge at its simplest level is just a collection of facts and data like those many of us memorized in grade school. We call that elementary knowledge. This type of knowledge includes facts like "The capital of the U.S.A. is Washington, D.C." and "Two times two equals four."

In general, physical work requires not only elementary knowledge, but also applied knowledge, such as "You twist this knob when the machine is out of alignment," "This is how you read a blueprint," or "This is how you machine a part." Knowledge work, however, relies not only on applied knowledge, but also on knowledge created specifically for the task at hand. An engineer, for example, may know the basic laws of mathematics (elementary knowledge) and the fundamentals of good computer software design (applied knowledge), but her project may also require her to do things that have not been done before. When she improves the processing speed of a new program by 30 percent, she is going beyond applied knowledge and creating new knowledge ("This is how you do something we haven't done before"). Or a doctor may know anatomy (elementary knowledge) and surgery (applied knowledge), but in virtually every operation he may find unique problems that depend on the condition of the patient. In such cases, the knowledge worker uses components of the elementary or applied knowledge but adapts, improvises, or creates something new for the specific work at hand.

You can use a musical metaphor to further illustrate these different types of knowledge. Elementary musical knowledge includes things like musical notation and harmony theory. All competent musicians amass a certain amount of elementary knowledge in order to be able to do their jobs.

When an orchestra actually plays a piece by Bach or Mozart, however, the musicians are utilizing more than elementary knowledge—they know not only what to do but how to do it. Where music theory is elementary knowledge, performance is applied knowledge. An orchestra may perform what was written by the composer on the sheet of music in front of them. But dynamics may vary considerably. Performances of the same piece by two different orchestras, or even performances of the same piece by the same group at different times, may differ so dramatically that it almost appears to be different music.

Applied knowledge is much more than the mechanical recital of fact. It requires interpretation, creativity, and skill. Different practitioners in the same field may distinguish themselves from others not by accumulating more elementary knowledge but by expertise in applying that knowledge. Two oil paintings of an apple, for example, may use the same art techniques, but differ so completely in their execution as to cause art critics to declare one a masterpiece and the other trash. Similarly, English poets may all use the same theories of rhyme and/or rhythm, and all are limited to the same 26 letters. Yet some of them go down in history as brilliant, while others are simply forgotten. But let's return to music to illustrate the last type of knowledge.

When a jazz combo does an improvisation, it uses not only elementary and applied knowledge but a different type of knowledge as well: what we call created knowledge. The musicians create new knowledge as they explore different harmonies and melodies together. While it may be true that they are mainly reassembling patterns and musical protocols determined from long years of practice, they are still making up the score as they go along. They go beyond creatively interpreting music to creating brand new music. This latter knowledge type, created knowledge, is typical of knowledge work. Thus, when physical workers use created knowledge, they are by definition doing knowledge work. When the knowledge work activities take a higher percentage of their time than their physical work activities do, they become knowledge workers. We will discuss this trend toward knowledge work and away from physical work in factories in Chapter 2.

Knowledge Work Defined

Considering these five key work characteristics, we suggest the following definition of knowledge work: Knowledge work is activity that frequently produces new knowledge. Its core task is thinking, its outcome is information, it is typically nonlinear in nature, and it requires mental skills to perform successfully.

Thus, the LFN professionals we opened this chapter with are knowledge workers rather than physical laborers. Although they perform both physical and mental tasks, their *core* work is thinking. They must make important decisions rapidly, using expert knowledge: What is the quickest route to the scene? What supplies and personnel are needed for this accident? Where can we land safely but as near to the victim as possible? What immediate medical attention does the victim need? What resources need to be available at the hospital when we return? They are highly skilled mentally, their work is mostly nonlinear, their key outcome is life-saving information, and they frequently produce new knowledge about how to deal with the unique situations they face regularly in the emergency rescue business.

Knowledge Workers Do Physical Work, Too

It is important to remember that knowledge workers perform both knowledge work and physical work. When a consultant writes a report on a computer, the thinking that leads up to the recommendations is knowledge work, but typing the report is physical work. When an attorney creates a deposition, determining the contents is knowledge work, but the production of the deposition is physical work. When the LFN team carries a stretcher into the helicopter, a surgeon cracks open a chest, a manager delivers a prepared presentation, or a work team publishes a strategic plan, that is physical work. What makes us knowledge workers is that the majority of our work is knowledge work (see Figure 1-5). In most jobs, the knowledge work content of our work is increasing. With the possible exception of highly theoretical fields, there are few knowledge workers who do only knowledge work. Conversely, there are few physical workers who do only physical work. In fact, there are few strictly physical workers at all anymore, as we will discuss in Chapter 2.

Knowledge Work Challenges

As more and more people become knowledge workers, it becomes increasingly important to understand and resolve the

Figure 1-5. Knowledge work as thinking work.

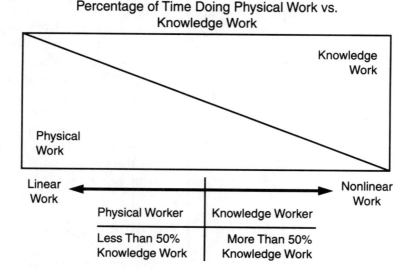

Percentage of Time Doing Physical Work vs. Knowledge Work

challenges that are typical of this work. Let's return to the Life Flight Network example to introduce some of these challenges, which we will be discussing in more detail throughout the remainder of the book.

Implementing Self-Management

The Life Flight Network has evolved over time to best accomplish its work. These changes have not only increased the commitment of employees but improved life-saving service to patients as well. For example, responsibilities such as decision making, which would have traditionally belonged to management, have moved to the team. As the LFN team has become more self-managed, team members have also taken on most of the administrative decisions. Workers in each specialty, for instance, find their own replacements when they are unable to make a shift. The manager is not involved in staffing decisions except when the team informs him of overtime, which the LFN team has worked hard to eliminate during the last year.

Developing Information Acquisition and Transfer Systems

Perhaps nowhere is the independence in decision making more critical or more evident than on-site during an emergency. More often than not, these are life-and-death situations. The team members must be able to act quickly and not be encumbered by a bureaucratic process that requires a manager's or doctor's approval. Often the accident site is out of radio contact, so real-time communication with doctors or hospitals is simply not an option. Therefore, confidence in one another's knowledge and an ability to quickly assimilate information from one another is absolutely critical to the timing and quality of patient care. There is a very high degree of interdependence among the various members of the LFN. Access to good information and reliable communication between parties is essential. This is a critical challenge. Information acquisition and transfer is the life blood of knowledge work.

Involvement in Areas Outside of Primary Expertise

All Life Flight team members are expected to participate in making decisions in a variety of areas. Not only are decisions on administrative topics such as staffing, overtime, equipment purchases, and budgeting made by the team, but so are flight-related decisions such as whether or not a flight goes. A typical LFN team, for instance, is composed of a pilot, nurse, and paramedic, with other specialty team members added as the patient's situation requires. Any member of the team can make the decision to terminate a flight. If a nurse or paramedic feels uncomfortable about a flight because of weather conditions, for instance, he or she can call for the flight to be aborted, even if the pilot feels that flying conditions are safe. This is sometimes a challenge for knowledge team members, who may initially be reluctant to participate in decisions outside of their special areas of expertise.

Appropriate Multiskilling

Similarly, the team makes decisions about on-ground safety. Until a couple of years ago, the pilot was the team member responsible for managing on-ground safety around the helicopter. In 1993, however, LFN acquired a new Bell 230 helicopter. The design of the Bell 230 did not allow the pilot to lock down the controls and leave the aircraft. To decide how to handle this change, the LFN team contacted other medical flight programs using similar helicopters to determine what procedures they had put in place to address this issue. Using this information, the LFN team made the decision to use the fire personnel on the scene to manage safety while the helicopter is on the ground.

This is an example of multiskilling. By using this technique, the team is able to be more flexible and responsive. As another example of multiskilling, nurses are responsible with the pilot for watching out for possible obstructions during landing and takeoff. Everyone is responsible for safety in flight. However, the extremely technical nature of their work assignments does not allow for full job rotation, as is common in advanced production teams. Nurses don't take a turn flying the helicopter, and pilots don't rotate through assignments where they treat patients. Importantly, pilots are actually restricted from participating in patient-care decisions so that they can retain their objectivity when making flight safety determinations. Finding the right level of multiskilling and applying the team concept has been another significant challenge for these and other knowledge workers. We discuss this in more detail in Chapter 4.

Changing Roles for Leaders

For the LFN team to function effectively and to save lives, team members must have the authority to take action, the resources and information to do so without error, and the accountability for taking reasonable action in the critical moment. This has required changes on the part of both team members and the management staff. Says LFN manager David Long, "I have had to make some changes in the way I manage the group. I no longer get involved in technical decisions. I let those who are the experts make the right decisions."

Challenges With New Members, Outsiders, and Limited Resources

The LFN team has run into a number of other challenges as well. When new people are incorporated into the team to meet special needs, they need a good understanding of how the rest of the team operates—a difficult problem to deal with when the composition of the team may not be finalized until minutes before the emergency rescue operation is in the air. Other parts of the hospital and medical establishment don't always understand the nonhierarchical nature of the LFN organization and are confused about how to work with the LFN team and who to contact. Developing not only the technical skills to complete their tasks, but also the "soft skills" necessary to work effectively as a team takes time—a very limited commodity in the life-saving business.

Other Knowledge Team Challenges

Although few knowledge teams face the sort of life-and-death situations that LFN faces, many other knowledge workers have challenges similar to those mentioned above. Some face additional ones as well. Design teams at Hewlett-Packard must coordinate the work of people from multiple locations across the world. Since the people involved aren't all located in one place, communication is extremely difficult. Product designers who are specialists in hardware, software, networking, chip design, or any of a number of other disciplines must also work effectively together without losing their individual expertise. Attorneys from the same company must find ways to communicate new contract provisions to one another rapidly before members of their team (several of whom are working on a number of contracts simultaneously) go to the expensive time and effort of recreating similar provisions in their own work. Knowledge teams at Amoco are often cross-functional teams. But where do technical specialists go for coaching and skill development if they report to someone who doesn't have experience in their discipline? Team members in Weyerhaeuser often find their E-mail and voice mail systems full. How then can they communicate effectively? All of these types of challenges are discussed in more detail in later chapters.

Summary

Knowledge work is challenging, as the Life Flight Network personnel can testify. It is hard to understand something that happens in the mind, perhaps the greatest miracle and mystery on earth. However we do know that knowledge work—even if it can't be completely explained—can be differentiated from physical work by looking at five work characteristics: type of knowledge used, work outcomes, typical work processes, critical skills, and core tasks. As we better understand knowledge work, we can improve our personal and organizational effectiveness. As more and more of our labor becomes knowledge work, perhaps we may come to better understand our own minds.

Notes

1. Michael Eisner, "Managing a Creative Organization: Never Being Afraid to Fail," *Vital Speeches of the Day* 62, no. 16 (1996): 503. Used by permission.
2. Peter Drucker, *Post-Capitalist Society* (New York: HarperBusiness, 1993), pp. 4, 8. © 1993, by Peter F. Drucker, HarperCollins Publishers Inc. Used by permission.
3. Drucker, *Post-Capitalist Society*, 6.
4. Cal Pava, *Managing New Office Technology* (New York: Free Press, 1983).
5. Richard McDermott, "Working in Public; Learning-in-Action: Designing Collaborative Knowledge Work Teams," in *Advances in Interdisciplinary Studies of Work Teams,* vol. 2, *Knowledge Work in Teams,* ed. Michael M. Beyerlein, Douglas A. Johnson, and Susan T. Beyerlein (Greenwich, Conn.: JAI Press, Inc., 1995), 36. Used by permission.
6. Walter Isaacson, "In Search of the Real Bill Gates," *Time,* January 13, 1997, 46. Used by permission.
7. Stephen Hawking, *A Brief History of Time: From the Big Bang to Black Holes* (New York: Bantam Books, 1988), vii. Used by permission.
8. R. Purser and A. Montuori, "Varieties of Knowledge Work Experience: A Critical Systems Inquiry into the Epistemologies and Mindscapes of Knowledge Production," in *Advances in Interdisciplinary Studies of Work Teams,* vol. 2, ed. Michael M. Beyerlein, Douglas A. Johnson, and Susan T. Beyerlein (Greenwich, Conn.: JAI Press, Inc., 1995), 122. Used by permission.

2

Brawn and Brains: Knowledge Work in Factories

"Cogito, ergo sum"
—Descartes

"We've got a problem," said Bim, a sense of urgency obvious in his voice. "You'd better get over to the tank farm." As a new team leader with the Procter & Gamble plant in Lima, Ohio, I had yet to hear a team member sound like this. Bim Guyton was an experienced technician with the factory. He had forgotten more about making fabric softener, bleach, and detergent than I would ever learn as his manager. "It looks like acid is spraying out of the hydrochloric tank," he panted. He jammed the headset into the cradle to sever the telephone call.

Adrenaline made my fingers hum as I dialed and let my boss know what was happening. Bolting out of my chair, I was out of the office, across the catwalk separating the packing building from the chemical mixing and storage operation, and down into the tank farm in a few seconds. There, among the large storage vessels that held the raw materials for Downy fabric softener, about a third of the team was donning acid suits and other safety paraphernalia. Members of the plant safety team, the plant chemical engineer, and other Downy process team members were en route.

In the center of the activity, I could see a stream of clear liquid about as big around as a pencil shooting out of the recently relined acid tank. Bim, Sam, and Tim—all nonexempt technicians—were shouting orders to the others. Although the cement pad under the tanks was containing the puddle, the acid was beginning to etch the concrete and could eventually eat through it. That would have to be stopped to avoid any potential contamination of the groundwater under the pad. The team leapt into action, each team member acting as a separate but integral part of a greater whole. They acted as though they shared a common mind—not like the movies that depict automatons intellectually enslaved to some giant brain, but as if each member of the team was somehow more free to do his or her best independent thinking without endangering the completion of the mission because they shared an understanding of the situation. It was as though they had a single distributed mind!

The problem was under control almost immediately. Within a few minutes the spray was stopped, neutralizing agents were spread on the acid puddle, and an investigation to determine what caused the incident was underway (apparently, when the tank was relined by contractors, the area around one of the nozzles hadn't been prepared properly).

Physical work was necessary to deal with the crisis, but it was knowledge work that made the difference between a minor problem and what easily could have become a major accident. Although this situation had been more urgent than the normal work of the Downy process team, it was not unusual. Increasingly, the nature of our work was evolving from predictable, routine physical labor to knowledge work. The technicians (the job title shared by all front-line employees) were no longer just the hands and backs of the operation; their primary contribution came from their minds. Technology had automated a great deal of the manual work, and increased empowerment demanded they do much of the work that had previously been reserved for managers. As project leaders, problem solvers, and decision makers, the technicians now bore little resemblance to the stereotypical factory worker of the past. And they were not alone.

Decline in Physical Labor

The workplace is rapidly evolving toward knowledge work and away from physical labor. The mix of work in contemporary economies has changed so dramatically that the actual numbers of physical workers are declining rapidly. Some experts predict that within the next few decades, purely physical workers will be only a small minority in the workplace in developed countries. For example, management consultant (and former economist) Peter Drucker suggests that "by the year 2000 there will be no developed country where traditional workers making and moving goods account for more than one sixth or one eighth of the workforce."[1] This is a far cry from only a few years ago, when physical work was the dominant job type in developed countries.

The nature of work is changing from mostly linear to mostly nonlinear and from requiring mainly physical skills to requiring mainly mental acuity. Jobs now usually produce more information than product and require more improvisation than rote, automatic application of process. While this trend is dramatic in a few cases, for most of us the change has been a slow, steady evolution of our jobs. We will illustrate this trend in this chapter and debunk the myth that knowledge work is only for the white-collar worker.

Most Work Is Knowledge Work

Knowledge work is rapidly becoming the dominant type of work in the postindustrial economy. Unlike the situation in most organizations of the past, where a worker's primary contribution to the organization was the strength of his or her hands and backs, the knowledge worker applies more mind than muscle to the task.

Knowledge workers are the fastest-growing and will soon be the largest segment of people in the modern workforce. Knowledge workers will soon outnumber physical laborers as the fundamental working class of modern societies. According to the Census Bureau, in the United States—often a forerunner for business changes across the globe—technical workers (medical technologists, technicians, paralegals, etc.) and professionals (accountants, scientists, engineers, doctors, etc.) alone already account for 16 percent of the American workforce. Experts project that this group will be the largest single segment by the year 2000, with 20 percent, or over 23 million people.[2] See Figure 2-1.

As Figure 2-2 demonstrates, if you include all knowledge workers, the demographic statistics are startling. In the 1970s, service work (which is mostly knowledge work) accounted for 55 percent of all U.S. private-sector jobs. By 1995, it accounted for 79 percent.[3] Today the U.S. economy is dominated by these knowledge workers. The U.S. Bureau of Labor Statistics projects that industries providing services will account for about four out of five jobs by the year 2005.[4] Some estimates run even higher.

Figure 2-1. Percentage of technical and professional jobs in America.

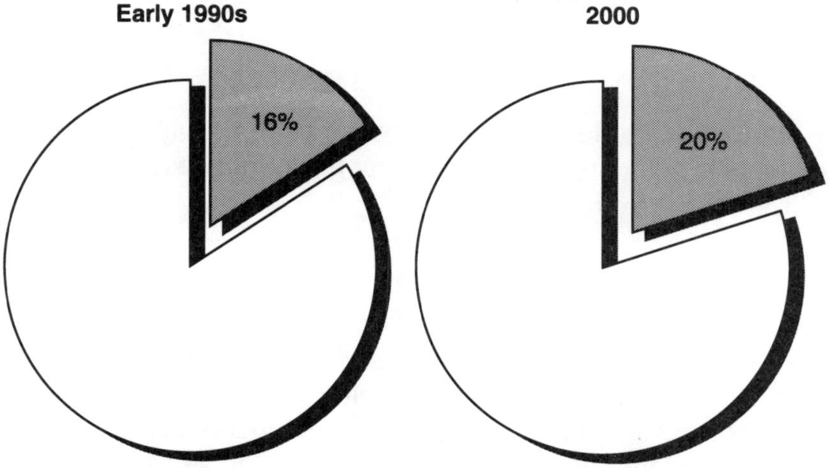

Technical and professional jobs will be the largest single segment in the workforce (23 million people) by the year 2000.

Source: U.S. Census Bureau.

Figure 2-2. Growing percentage of service jobs in the United States.

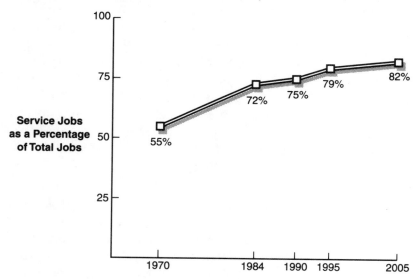

Source: Occupational Outlook Handbook, 1992–1993 edition, U.S. Department of Labor, Bureau of Labor Statistics and Office of Employment Projections (1995). *ftp://stats.bls.gov/pub/news.release/ecopro.txt*

According to economists such as Nuala Beck, roughly 97 percent of all employment growth is coming from knowledge work.[5]

I Work, Therefore I Think

Descartes, the French philosopher and mathematician, once suggested that our ability to think was clear evidence of our sentient existence in the famous observation that opens this chapter: "I think, therefore I am." With an admittedly perverse adaptation of the great scholar's quote, we suggest that this is the first period in human history where the fundamental nature of work has changed so completely that virtually everyone in the workforce can say, "I work, therefore I think." This affirmation was not always true in the past, when many employers asked workers to "leave their brains at the door."

Physical Work in the Days of Henry Ford

Said Henry Ford of the workers at his plant, "The average worker, I am sorry to say, wants a job in which he does not have to put forth much physical exertion—above all, he wants a job in which he does not have to think."[6] In many ways Ford was more progressive than his contemporaries—he strongly believed that service was more important than profits, for example, and that restrictive titles and red tape should be avoided. But even Ford admitted that the jobs of his day didn't require all the skills and attributes of the workers. They didn't even require a "whole" person. He notes that in an analysis of the 7,882 jobs in one factory, it was found that "949 were classified as heavy work requiring strong, able-bodied and practically physically perfect men; 3,338 required men of ordinary physical development and strength. The remaining 3,595 jobs were disclosed as requiring no physical exertion and could be performed by the slightest, weakest sort of men. In fact most of them could be satisfactorily filled by women or older children."

The company also found that "670 could be filled by legless men, 2,637 by one-legged men, 2 by armless men, 715 by one-armed men, and 10 by blind men."[7] It goes without saying that physical strength, not mental acuity, was the primary requirement for factory jobs, an observation reinforced when one reviews the typical training required for proficiency in these tasks: "43 per cent of all the jobs require not over one day of training; 36 per cent require from one day to one week; 6 per cent require from one to two weeks; 14 per cent require from one month to one year."[8] Only 1 percent of jobs (high-skill crafts like tool and die making) required more than one year of on-the-job training.

Part of this work transformation that has occurred since the days of Henry Ford is due to a shift in the predominant types of modern companies. A bellwether of this change occurred when the *Fortune* 500 list of the largest companies in the United States included knowledge work companies like Microsoft in the list, which had previously been reserved for heavy industrial monoliths like General Motors—the prototypical symbol of big business.

Brain Power Industries on the Rise

Traditional smokestack organizations like automobile, steel, mining, and chemical operations have been in decline for years, whereas brain power organizations like software development, technology design, and consulting have been rising. But even inside GM there is a shift away from heavy manufacturing to high-tech computer design and installation. One of the world's largest users of computers—if not *the* largest—is the automobile industry, which employs innumerable high-tech gadgets to monitor and control the sophisticated operating systems of the modern car. These components require more knowledge to assemble and test than was necessary to put nuts on bolts as partially assembled automobiles sped down the assembly line. There are a number of other changes affecting operations that traditionally have utilized physical work that also deserve some elaboration. See Figure 2-3.

Figure 2-3. Selected trends affecting knowledge work in factories.

Trend	Key Implication
The automation of physical work	Remaining work is knowledge work
Work becoming increasingly complex	Workers need more technical knowledge
Unions more involved in decisions	Workers need more business knowledge
Increasing empowerment of workers	Workers spend more time on knowledge work rather than physical work

Knowledge Work in Factories

Larry Neihart, former president of the Diesel Workers Union, confirms the trend toward knowledge work in manufacturing enterprises on the eve of his retirement from Cummins Engine, makers of high-quality diesel engines for trucks and tractors. "The technologies here have been increasing at an incredible rate. You just about need a technical master's degree to operate the machinery we use to make engines today. It is much more complicated than when I started with the company." In one Cummins Engine plant in Indiana, employees now receive a minimum of 292 hours of training, including 72 hours of math, 36 hours of statistics, and 56 hours of process and product technology. This technical knowledge work is becoming increasingly common in many production jobs.

Neihart has also seen a welcome evolution in management and union relationships over his career. These changes have increased another type of knowledge work: business knowledge work. "We work together now to make management decisions," he says. This partnership in decision making and problem solving requires a much more sophisticated level of business literacy than workers were expected to have only a few years ago.

The Saskatoon Chemical plant in Saskatoon, Canada, boasts a workforce in which almost one-third of the workers are college graduates. In spite of having this relatively well-educated production workforce, the company added a fifth work shift to facilitate coverage for several additional weeks of technical and business training required for each employee annually. This training teaches employees how to use the increasingly complicated computer systems that monitor their equipment. The training also covers business issues, such as financial, quality, economic, and interpersonal skills. Everyone (including the vice president/general manager) has a training and development plan that is kept on a server accessible to anyone. This is an expensive investment that the company believes is justified because of the need for everyone to do more knowledge work.

For similar reasons, some Intel fabrication plants require workers to have much more education than they did just a few years ago. In one wafer production fab in Hillsboro, Oregon, for example, all new manufacturing hires must be college graduates because of the increased operator responsibilities. Current employees are also expected to work toward a degree.

Empowerment Creates Knowledge Work

Many empowered manufacturing teams on today's shop floor make decisions that were previously reserved for middle-level management. We have witnessed some of this transformation firsthand. Before we started our consulting firm, we both worked in Procter & Gamble manufacturing facilities—one of us as a manufacturing manager in the team-based plant in Lima, Ohio, and the other as a contract employee in the then top secret soft cookie start-up facility in Chicago.

Most Procter & Gamble soap, paper, and food plants use what they call "technician systems." Workers in these team-based operations set their own schedules, manage their own projects, rotate through multiple technical positions, hire their own team members, and participate in goal setting, peer evaluation, and daily management meetings. As a percentage of their time, their knowledge labor has now surpassed their physical labor.

The bottom line is that even the most traditional factory work is rapidly shifting away from assembly-type linear work to nonlinear physical work, or in many cases to knowledge work, as illustrated in Figure 2-4.

Says Bob Wroblewski, director of human resources for the Weyerhaeuser Company,

> "It is becoming increasingly difficult to differentiate between knowledge work and manual labor. There is a blurring of management and nonmanagement work, for example, as we redistribute power and responsibility from managers to the workers in our plants and mills. The model we are using drives us in the direction of having manufacturing employees do much more nonroutine, nonlinear, knowledge-type work that used

Figure 2-4. Shifting job trends.

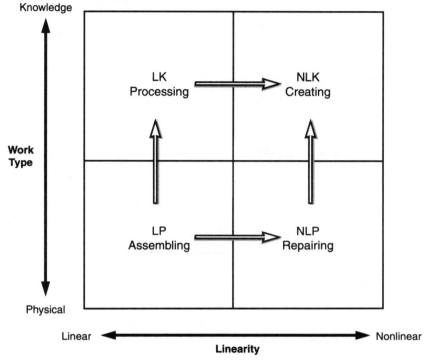

to be done by managers or staff professionals. That will continue. It has to continue for us to be competitive."

The same is true in many manufacturing operations at Corning, Cummins Engine, Ford, General Electric, Champion Paper, Nucor Steel, Allied-Signal, Rockwell, Apple Computer, Hewlett-Packard, Monsanto, Motorola, and countless other companies. We are not aware of a single *Fortune* 100 company that isn't moving to team-based systems in a significant portion of its production facilities. In today's environment there is little competitive advantage to purely physical work. Developed countries have higher wage rates than less developed countries and therefore cannot afford to compete on physical labor without a significant knowledge work component. Strong backs and arms are cheaper elsewhere. Yesterday's factory is rapidly becoming today's university. It has to complete this evolution to survive. Thus "laborer" as a synonym for "employee" is now obsolete.

Summary

Not all of the implications of the mass transition from physical work to knowledge work are clear. But a few things about knowledge work are more apparent than they were a few years ago. One is that knowledge work is moving toward team-based structures with limited traditional supervision. Another is that manufacturing work, which has traditionally been mostly physical work, is rapidly being transformed into knowledge work. We know that work in general is transitioning to knowledge work as a result of increasing movement toward service jobs, increases in technology, and changes in contemporary work design. Thus many of the work systems and organizational designs created for physical work are now obsolete, as we shall see in Chapter 3.

Notes

1. Peter Drucker, *Post-Capitalist Society* (New York: HarperBusiness, 1993), p. 5. © 1993, by Peter F. Drucker, HarperCollins Publishers Inc. Used by permission.
2. Walter Kiechel III, "How We Will Work in the Year 2000," *Fortune* 127, no. 10 (1993): 44. © 1993 Time Inc. All rights reserved. Used by permission.
3. Richard McDermott, "Working in Public; Learning-in-Action: Designing Collaborative Knowledge Work Teams," in *Advances in Interdisciplinary Studies of Work Teams*, vol. 2, *Knowledge Work in Teams*, ed. Michael M. Beyerlein, Douglas A. Johnson, and Susan T. Beyerlein (Greenwich, Conn.: JAI Press, Inc., 1995), 36. Used by permission.
4. *Occupational Outlook Handbook*, 1992–93 edition, U.S. Department of Labor, Bureau of Labor Statistics, Bulletin 2400, May 1992.
5. "Managing in an Information Highway Age," *Business Quarterly* 58 (Spring 1994): 73.
6. Henry Ford, *My Life and Work* (Garden City, N.Y.: Doubleday, Page and Company, 1926), 103. Used by permission.
7. Ibid., 108.
8. Ibid., 110.

3

Knowledge Work Teams: Organizing for Empowerment

"Tomorrow's dynamic, growing organization will have a very strong team orientation. Such an organization will build cross-functional teams. For example, each of the design/build teams we put together on the 777 program had manufacturing, design engineering, finance—and customers and suppliers on the team. As a result, the design released from these teams reflected customer needs and manufacturing needs."[1]

—Philip M. Condit, President, The Boeing Company

On May 15, 1995, Boeing delivered its first 777, currently the largest twin-engine long-distance jet in the world. In accordance with its promise not only to produce a whole new class of airplane but to do it in a whole new way, the Boeing triple seven design team included an unusual mix or engineers, maintenance, and manufacturing technicians. In addition, engineers from United Airlines, one of Boeing's largest customers, served on the design team from the start. Other part-time members of this knowledge work team included representatives of the FAA, who must authorize the long-distance, overseas certification.

The team's results are impressive. United spokespeople have excitedly announced that the company's participation has resulted in more benefits for fliers, including flatter floors, more luggage space, and in-seat video technology (results that we can personally corroborate from a trip on the 777 between Washington, D.C., and Frankfurt). The FAA certification occurred more quickly than normal because of more strenuous testing during development, including multiple single-engine landings, which are not part of the normal development process. Without the FAA's active participation, these tests probably would not have been made. The plan is also easier to manufacture and service because of the early involvement of technicians. For example, to reduce weight, structural engineers proposed eliminating a service door that would normally be located aft of the cockpit. It was retained when maintenance technicians argued successfully that eliminating the door would make servicing certain equipment nearly impossible.[2]

Like the Life Flight Network team mentioned in Chapter 1, the Boeing Triple Seven development team was a team because every knowledge worker shared a common purpose: to create a new long-distance jet. This common purpose differentiates a team from other organizations of people that are not teams. But clear purpose alone does not account for the success of a knowledge team, nor does it help us understand how the characteristics of knowledge teams generally differ from those of the more traditional teams that have been in vogue for the last several years. In this chapter we will explore work teams more fully in order to better understand them and to show how they differ from non-team-based operations.[3] We will also introduce the ways in which self-directed work team concepts must be adapted for knowledge work, a topic we will examine in more detail in Chapter 4.

Teams Smeams

Under the heading "A Team Effort," an article naming Dr. David Ho the 1996 *Time* Magazine Man of the Year noted that Ho alone could not take all the credit for his discoveries about AIDS. His work built on a number of sources: Michael Gottlieb, who reported the first cases; the U.S. Centers for Disease Control, which showed how the infection was transmitted; Dr. Luc Montagnier's laboratory at the Pasteur Institute in Paris, which isolated the virus; Dr. Robert Gallo at the National Cancer Institute in Bethesda, Maryland, who produced it in the lab; the National Institutes of Health, which funded basic research; and drug companies like Burroughs Wellcome and Merck, which brought anti-HIV drugs to the market.[4]

The article explains how in this age of technological complexity, it is difficult for a single knowledge worker—even one with extraordinary talents—to accomplish significant work without the help of others. But are the people mentioned in this article really a knowledge team?

What Is a Work Team?

To understand knowledge work teams, we first need to understand teams in general. The lack of common terminology concerning teams makes a discussion about them difficult, but there are some generally accepted working definitions that are helpful. The word *team* itself, for example, most commonly refers to a collection of individuals who share a common purpose.[5] This is what differentiates a *team* from a *group*, which is any collection of people. Thus people with red hair are a group simply because they can be distinguished from other people. But they would not be a team unless they got together for some common purpose, say to set up a foundation to study the historical contributions of people with red hair.

Common Understanding and Commitment

Using only this very simple definition of a team, it is already obvious that some organizations that call themselves teams are not teams at all. If a group doesn't have a clear purpose, it cannot by definition be a team. Moreover, if the participants in a group do not have a *common* understanding and commitment to that purpose, the group is not a team.

In the case of the AIDS researchers, although the scientists and doctors mentioned share a common desire to discover a cure for AIDS, the independent organizations pursue different specific initiatives and theories depending on their staffing, funding conditions, and interests. They may collaborate from time to time, and they keep up with one another's work through publications, conferences, and telephone calls. But they are not a team. They are a talented group of people with similar interests, in much the same way that American football players on the San Francisco 49ers, the Dallas Cowboys, and the Green Bay Packers are a group of people with similiar interests who are not on the same team.

From time to time we will gather so-called team members from an organization and ask them individually to describe the primary purpose of their particular "team." It is not unusual to get *very* different answers from participants. In one such exercise with a group of engineers from a high-tech company, some said that their primary purpose was to bring leading-edge technical products to the marketplace, while others said that their purpose was to design more cost-effective products. These two factions were, of course, frequently at odds with each other because their purposes were often mutually exclusive. To muddy the water further, still other engineers in the group described their purpose in terms of a customer focus, such as creating state-of-the-art, user-friendly products or solving customer problems. This engineering group had internal disagreement about its fundamental purpose, creating an underlying confusion that made it difficult for the engineers to agree on product parameters. Regardless of what they called themselves, these engineers were a group rather than a team.

Team Babel: A Confused Language

Understanding teams is not as simple as it may appear. What do managers mean when they say they want a "team-based operation"? Are they simply saying that they want people to have common goals? Usually not. Is there only one kind of team-based organization? No. So what do they mean when they say they want teams?

Unfortunately, they may mean several different things. People have used "team" terminology in seemingly contradictory ways. For example, while some managers use the word *team* to describe a participative workplace (as in, "Let's not make a unilateral management decision on this one; we'll take it to the *team*"), others use the same terminology to reinforce the traditional autocratic paradigm (as in, "Don't rock the boat, we need you to be a *team* player"). It's no wonder that some people are confused when organizations say they want to create teams. As evidence of this, you have only to look at the rising popularity of Scott Adams's Dilbert cartoons, which (in addition to poking some well-deserved fun at consultants) offer insightfully scathing observations about the hypocrisy with which some organizations use the team terminology to manipulate workers into doing whatever management wants them to do.

Teams as Vehicles for Empowerment

When most contemporary organizations talk about teams, they are describing something that is much more than a purposeful organization. Whether they are using teams for physical work or for knowledge work, they are usually talking about a particular organizational structure that is commonly used as a vehicle for employee empowerment. Thus, while certain organizations could technically be called teams because they meet the first two criteria we have discussed (clear purpose and common agreement to achieve the purpose), those characteristics alone do not distinguish classic bureaucracies from what are currently called team-based operations.

For the purposes of this chapter, we will employ what is becoming the more common usage of the term in organizations: Teams are nonauthoritarian work structures with shared responsibility for decision making, problem solving, and organization design. More succinctly stated, the third criterion for team operations is that they are work structures based on a commitment (rather than a control) paradigm.[6] That is, team operations are constructed and facilitated to elicit the commitment rather than the compliance of the workforce.[7] For an illustration of the differences between a control-based organization (where the management and organization structures are focused on controlling the workforce) and a commitment-based organization (where the organization structure and processes focus instead on creating a culture of employee commitment), see Figure 3-1.

Using these characteristics to define teams narrows the scope of our discussion from all so-called teams (including some of the boot camp teams in the military or some of the sports teams managed by authoritarian coaching staffs) to only those teams built on a foundation of empowerment. Teams are often described as a structural manifestation of an empowered work culture. To understand these kinds of contemporary teams, therefore, we need to better understand the emerging movement to empower employees.

The Empowerment Revolution

Today it is estimated that virtually every major corporation in North America and Western Europe is using various forms of empowerment somewhere in the organization. This workplace

Figure 3-1. Comparing control-based organizations with commitment-based organizations.

Control-Based Organizations	Commitment-Based Organizations
• Management gets compliance	• Leadership develops commitment
• Authoritarian practices	• Nonauthoritarian work structures
• Management solely responsible for managing	• Shared responsibility for decision making, problem solving, goal setting, results, and organization design
• Reliance on policies, rules, or regulations	• Reliance on principles, philosophies, or values
• Hierarchy culture	• Empowerment culture

transformation has already been dubbed the "second industrial revolution" because it challenges the fundamental assumptions of work structures of the first industrial revolution.[8] Although it goes by a number of names, including socio-technical systems, employee empowerment, high-performance work teams, and the like, the workplace transformation in contemporary organizations is commonly known by the generic label team-based organizations.[9] A number of organizations are using a particular kind of team called a self-directed work team, which is a very advanced form of structured worker empowerment discussed later in this chapter.

Team-based workplaces differ from traditional operations. In stark contrast to common operations of the past, many contemporary organizations have created work structures that are more democratic and flexible in nature. Team members have responsibilities once reserved for management. The trend in these operations is toward less authoritarian processes. These operations share a common underpinning philosophy of sharing responsibility for results and decisions between management and individual contributors. They rely on employee empowerment rather than management direction. See Figure 3-2.

Empowerment Continuum

Empowerment gives people more power to influence their own workplace. But obviously, varying degrees of empowerment are

Figure 3-2. Characteristics of team-based operations.

Team-Based Operations

- More democratic
- More flexible
- Distributed management responsibilities
- Fewer authoritarian processes
- Improved labor relations
- Principle-based contracts
- Shared responsibilities for results
- Shared decision making
- Empowered rather than management-directed

possible even within team-based operations. Any kind of team, whether knowledge or physical, can be dominated by management (lower empowerment) or entirely self-directed (high empowerment). One way to explain this is to visualize empowerment as a continuum of employee involvement, with lower-empowerment techniques like selected employee input on projects on one end, ongoing employee task forces in the middle, and higher-empowerment processes like self-directed work teams (SDWTs) on the other end.[10] See Figure 3-3.

Self-Directed Work Teams

What are self-directed teams? Let's use a slightly modified version of the definition used by The Association for Quality and Participation for its study on the subject:

> *Self-directed team* (noun): A group of employees who have day-to-day responsibility for managing themselves and the work they do with a minimum of direct supervision. Members of self-directed teams typically handle job assignments, plan and schedule work, make operational decisions, and take action on problems.[11]

These teams have been popular in the physical workplace for decades and have become increasingly common in knowledge work applications over the last several years. Consider a

Figure 3-3. The empowerment continuum.

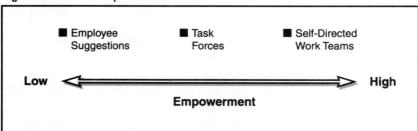

Source: Adapted from "The Involvement Continuum" © 1989 Belgard•Fisher•Rayner, Inc. Influenced by the work of John Sherwood.

few examples. Aid Association for Lutherans (AAL) uses self-directed cross-functional teams, with each team having within its ranks the necessary skills to process an application from start to finish. AAL credits these teams with major improvements in results, including the following:

- ► Insurance application processing went from twenty days to five days—a 75 percent reduction in processing time.[12]
- ► Productivity increased by 20 percent in 1990[13] and 40 percent by 1993.[14]
- ► Three hierarchical layers were eliminated.[15]
- ► Increased assets now total $11.2 billion, placing AAL in the top 2 percent of life insurers.[16]
- ► Field workers who believed that the home office understood their needs and problems increased from only 27 percent in 1985 to 57 percent in 1990.[17]
- ► Customer satisfaction increased on the company's five-point scale from 4.12 to 4.85.[18]

At the Mayo Clinic, self-directed physician teams are used in parts of the hospital.

- ► When a patient is first diagnosed, an appropriate mix of doctors is temporarily assembled to serve as the patient's team. Members of this team consult with one another to provide the patient with the best possible care—"two heads are better than one, and three are even better." Mayo is the world's oldest and largest multispeciality group practice.
- ► When information systems are designed, doctors are part of the development team to ensure that the systems are appropriate.
- ► The Mayo Clinic's board of trustees is partially composed of the clinic's doctors to ensure that all policies are realistically suited for everyone. Consensus is also used, as opposed to a majority rules system.

The clinic believes this has resulted in the following

- ► Per person costs are 15 to 22 percent below the national average.

► The Mayo clinic is currently ranked second by *US News & World Report*. According to this study, the Mayo Clinic scored in the top ten among U.S. hospitals in fourteen of sixteen possible areas, including AIDS, cancer, and cardiology.

In 1984, Shenandoah Life Insurance implemented a team-based structure, placing knowledge workers in a cross-functional system that includes new policy issuing, accounting, and policyholder service. By 1990, twenty-two workers were participating in this system. As a result:

► Processing of service requests dropped from 4.97 days in 1985 to 3.15 days in 1989.
► Although there were one-third fewer employees, the workers handled 40.5 percent more service requests.
► Eighty-eight percent of field agents who submit forms to the team found their service "very good," while 11% rated it "satisfactory."[19]

At Microsoft, David Pritchard is the team leader of recruiting teams responsible for filling the staffing requirements of the rapidly expanding giant. He explains the transition to SDWTs.

"My group is responsible for all technical hiring of people for our product teams. This group consists of recruiters, event coordinators, and headhunters. We go out and look for the best and brightest people around the world. About February of 1994, we realized we could use self-directed teams to build a more flexible organization to meet business needs. So we took a group of employees—those currently involved in all areas of recruiting—and brought them together in a team-based environment by April of 1994. During that period of time we had a horrendous amount of new positions to fill within the company, because we were growing so rapidly. We had to proceed with work as usual while bringing together all of these recruiting groups, which had been previously structured as separate, inflexible, hierarchical teams. Within each group, there are no formal leaders. It is a shared responsibility. For example, I have over forty direct reports.

"We have increased productivity well over 50 percent during the last year. We were able to hire twice as many people. We basically blew every metric we had out of the water. Self-directed teams have really empowered people to do things they were never able to do before. In terms of diversity (age, ethnicity, etc.) our hiring metrics all increased well over 50 percent. Also, with regard to employee attitudes, they all vastly improved, but we won't know the specifics until September when we administer a more complete employee attitude survey. In terms of our customers (the product groups within Microsoft), we have people saying, 'I thought we were getting great people last year, but this year they were even better.' But the success has not come overnight, and it has not come without a lot of pain.

"Initially, there was some push-back, but since then things have really changed. This time last year, for example, while we were conducting performance reviews, there was a lot of negative feedback about this new structure. And I think a lot of it had to do with the fact that we just pulled the switch, and the transition hadn't really been planned well. But since then, the feedback has been overwhelmingly positive. People make comments like, 'I've never felt so empowered before.' They've never felt like they've had so much freedom and independence to get things done, and they've never felt so much support. We have some really supercharged people who a year ago were thinking they would like to do something new (change departments) within a few years. Now, these people really want to stay in their same jobs, because they like the new processes. We're now doing some refinement of the organization, and we have people saying, 'I don't care what we do in terms of refining the organizational structure, but I hope we still foster the self-directed teams, and I hope we continue to have leaders in the organization like you, David, who let us do what we need to do to get the job done, but at the same time was off on the side coaching us. We want that to remain the same.' To me, that says a lot about the success of self-directed teams.''

Where traditional work groups typically are organized into separate specialized jobs with rather narrow responsibilities, members of SDWTs are usually jointly responsible for whole work processes, with each individual performing multiple tasks.[20] These are common elements of SDWTs. As we will mention later, this is one area where knowledge teams differ somewhat from physical work teams. For other key differences between self-directed work teams and traditional organizations, see Figure 3-4.

Common Misconceptions About SDWTs

A couple of caveats are in order when defining SDWTs. First, some organizations apparently believe that the teams are the

Figure 3-4. SDWTs vs. traditional organizations.

Self-Directed Work Teams	Traditional Organizations
Customer-driven	Management-driven
Multiskilled workforce	Workforce of isolated specialists
Few job descriptions	Many job descriptions
Information shared widely	Information limited
Few levels of management	Many levels of management
Whole business focus	Function/department focus
Shared goals	Segregated goals
Seemingly chaotic	Seemingly organized
Purpose achievement emphasis	Problem-solving emphasis
High worker commitment	High management commitment
Continuous improvements	Incremental improvements
Self-controlled	Management-controlled
Values/principle-based	Policy/procedure-based

Source: Kimball Fisher, *Leading Self-Directed Work Teams: A Guide to Developing New Team Leader Skills* (New York: McGraw-Hill, 1993), p. 16. Used by permission.

end instead of the means to an end. In the most successful operations, SDWTs are viewed as a method of improving results, not as a substitute for them. The means/ends inversion commonly results in less than satisfactory performance; organizations lose sight of their purpose and focus on the care and feeding of the structures instead ("Sorry, our poor customer service is caused by the fact that everyone is in a team meeting right now"). This is obviously a bad mistake. Our experience suggests that if the organization uses measures that focus on key result areas, such as customer satisfaction or market share, it is more likely to be successful than if it uses measures such as number of teams, frequency of team meetings, or numbers of hours of team training. This observation can be supported by the numerous contemporary business books that illustrate the problems many companies have had with the team concept. More often than not, the reason for these problems is a flawed implementation process in which the team concept somehow takes precedence over business effectiveness.

The second caveat when defining SDWTs is not to overemphasize the "self-directedness" of the teams. We have often argued that the name "self-directed work team" can be misleading. Some believe that it connotes a complete absence of management personnel (which is inaccurate). In the most successful implementations of both physical and knowledge work teams that we have seen, SDWTs mean a change in the role of management, not an elimination of all supervisors and managers. Those who use SDWTs as a means of downsizing management staffs almost always harm the teams by stripping them of essential coaching and training resources. Both Procter & Gamble and Tennessee Eastman Kodak, for example, found it necessary to add management personnel back into team-based organizations from which they had been removed earlier. They did this in order to support the high development needs of the team members—not to add back directive and controlling bosses.

Another misconception created by the name SDWT is the implication that the team has complete latitude to do whatever it wants (which is equally inaccurate). All teams operate within certain boundary conditions. Probably a more accurate term would be *work-centered teams*. Simply stated, in these teams, skilled, well-informed people take direction from the work itself rather than from management.

Types of Teams

Although teams are not a new phenomenon, they currently are a popular way for organizations to provide a structure that facilitates empowerment. Says John Tysse, an attorney with McGuiness and Williams, "Teams will spread into more and more levels of the organization—both higher and lower. Twenty-five years from now there will be employee teams everywhere, in meetings with vendors, suppliers, and customers. There will be assembly teams, design teams and management teams."[21]

There are several different kinds of teams used today in either knowledge or physical work settings that differ in their tasks, membership, or scope. An average employee, for example, can be a member of multiple teams. She may be a member of her natural work team, a cost-reduction team, a new product development team, an overall company team, a new equipment procurement team, a supplier relations team, an organization redesign team, and an intraorganizational volleyball team all at the same time. This is all pretty common and very confusing.

Generally speaking, teams can be separated into different categories on the basis of their duration and scope, as seen in Figure 3-5. There are teams that have ongoing responsibilities, and others that are only temporary and will be disbanded after the team's task is accomplished. There are also teams that work within smaller organizational borders, and others that cross multiple organizational boundaries. If we put these variables into a 2-by-2 matrix, we can divide teams into four general types: (1) natural work teams, (2) cross-functional teams, (3) small-project teams, and (4) special-purpose teams. Each of these deserves some elaboration.[22]

Natural Work Teams

Natural work teams are the collected individuals that form around normal work processes. They are subsystems of an orga-

Figure 3-5. Types of teams.

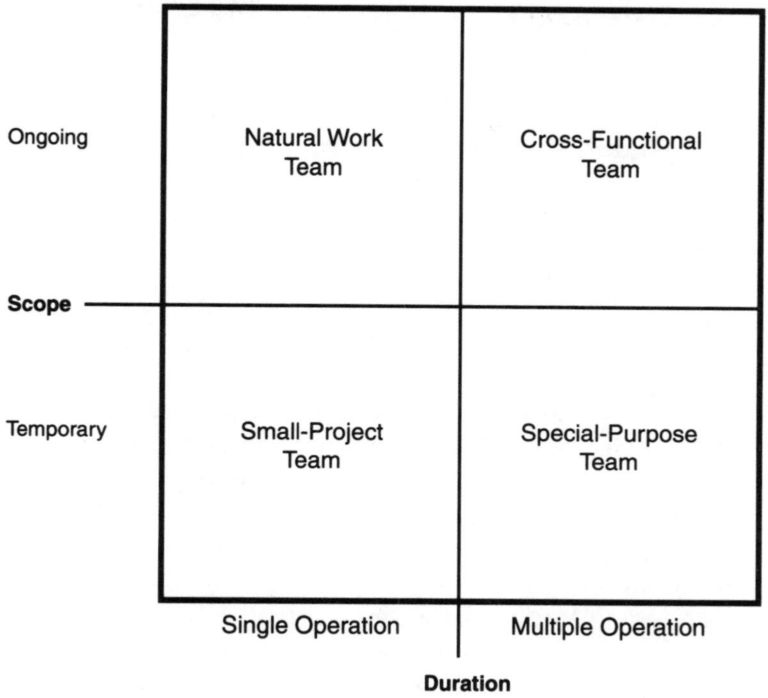

	Single Operation	Multiple Operation
Ongoing	Natural Work Team	Cross-Functional Team
Temporary	Small-Project Team	Special-Purpose Team

Scope (vertical axis) / Duration (horizontal axis)

Source: "Diagnostic Issues for Work Teams," by Kimball Fisher in Ann Howard and Associates, *Diagnosis for Organizational Change: Methods and Models* (New York: The Guilford Press, copyright 1994).

nization, as the Life Flight Network is to the Legacy Health System Hospitals or as a long-distance sales team is to one of the Baby Bells. They generally are composed of a small group of people (ideally less than ten) who work together regularly in the same organizational unit. These teams have an ongoing operational responsibility to provide some products and/or services. They are as the family unit is to society as a whole—a group of people who work and live together on a regular basis. Also referred to as work teams or functional/department teams, these are the units that are the most likely to become self-directed work teams because they have the most sustainable influence on organizational results and because they endure long enough to justify the inevitable investment in training and communication infrastructure. In knowledge teams, however, there is a trend toward redesigning natural work teams into business- or customer-oriented teams, rather than maintaining the traditional functionally oriented or job-oriented groupings. Thus, many knowledge workers now find their natural work team—the people they spend most of their time with—includes people from a wide variety of technical disciplines.

Cross-Functional Teams

Cross-functional teams are organization units with an ongoing purpose that crosses multiple natural work teams. Parts of P&G and Tektronix, for example, use teams with representatives from each natural work team for communication and administration. These teams meet on a regular basis, weekly or daily, to review systemwide issues and to coordinate ongoing activities such as project staffing and scheduling. This P&G group in Lima, Ohio, is called the core group. The core group discusses issues that affect the whole facility, including such things as training and development, hiring practices, administrative discrepancies between teams, integration of team goals and activities, personnel policy application, and general plantwide planning and problem solving. The core group reviews information and solves problems normally reserved for senior managers in more traditional P&G locations. Participation in the core group is limited to a specific term. When a participant's term is completed, that person's natural work group team selects a different representative. This makes core group participation a rotated responsibility rather than allowing it to devolve into a permanent hierarchy of straw boss employees. Terms are staggered to avoid continuity problems for the core group.

Cross-functional teams are like community organizations or representational government groups are to society as a whole. They represent multiple constituencies and have a long-standing responsibility for integrating and coordinating diverse viewpoints. Other examples of cross-functional teams might be safety teams, employee relations teams, or pricing teams, which have a standing task that affects the whole hospital, store, firm, or division. Although cross-functional teams are typically representative in nature, with rotating membership to allow maximum opportunity for everyone in the operation to serve on the team, some operations use the whole organization as the cross-functional team for decision-making and problem-solving activities.[23] Thus the membership of a cross-functional team can range from a few people (representative) to several hundred people, or even to a whole system (a site, a sector/division, a company, etc.), depending on the task.

Small-Project Teams

Small-project teams are temporary collections of people that are formed to work on a particular task until it is completed. After the work is done, they disband. The task in this case is confined to the limits of a single natural work group and usually does not require participation from everyone on the natural work team. When a family plans a special vacation, works to solve a financial crisis, or puts together a retirement savings program, it may create this type of team. Usually composed of a few family members, the team forms when needed and then dissolves after the work is completed. Examples of work projects include tasks such as creating personnel development plans, resolving equipment problems, making certain staffing decisions, evaluating equipment purchases, writing reports, developing proposals, etc.

As subgroups of the natural work team, small-project teams usually have only a few people (ideally five or fewer). If these teams are properly focused and trained, they should be able to make and implement good decisions rapidly. People are seldom assigned to project teams full-time. A single team member will often serve on several project teams concurrently, with these projects consuming only a few hours a week. Small-project teams can be used for either physical or mental work, but their work more commonly has a large knowledge component.

Special-Purpose Teams

Special-purpose teams are another kind of temporary organization that disbands upon the completion of the task. The scope of the tasks, however, is bigger than that of a small-project team, with implications that cross multiple natural work groups. In society, these teams might be sponsored by churches, schools, or community groups. Planning a community picnic, raising money for a new athletic field, or creating a coalition to support or oppose legislation might be examples of special-purpose team tasks. On the work side, such things as vendor or customer problem-solving activities are normally done in special-purpose teams. New product development, new technology investigation, future search conferences, organization redesign, and similar activities are typically handled by these teams as well. The 777 development team was this type of organization. These teams require more time and support than small-project teams. They often demand intense commitment from participants for several weeks or months, and it is difficult for a team member to be on more than one of them at any given time.

These teams are used in a variety of circumstances. Phil Barber, for example, has helped the twenty-eight schools in Bellevue, Washington, use special-purpose teams to design annual school programs, including curriculum and certain class structures. The school district calls these teams program delivery councils (PDCs). They are composed of teachers, parents, students, and school administrators. Explains Barber,

> "The councils are looking for diversity—those individuals who have alternative points of view about what education is about. We need individuals who are diverse, but are still willing to participate in a collaborative process. We also like representative ratios of teachers, staff, parents, and students. It would be ineffective to have thirty parents on the PDC and only two teachers.
>
> "Each team has a facilitator and/or chair. In a small number of cases the principal has filled this role, but they have found that since the principal is a stakeholder, he or she can be accused of manipulating the process. So this is a rotating position that changes as individuals filter in and out of the teams."

These special-purpose knowledge teams have produced some very interesting successes, says Barber.

> "It's real hard to quantify our results, but I can point to two or three schools that have completely revised their school program. In one case, the school has changed its hours and reduced class size by eight to nine students per class by shifting some of its specialists' time. I'm confident that the school was able to achieve this because of both buy-in and ownership of the changes. The parents, staff, and administrators were part of the creation of these changes. It was a significant amount of restructuring that continues even now. I point to this school as a typical example of how the PDCs can work effectively.
>
> "But I'm really thinking that the significant victories that are going on are not big changes in test scores or program changes like the above-mentioned school experienced. I was at another elementary school consistently last year. I was present at eight or nine of its meetings doing some facilitating, observing, etc. It was a contentious group two years ago, but through its own efforts—its own attention to process and relationships—it's a much better functioning group and is now making some decisions about integrated curriculum and multiage classrooms that it would not have been able to make just a few years ago. I think these victories are not measurable. But they are significant."

Common Characteristics of Team-Based Organizations

Regardless of the type of team used, in both the physical and the knowledge workplace, team-based organizations tend to have certain characteristics that distinguish them from organizations that aren't team-based. Although team-based operations have increased dramatically over the last few years, they have not yet become the predominant organization type. Most organizations, even knowledge work organizations, are still based on the hierarchical model. See Figure 3-6 for a comparative list of the characteristics of hierarchical and team-based organizations.

Hierarchical organizations rely on management direction and organizational departmentalization to provide order and consistency. Rules (written or unwritten) and auditing processes are important means of control. Employee roles and responsibilities tend to be very specialized, and information typically goes to management rather than to employees. Hard work is encouraged more than a balance between work and home life. Conservative improvement tends to be the norm because organizational controls typically inhibit risk taking. Team-based organizations' characteristics are often the converse of these—the focus is on global, rather than departmental success; there are minimum rather than maximum controls; defects are controlled at the source rather than by a separate policing function; information goes to employees; work balance is emphasized over long hours; and continuous improvement is more important than conservative improvement. Team-based operations also focus on creating multiskilled team members.

Where a traditional organization might be divided into groups of functional specialists, in team-based organizations a team (especially an SDWT) is usually responsible for delivery of an entire service or product, or for a geography or customer base. This is done to create (wherever possible) small self-sustaining businesses that can be jointly managed by their members.

Summary

Team-based operations have a number of characteristics that differentiate them from operations that aren't team-based. There are a number of different types of teams, including natural work teams, cross-functional teams, small-project teams, and special-purpose teams. Self-directed work teams are a special type of team with extraordinary levels of empowerment. All teams, of

Figure 3-6. Comparing hierarchical organizations with team-based organizations.

Hierarchical Organization	*Team-Based Organization*
• **Hierarchical Order:** Order and consistency are maintained by a hierarchy of management.	• **Information Order:** Order and consistency are maintained by a hierarchy of information.
• **Local Optimum:** Energy is focused on how to maximize the performance of a subunit.	• **Global Optimum:** Energy is focused on how to maximize the performance of the entire organization.
• **Maximum Specification:** To the greatest extent possible, all aspects of the jobs and methods are specified.	• **Minimum Critical Specification:** Only the most critical aspects of jobs and methods are specified.
• **Functional Defect Control:** Defects, if they cannot be eliminated, are controlled by a specialized function (e.g., quality control inspector).	• **Source Defect Control:** Defects, if they cannot be eliminated, are controlled as near the point of origin as possible.
• **Specialized Skill:** Employees are highly specialized with a narrow skill set.	• **Multiskilled:** Employees are cross-trained, multiskilled, and highly flexible.
• **Vertical Information Flow:** Information goes up the management hierarchy.	• **Source Information Flow:** Information goes directly to the point where action is taken.
• **Work Ethic Value:** A core organizational value is that working hard is important.	• **Work Life Value:** A core organizational value is to provide a high quality of work life.
• **Conservative Improvement:** The organization improves through a formal process of management's carefully planning out and instituting policy, procedural, and method changes.	• **Continuous Improvement:** The organization is continuously improving its performance through the redesign of work, experimentation, and risk taking.

Source: © The Fisher Group, Inc. 1996. All rights reserved. Adapted from the control and commitment paradigm-based organization comparison by BFR. Influenced by the work of Albert Cherns, Eric Trist, and Fred Emery. Used with permission.

course, require a clear shared purpose to be effective. As we will see in Chapter 4, however, there are also a number of very specific differences between knowledge teams and the types of teams that have typically been used in business. Understanding those differences will help us make these unique operations more effective.

Notes

1. Philip M. Condit, "Focusing on the Customer: How Boeing Does It," *Research Technology Management*, January–February 1994, 36.
2. As reported on "Morning Edition," a news report program on National Public Radio, May 15, 1995.
3. Much of this chapter has been adapted from Kimball Fisher, "Diagnostic Issues for Work Teams," chapter 11 in Ann Howard and associates, *Diagnosis for Organizational Change: Methods and Models* (The Guilford Press, New York © 1994). Used by permission.
4. Christine Gorman, "The Disease Detective," *Time*, December 30, 1996/January 6, 1997, 57. Used by permission.
5. Jon R. Katzenbach and Douglas K. Smith, *The Wisdom of Teams* (Boston: Harvard Business Press, 1993).
6. R. Walton, "From Control to Commitment in the Workplace," *Harvard Business Review*, March–April 1985.
7. K. Fisher, "Managing in the High Commitment Workplace," *Organizational Dynamics*, Winter 1989. Reprinted by permission of the publisher, from ORGANIZATIONAL DYNAMICS WINTER 1989, © 1989. American Management Association, New York. All rights reserved.
8. E. Trist, "The Evolution of Socio-technical Systems: A Conceptual Framework and an Action Research Program," *Issues in the Quality of Working Life*, no. 2, A series of occasional papers, Ontario Ministry of Labour and Ontario Quality of Working Life Centre, June 1981.
9. J. Hoerr and W. Zellner, "The Payoff From Teamwork," *Business Week*, July 10, 1989, and Susan Albers Mohrman, Susan

C. Cohen, and Allan M. Mohrman, Jr., *Designing Team-Based Organizations: New Forms for Knowledge Work* (San Francisco: Jossey-Bass, 1995).

10. K. Fisher, *Leading Self Directed Work Teams: A Guide to Developing New Team Leader Skills* (New York: McGraw-Hill, 1993).
11. Richard Wellins et al., "Self-Directed Work Teams: A Study of Current Practice," *Industry Week,* The Association of Quality and Participation, and Development Dimensions International Study, 1990.
12. D. J. McNerney, "Compensation Case Study: Rewarding Team Performance and Individual Skillbuilding," *HRfocus* 72, no. 1 (1995), 1, 4.
13. M. Hequet, "Paying for Knowledge in 'Paper Factories,' " *Training* 27, no. 9 (1990), 75.
14. N. K. Austin, "Reorganizing the Organization Chart," *Working Woman,* 18, no. 9 (1993), 26.
15. Ibid.
16. Ibid.
17. Hequet, "Paying For Knowledge," 70.
18. Ibid.
19. Ibid., 70, 74.
20. Fisher, "Managing in the High Commitment Workplace."
21. Michael A. Verespej, "A Workforce Revolution?" *Industry Week,* August 21, 1996, 24. Reprinted with permission from *Industry Week,* August 21, 1996. Copyright Penton Publishing, Inc., Cleveland, Ohio.
22. Fisher, "Diagnostic Issues for Work Teams," 247, 248. Used by permission.
23. Reprinted with permission of the publisher. From *Discovering Common Ground,* copyright © 1993 by Marvin R. Weiskord, Berrett-Koehler Publishers, Inc., San Francisco, CA. All rights reserved.

4

Jack of All Trades, Master of One: Vertical Multiskilling and Other Unique Characteristics of Knowledge Teams

"The term generalist implies a "jack of all trades master of none," and, in the world of product development, expertise is required. In fact, many professionals who are assigned to cross-functional teams are concerned that they may lose their "professional identity" and that there will be an expertise dilution as they move out of their functional homes."[1]

—Janice A. Klein and Patrick M. Maurer,
Massachusetts Institute of Technology

The Administrative Center for Corning, Inc., has 135 employees and is divided into 17 self-directed teams that have been in operation since 1990. It provides several services for the business units across the $5 billion company, including various employee services, customer services, and communication services.

Before the teams were developed, the administrative services work was done very differently. Explains Bob Condella, leader of the Administrative Center: "All of the services that now make up the Administrative Center used to be scattered across what we call the Corning Valley. They were located in five different divisions. We decided to bring all of these different groups together and house them under one roof. The basic objective was to implement high-performance work systems in order to improve customer service, streamline operations, and reduce cost."

The change process wasn't easy. Employees had been ingrained with the traditional knowledge work practices that are common even in a well-managed company like Corning. At the time of the change, the average length of previous service for employees in the new division was sixteen years. Says Condella, "First, we had people saying, 'You want me to do what?!' and 'Tell me again what this high-performance stuff is all about.'" Corning also did cross training to broaden people's perspective and skills. This brought to the surface a phenomenon that Condella calls the "key person" syndrome. Individuals with this syndrome are convinced that no one else can learn to do their jobs. They might say, "Nobody can do the job as well as I can do it" or "There's no way I could ever cross-train and learn somebody else's job." Much of this concern proved to be unjustified as knowledge workers learned about how other team members provided certain services.

When asked if the knowledge work teams have become fully self-directed, Condella says,

> "I wouldn't say that you ever arrive at an endpoint, but about a year ago we got to the point where we began the renewal phase. So, yes, we are self-directed, but we're still working to maintain and improve it. If you went back to 1990 when we started and tried to pinpoint a date when teams had full responsibility for operations and they were doing their own performance reviews and comparable actions, it was probably

around mid-1993. The process took about three and a half years before we felt we were far enough along to say we had a self-directed team environment. They absolutely assign the work themselves now. They have responsibility for their particular operation. They build a skills matrix and use that to assign work as individuals come up to speed. They work out vacations, days off, sick leave, etc., themselves. They handle discipline themselves. If there is an issue on a team that the team is having a problem with—a particular team member, for example—we have an HR person go in and work with the team and facilitate a process to deal with it. The team then takes it from there. On the rewards side, we have what we call a goal-sharing plan. Each team has specific goals—new ideas, cost goals, process goals—and we track these goals on a monthly basis. At year's end we pay out a percentage of the team members' base salary based on how they achieved these goals. The amount ranges from 0 to 10 percent, with a goal amount of 5 percent."

The results of this effort have clearly been very positive, says Condella.

"Our initial goal was to save $2 million in costs over a five-year time frame, and we actually ended up saving in excess of $3 million. There are also a number of other things that we measure. For example, all of the teams have what we call process efficiency and customer satisfaction goals. In our medical claims area, we had a turnaround time of sixteen days, and the team established a goal of ten days. That then became a measurement. The team then established goals for error rates. All of the teams have established performance goals that they are measured against, and they have met those."

Many of the goals, confides Condella, were more aggressive than the managers of the previous operation would have ever thought possible.

"What they do really well is provide a level of customer service that most businesses aren't accustomed to. Additionally, because of cross training, whoever picks up the phone can help that customer. This makes the customers feel like we are more responsive than an operation that has to shuffle them around to a variety of people to get their questions answered. There is also excellent communication across teams; they run their particular business units far better than they could ever have been run in the old environment."

It isn't easy. Continues Condella, "Team members need to stay current in the service they provide by attending the appropriate seminars or reading the appropriate materials. They also need to know what the company's goals are and drive hard to achieve them."

Knowledge Work Teams

As this short case study illustrates, effective knowledge work teams can have many of the characteristics of teams mentioned in Chapter 3. Like other teams, they require a shared understanding of their purpose and are based on the commitment paradigm. They can vary on the empowerment continuum from low empowerment to the highly empowered teams at the Corning Administrative Center. The Administrative Center, in particular, uses all four types of teams mentioned earlier: natural work teams, cross-functional teams, small-project teams, and special-purpose teams. It is a nonauthoritarian operation where the teams operate as SDWTs. Team members are multiskilled and able to perform a variety of tasks. There have been clear benefits in improved organizational results. These are all common elements of team-based organizations.

But not all knowledge teams can apply the traditional characteristics of SDWTs as nicely as the Administrative Center. In our experience, knowledge teams have few problems assuming the responsibilities for self-direction. Many knowledge teams do much of that already, since their managers seldom have deep enough or current enough technical knowledge to direct their tasks. But there seem to be other differences in applying traditional team practices.

Common Characteristics of Knowledge Teams

Consider a few vignettes to illustrate how knowledge teams require some unique alterations from the way many companies have used the team concept before. In the Montana Power Company, for example, there is a group of about thirty people who, among other things, write software and provide applications support for the financial systems (such as accounts payable and accounts receivable) and human resource systems (such as payroll) for the utility's gas, electric, and telephone companies. Even though they are on an "applications team" with other software experts, their primary work is done with internal clients or with other technical experts in database management, networking, or technical writing. Said one knowledge worker, "Even though we report to the applications director and work on the applications team, 90 percent of our work time is spent with people who aren't in applications." Their real natural work team changes from project to project, regardless of what the formal structure implies is the team. This creates a team where the membership is fluid and the workers have very diverse skills.

The 777 team example highlighted in Chapter 3 also required a fluid team. The Boeing team included people from a plethora of different specialties from both inside the company (engineering, maintenance, management, and manufacturing people) and outside the company (the FAA and United). Some of these people were full-time team members, and some of them worked as part-time team members. When the team had accomplished its task, it was dissolved and members went on to other tasks. Similarly, a Hewlett-Packard professional services team now may include HP salespeople, HP engineers, contract software developers, consultants on leading-edge technologies, and representatives from other companies whose hardware or software products are included in the customer's system. These teams often are temporary.

As an extreme additional example of this phenomenon of short-duration knowledge teams, there are flight attendant teams at South African Airlines (SAA) that may only last for the duration of a single two-hour flight. As an SAA flight attendant explained, "We often don't even know the other attendants when we show up for a flight. Within the time required to complete the flight, we have to get to know each other, coordinate assignments, and provide service to the passengers. It can be tough to operate like a team when you're only with the other attendants for two hours."

Five Key Differences Between Knowledge and Physical Teams

Knowledge teams typically differ from physical work teams in five significant ways:

1. By definition, of course, the primary work has a larger component of mental labor than physical labor.
2. As a result of the complexity of their work, the teams are frequently composed of multiple specialists rather than multiple skilled generalists.
3. Team representatives are often from several different organizations, sometimes even different companies.
4. The composition of the team may change from time to time depending on the task at hand.
5. Many of these teams never deal with the same job twice, unlike physical work teams, which may have ongoing responsibilities for repetitious processes (see Figure 4-1).

In Chapter 7 we discuss a number of these characteristics and suggest how companies such as Hewlett-Packard deal with the special challenges they present. But in this chapter we would like to focus special attention on the second point, the specialist versus generalist issue. This is an important characteristic differentiating physical work teams and knowledge work teams. It

Figure 4-1. Comparing "typical" physical work teams with knowledge work teams.

Typical Physical Work Teams	Typical Knowledge Work Teams
• Physical labor	• Mental labor
• Multiple generalists	• Multiple specialists
• Inside single organization	• Across multiple organizations
• Fairly stable membership	• Shifting membership
• Repetitive responsibilities	• Single-purpose responsibilities

affects the ability of a team to do multiskilling (the practice of learning multiple skills). This practice often requires a significant adaptation if a knowledge team is going to be successful.

Multiskilling

The typical SDWT member in a production organization is a multiskilled generalist who has mastered several distinct work skills. A specialist in a manufacturing plant, for example, may be able to operate only one machine, whereas a multiskilled team member in the same plant can operate several. Or, a specialist in the plant may be competent only in chemical analysis, whereas a multiskilled generalist may be able to perform not only analysis but procurement, chemical mixing, boilerhouse operation, and rudimentary maintenance, as is the case in the Lima, Ohio, P&G Downy process team. In this facility, a technician is not "fully qualified" until she or he has mastered all five of these skills, which normally requires a two-year rotation in each of these job skill areas. Thus, over a ten-year career, technicians become fully multiskilled. This enables them to perform any of the five jobs with sufficient proficiency.

In some Cummins Engine plants, for another example, a team member on a diesel engine assembly line knows and performs multiple jobs (component insertion, selected machine maintenance, torque testing, and so forth) that would normally be separated into department or job groupings in a traditional plant that did not use the team concept. These kinds of work systems are often supported by pay-for-skill programs that compensate team members for the number of skills they master, as seen in companies like P&G, Cummins Engine, Weyerhaeuser, General Mills, Corning, and a host of others.

Multiskilling has obvious advantages for the physical portion of manufacturing work. When people can perform multiple jobs, the work team has increased flexibility and responsiveness. It is easier to cover during vacations or illnesses, and to free up team members for immediate assignment changes. Multiskilling virtually eliminates the problems that can occur between jobs. As the Native American axiom that you should hold off on judging others before you "walk a mile in their moccasins" suggests, you see fewer problems that are caused by "the other shift," "the other guy," or "the other function" when people understand and rotate through these assignments. Problem solving is facilitated when people have a better grasp of the big picture. Coordination of multiple tasks improves as people better understand how the jobs interface with one another and how certain activities can unintentionally cause problems for someone further down the value chain.

Multiskilling in Knowledge Teams

Multiskilling can also be helpful for the knowledge portion of work. Many factories, like those mentioned above, have found that as jobs have come to involve higher percentages of knowledge work, their multiskill work designs have continued to be useful as a way to develop flexibility and break down what might otherwise become rigid functional stovepipe perspectives. In P&G, when the Downy team was commissioned to solve special problems or to manage complex projects (assignments that are more knowledge work than physical work), the multiskilling gave team members a broader knowledge of the whole operation and a type of empathy for all the jobs that was helpful in completing the knowledge tasks. There were no "we/they" distinctions or "that's not my job" problems. Responsibility gaps and overlapping jurisdiction problems, which are common in functional stovepipe organizations, virtually disappeared because of multiskilling.

We also saw in the Corning example that multiskilling provided some advantages from the customers' perspective. Customers could talk to anyone about their problems rather than having to be referred to this specialist on this question and that specialist on that question—a convenience appreciated by customers conditioned to being put on hold to wait for the answers to their questions. Similarly, Procter & Gamble has found that the stores that are their customers are vastly more interested in dealing with one multiskilled salesperson who can coordinate orders and shipments from all P&G brands than they were in the previous approach where the major brands (called the seven dwarfs by retail grocery chains) each had its own representatives. Prior to 1996, each of these sales reps often had his or her own policies and approaches, and shipments and orders could not be coordinated.[2] The Life Flight Network team also found that having nurses and paramedics learn and become proficient in certain aspects of flight safety was beneficial to the team because the safety of crew and patient became a shared responsibility.

But multiskilling can have diminishing returns in many other knowledge work situations. Sometimes these drawbacks occur in different situations in these same companies. Should P&G sales team members also become multiskilled in marketing and advertisement writing? Having LFN nurses master helicopter flight as well as retaining their medical expertise may be impractical—perhaps even dangerous. In one Hewlett-Packard facility, engineers informed us that if their development teams became fully multiskilled like the teams they saw on the manufacturing floor, there would be more problems than benefits. "The half-life of a software engineer in this specialty," one team member told us, "is now about eight months." That means that half of what the engineer knows will be obsolete in eight months. "If we rotated out of software development for long enough to be proficient in hardware design, we would be virtually worthless to the company when we returned to our specialty." The same is true in many areas of medicine, law, and technology.

Multiskilling, in the way it has traditionally been used for physical work, can be tantamount to de-skilling for certain knowledge workers who must stay actively engaged in their specialties just to keep up with their rapidly evolving fields. Some organizations have found this even in factories, when attempts to have all skilled trades and maintenance people engage in full multiskilling activities gave the organization increased flexibility at the cost of important specialized knowledge. When electricians became pipe fitters became welders became operators became electronics repairers, something had to give. Team members in one forest products plant located in North Carolina describe what they call the "multiskillmania," the belief that everybody should be able to do everything—an unrealistic expectation that was modified into a more selective multiskilling approach. In other operations in Cummins Engine, Rohm & Haas, and other plants with increasingly complex manufacturing technology, people are finding that certain operations within the factory don't fit well with the total multiskilling concept that has been so successful in many team approaches elsewhere before the evolution to knowledge work.

Interestingly, as the P&G Lima Downy physical work team took on more knowledge work assignments, the team composition and assignments also changed appropriately. When we worked on a new product formulation, for example, our work team expanded temporarily to include product development engineers from corporate headquarters in Cincinnati. For the duration of the project, these Ph.D. chemical specialists worked with representatives of our natural work team as a special-purpose knowledge work team with the mission of bringing the new formula online. But the chemists never became multiskilled in plant operations, nor did the technicians (as we called manufacturing team members) become multiskilled in advanced chemical engineering. Similarly, when a new packing technology was developed in another part of the plant, technicians joined with corporate resources and vendor representatives from a company in France to create a special-purpose knowledge work team that was later disbanded when the mission was accomplished. This team displayed the typical attributes of knowledge teams, including the lack of full traditional multiskilling.

A Different Kind of Multiskilling

Perhaps a more accurate way to discuss this dilemma is to describe it not as an absence of multiskilling in knowledge work applications, but as a different emphasis. To be fair, we need to mention that knowledge teams often do a certain amount of traditional multiskilling, as illustrated by some of the examples we have already discussed. But it is often more limited. There are three significant differences in the way this practice is used in many knowledge work teams. These differences are described in Figure 4-2. First, a knowledge team tends to be multiskilled as a team rather than being a collection of multiskilled individuals in the traditional sense. Second, the multiple skills that individual knowledge workers emphasize tend to be what we call vertical skills, which are more oriented toward business than technical skill. And third, integration between specialists on the team is a key focus area. We will consider each of these points in more detail.

Team Multiskilling

Multiskilling for each individual (in the way the practice has traditionally been used) tends to be less important for knowl-

Figure 4-2. Comparing multiskilling in physical work teams and knowledge work teams.

	Physical Team	Knowledge Team
Primary multiskill target	Individual	Team
Individual skill emphasis	Vertical and horizontal skills	Mostly vertical skills
Job design	Generalist	Integrated specialist

edge teams than putting together the right team of people who collectively have multiple skills.

Horizontal (Technical) vs. Vertical (Business) Multiskilling

Traditionally multiskilling has emphasized learning multiple jobs at the peer level. This is what we call horizontal multi-skilling. The emphasis in this approach is to become proficient in many, if not all, of the jobs performed by team members, as in the P&G examples. These team members are multiskilled technically. Vertical multiskilling involves learning leadership and business skills that have normally been reserved for managers or other staff professionals outside of a particular technical discipline.

It is becoming common practice in many knowledge teams to involve team members in hiring, giving feedback on performance appraisals, project staffing, interacting with customers and vendors, and other vertical tasks. Design engineers, for example, may learn how to assess customer needs and visit customers directly instead of just receiving reports from marketing. Team members may take on the responsibility of monitoring their own finances, rather than having that done by accounting or management. Participation in goal-setting, decision-making, and problem-solving activities previously reserved for management involves vertical multiskilling. When team members learn and apply these kinds of management and business skills, they are becoming multiskilled in a different way. They develop multiple business skills rather than multiple technical skills. They may or may not use horizontal multiskilling.

To be sure, even if they don't require horizontal competency, knowledge teams often insist that team members learn about several other technical skills represented on the team, while retaining deep proficiency in their own. Software engineers and hardware engineers often learn enough about each other's disciplines, for example, to ensure that the software and hardware work is compatible. The coauthor of the quote that opened and named this chapter, MIT professor Janice Klein, refers to this as being a "Jack of all trades, master of one."[3] When Port of Seattle team members are familiar with basic contract, labor, and environmental law, that helps them avoid costly mistakes later on. But they don't have to be able to pass the bar exam. When they understand how the financial reports are developed, they know better how to spot opportunities for cost savings. But they don't have to become C.P.A.s. When they are familiar with the progress of other projects in the line of business they support, they can coordinate with other engineers to meet schedules and save time, effort, and rework. But they don't have to be able to step in and perform every design specialty in civil engineering. For additional illustrations of vertical and horizontal multiskilling, see Figure 4-3.

Generalists vs. Specialists

Effective knowledge teams focus heavily on integrating specialists into the team in such a way that they feel responsible for the whole project and completely understand how their work affects everyone else on the team. This is necessary if the team is to operate as a team instead of as a group of isolated specialists. Think of the specialists as the bricks in a wall. The individual bricks are strong, but not as strong as they can be together. The integration activities are the mortar that holds them together and gives the wall strength. Integration is the minimum require-

Figure 4-3. Comparisons between vertical and horizontal multiskilling.

Vertical Multiskilling	Horizontal Multiskilling
• Focus on leadership (up) skills	• Focus on lateral (sideways) skills
• Emphasizes business skills	• Emphasizes technical skills
• Frequent communication about jobs	• Frequent rotation of jobs
• Learn about many peer jobs	• Learn to perform peer jobs
• Cross-train in some peer skills	• Cross-train in peer skills

ment for creating the distributed mind. Regular cross training and team communication meetings help to do this. It usually also requires special team start-up and maintenance activities, which will be detailed in Chapter 11.

The following examples will further illustrate the multiskilling issue in knowledge work teams.

NBTel Service Teams

NBTel is the seventh largest telecommunications company in Canada. It has a workforce of about 2,378 with 616 management professionals and supervisory staff. The company has approximately 776 union technical staff and 936 support staff and has been known over the years as being very progressive technologically. The first telecom company in North America to become 100 percent digital, NBTel provides customers with access to the latest services and features. Nancy Tyler, internal consultant, explains that historically the company was very functionally oriented. But with the development of interdependent knowledge work teams, this has started to change: "In the service department one team with twenty-four members now has one team leader." Before we went to the team structure, those twenty-four members would have served under eight different functional leaders. So, you can see, we were a pretty functionally divided company."

That began to change some time ago. "Starting in the late 1980s and early 1990s," she recalls, "we began some quality initiatives, but we never got the anticipated payback. Larry Travis, a middle manager at the time who had some socio-technical experience, began to experiment with the supplies department, with some very powerful results."

Socio-technical systems (STS) was the name given to the process of creating self-directed-team-based operations by Eric Trist and his colleagues at the Tavistock Institute in the United Kingdom. The STS approach has had a remarkable track record in improving business results in a variety of industries for more than four decades. NBTel Supplies was no different. When the

Supplies effort proved successful, Travis began to apply the same approach to the service teams he now led. Although the process hasn't been completed—there is still some process redesign work the teams want to do—early indicators are positive, Tyler notes.

> "The eight teams that we have up and operating right now are getting very impressive results. For instance, after less than a year, one team's revenues are up 20 percent compared to 10 percent with the rest of the region. Long-distance sales plans are up 65 percent over the rest of the regions. Troubles are down over 30 percent, and repeat customer trouble is down over 40 percent. Inventory has been cut in half, and overtime has decreased by 30 percent. And along with these hard numbers, employee morale is greatly improved and the training has more than tripled.
>
> "We haven't really done any process improvement yet. Most of the results we're realizing come from the increase in social contact. Team members get together and talk about their problems and talk about shared goals. Now if we can integrate the improved communication with appropriate process flows, I can see these teams growing by leaps and bounds."

However, employees who designed the service teams decided to modify a practice that is common in STS physical work design. Instead of making everybody a generalist and no one a specialist, they found that a certain level of specialization was required to perform their knowledge work properly. The teams do have far fewer functional distinctions and significantly more cross training than before. This eliminates many of the "we/they" problems. But a complete elimination of these distinctions was deemed impractical.

Says Tyler,

> "The design teams have taken the process flow between specialized groups and looked at where problems occur. For example, after engineers develop a

product, it is given to the installers to put in place with the customers. We've found that there is often miscommunication during this 'hand-off,' so we want to have the installers work on the same team with the engineers. Now it's true that the installers may not learn everything the engineers know, but they can learn those crucial *portions* so that a smooth flow occurs with no lapse in communication. There will always be specialists in our organization, but bits and pieces of everyone's knowledge can be shared and learned."

Other knowledge teams have had similar experiences. Let's discuss one of them in sufficient detail to reinforce more of the unique characteristics of knowledge teams.

The Strategic Alignment Services Team Case Study

Stu Winby is the leader of an elite team of consultants that work quietly inside Hewlett-Packard (HP). A lanky blond, Winby appears to be the perfect mix of Texas cowboy and California surfer. He is witty, charming, and bone-practical about his team. It has a critical mission. The group of well-educated experts is in high demand. They don't build computers, they don't service printers, and they don't qualify parts vendors. They help HP organizations around the globe transform themselves into faster, more effective, and more flexible operations. Their product is knowledge—special knowledge about how people and organizations work most effectively. Their consulting team, composed of technical specialists in the fields of organizational design and change, systems modeling, business analysis and strategy, and action research, is one of the best in the business. The skills of each member are both distinct and necessary if the whole team is going to accomplish its mission. The team has recently been renamed Strategic Alignment Services (SAS), and if history is any indicator, it may well be reconfigured several more times

before you read this case study. Most of the following comments
will be in Winby's own words.

HP Background

Hewlett-Packard is about a $40 billion company with about
100,000 employees all around the world. It provides high-technology products and services in computing, communications,
and measurement. Product innovation, time to market, performance, lean cost structures, customer focus, and a culture that
fosters cross-boundary integration, communications, and teamwork drive the operations. More than 65 percent of HP's revenues come from products developed in the last two years. Thus,
the R&D and product generation segments of HP are essential.
"That's the heart and soul of the company," notes Winby.
"Growth continues to migrate to service and value-added areas.
HP has always been a company that views people, technology,
and business as integrated and mutually reinforcing sources of
its success. There have been a few periods where employee reductions were used in order to maintain profitability, but that's
not generally done. The company is generally seen as being both
employee- and business-oriented."

SAS Operations

Winby's style promotes self-directed work teams.

> "The management style is high involvement. People
> need to participate and get involved. All of our proc-
> esses, including overall strategy and individual respon-
> sibility and assignments, are done participatively, so
> there is an environment where people have a lot of
> ownership, commitment, and knowledge of how
> things work. A good example is our hiring process. We
> don't have a traditional hiring process. When we have
> a need to hire, we identify the requirements and talk to
> the appropriate people. When we narrow in on some-
> one, we invite that person to an off-site and get to know
> them. It's easy enough to see if the person has the nec-

essary skills, but the most important fit is the values of the individual."

Most of the work done in SAS is project work where there are discrete outcomes and activities. Projects range from individual consulting engagements to large projects that include members from multiple areas. SAS is funded by HP clients. Fees are approved by customers, and projects are subject to internal and external competition.

Winby explains the operation of SAS:

> "There is a portfolio of projects that we work on, a percentage of which we call action research projects. They're projects that require new knowledge. We refer to these as R&D projects. The remaining projects are core projects—things we've done before. We continue to work on these, because they have high change value to the company.
>
> "Projects are initiated with MOU (memo of understanding), which is similar to a project proposal but more like a joint project plan. The MOU defines the project goals and objectives, measures of success, economic justification such as an estimated ROI or value, schedule, technical risks, etc. The project is managed against the MOU and then at completion evaluated for learnings and for value to the customer. A roll-up of project performance can provide an estimate of the value SAS is providing to the company."

The Evolution of SAS Work

Notes Winby, "When I first joined HP in 1989, we focused on a few key projects that would have an action research flavor to them. That is, we focused on results, creating new knowledge, and learning. The basic principle was to jointly invent new organizational and management solutions with the customer and for the customer, consider these prototypes, and then diffuse these new knowledge-based prototypes throughout the company. We started a diffusion process called the 'Work Innovation Network'

(WIN), which would provide real practical case examples. The HP businesses would present reviews of projects including all of 'the good, the bad, and the ugly' to ensure the accuracy of the learning diffusion. We were just as interested in failures as raving successes. Frequently, second generation projects would start as a result of listening to first generation projects during WIN."

The WIN conferences have been created to share best practices across the company. Normally a two- to three-day activity, a conference includes an invited outside keynote speaker and several presentations from HP businesses. Business representatives, not consultants, make the presentations and answer questions from network participants. People then gather in what HP calls "neighborhoods"—smaller groups of people who are interested in special topics—to discuss selected issues in more detail.

WIN has evolved into a network of specific special interest groups such as a SAP implementation group or a Customer WIN group. Innovations spread on the basis of who is interested in participating in these groups and applying their learnings back home. Those that are of value spread rapidly. Says Winby, "HP businesses pull the knowledge and technologies they want and adapt these new business processes to their own unique circumstances, thus creating new innovations—worthy of sharing during a future WIN session. Soon many innovations gain a life of their own. Instead of a centralized company program, the notion of WIN is to spread innovation in a distributed way through the line organization."

Team Challenges

Winby notes that one of the primary challenges of the SAS team is effective communication. The consultants work all over the world and are seldom in the office. Although consultants will work with others in their practice area team, they also complete a number of assignments alone with the client. How do they keep up with what is happening in their practice area and elsewhere in SAS? How do they develop relationships that will foster the trust and commitment they need in order to work effectively with their SAS teammates? Winby answers:

"There are a few mechanisms that enhance communication and relationships. The first mechanism is the quarterly off-site. We meet for three days and do project review, business development, and team development. We look at the financials, the quality of our projects, and customer satisfaction. We also look at areas that we are learning about and might bring in a colleague for a day to chat with. If we're looking at network organizations, for example, we might ask an outside expert to join us and chat with us about that concept.

"During that time there is a lot of integration. It's a really participative design where people are responsible for sections of the off-site around a specific objective on different days."

Consultants review one another's projects and participate in the development and selection of new projects.

"People need to be satisfied with the work that they are doing. The off-sites help a lot, because there is a lot of work, play, and integration.

"The second area of communication is voice mail. People talk to each other twenty-four hours a day through voice mail, a lot of work gets done that way. To further promote communication, we try to double up on projects whenever possible. There are teams within the group that get together regularly to share ideas."

Summary

From this rich HP study we learn much about effective knowledge teams. We will return to it several times to reinforce what we have learned about information distribution, virtual teams, and other topics. But it helps to illustrate several key points of this chapter. Most knowledge teams, like the Strategic Alliance Service consulting team, do not use multiskilling in the traditional sense of everybody rotating through everybody else's job. Rather than generalists, they use specialists who are highly integrated into a team that has multiple skills represented on it. Like the NBTel example and the vignettes from the Port of Seattle and other knowledge teams in Cummins Engine and Procter & Gamble further illustrate, these teams often use vertical rather than horizontal multiskilling, emphasizing business rather than technical skill diversity.

These different approaches to the common team-based approaches are necessary to knowledge teams because of the five ways in which they differ from physical work teams. In Chapter 5 we discuss the paradigms and metaphors needed to create successful knowledge teams.

Notes

1. Janice A. Klein and Patrick M. Maurer, "Integrators, Not Generalists, Needed: A Case Study of Integrated Product Development Teams," in *Advances in Interdisciplinary Studies of Work Teams*, vol. 2, *Knowledge Work in Teams*, ed. Michael M. Beyerlein, Douglas A. Johnson, and Susan T. Beyerlein (Greenwich, Conn.: JAI Press, Inc., 1995), 94.
2. Raju Narisetti, "P&G Overhauls Its Marketing Tactics," *The Wall Street Journal*, January 15, 1997, p.1.
3. Klein and Maurer, "Integrators, Not Generalists, Needed."

5

The Learning Lattice: Evolving Organizational Forms for Knowledge Work

"The reality is that professionals and specialists must work together to be effective. Marketing professionals and specialists themselves cannot deliver a valued product to customers; informational specialists cannot use their programs to create cost reports; training personnel cannot make managers skilled. Specialists who try to do it all are not specialists. They must apply their specific skills in conjunction with other professionals and employees. They can only be successful together."[1]

—Dean Tjosvold and Mary M. Tjosvold,
Researchers and Authors

Mark Reis was the team leader for the Port of Seattle Capital Management System (CMS) redesign team for the one-and-one-half-year process that began in 1995. Educated at Harvard's Kennedy School, Reis found the leadership of the team to be one of the more challenging assignments of his career. He and his team were charged by Mic Dinsmore, the Port's executive director, to reengineer the way major capital projects were done so that the Port could be more responsive to the taxpayers and communities who fund its efforts. These projects range from small improvements in the airport parking structure to huge additions to the seaport or airport that can cost hundreds of millions of dollars.

The redesign team was a special-purpose knowledge team composed of representatives of the functional departments that work on capital projects, including project managers, civil engineers, finance people, human resources specialists, communications and organizational development representatives, accounting and systems people, and a host of temporary resources. Their goal was to find a way to increase capacity by 20 percent without increasing cost. The team used both an internal Port consultant named J. Loux and external consultants to help with the effort.

The capital management team began its assignment with a systematic and thorough review of the existing CMS process. As a result of this analysis, the team discovered that the only way to achieve the major improvements required by the steering committee that commissioned it was through a fundamental culture transformation. This required a shift from functional to business thinking. It required numerous changes, not the least of which was a new knowledge work organization that moved the Port away from the traditional functional silo design, in which, for example, all the engineers and project managers were located in and reported to a centralized engineering department (see Figure 5-1) with multiple levels of hierarchy.

These silos had unintentionally caused some bottlenecks and inefficiencies in project flow. Reviews by function leaders, for example, often slowed project progress because team members had to use valuable project time to prepare for and follow up on these activities. Sometimes elements of the projects had to be changed in midstream when functional managers who were separated from the day-to-day reality of the operations made unrealistic commitments relating to project time or expense. Costly rework after project completion to rectify these fit or scoping problems was not uncommon. Overall coordination

Figure 5-1. The Port of Seattle design prior to redesign.

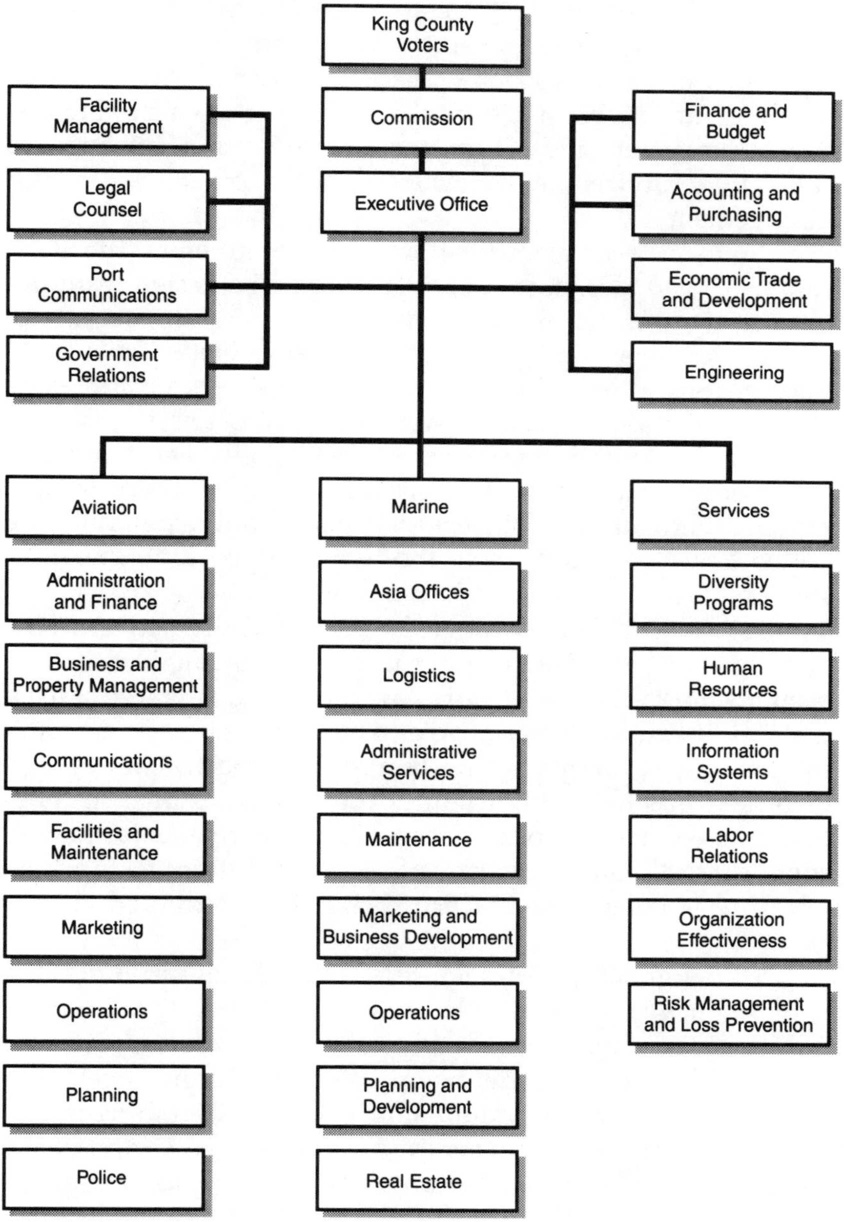

and, perhaps more importantly, a feeling of personal responsibility for the projects had mostly been limited to very senior managers. Senior management was the only place where all functional perspectives came together, requiring their personal involvement in most decisions. This often resulted in potential cost improvement ideas from the people working on projects being underutilized or overlooked, and it overloaded senior management.

Problems with coordination between different functions and levels had also slowed project efforts. The design team uncovered the fact, for example, that the payment of external design consultants required about twenty-five steps, when only three or four were really necessary. The businesses complained that the centralized services were sometimes unresponsive to their requests and didn't prioritize projects in the way that made the most financial or operational sense. The matrix type organization, where knowledge workers report to a function but have dotted-line responsibilities to those they support, wasn't sufficient to fully integrate them into the businesses.

But the CMS team struggled with viable alternatives to the existing structure. The functional silo design might not have been the most effective way to allow projects to flow through the Port, but it had a number of advantages, including good technical quality control on each portion of the project, skill development and coaching opportunities for each functional member within his or her area of expertise, clear career paths for knowledge workers, and consistency of approach within the function, which resulted in best practices being spread throughout the Port.

After a great deal of deliberation, the design team decided to build on what the Port called a line of business (LOB) orientation, a concept that had already been discussed and received support. The primary orientation of the project managers and engineers, particularly, would shift from function to LOB allegiance. The redesign team believed that this would improve the efficiency and effectiveness of projects. The team also thought it would enable the culture shift toward customer- and business-focused projects rather than projects focused primarily on technical elegance.

To fully implement the LOB concept, the divisions organized resources and leadership responsibilities around specific lines of business. The Marine and Aviation divisions each identified a few specific LOBs, such as the airport parking business or the marine container business, that would focus knowledge workers on specific projects that would help a small stand-alone business enterprise. Project managers (PMs) were transferred from centralized functions and organized into a Marine PM team and an Aviation PM team. These new PM teams selected their own team leader from among their peers and included some people from the old services organization who had not previously been eligible for PM positions, which had been reserved for engineers. Project managers were selected from this service team by the LOBs rather than being assigned and managed by the PM team leaders. The team leaders became career coaches, communicators, counselors, and marketers of the team. Their responsibilities were developmental rather than hierarchical. They developed both the new practice and the people, acting more like a managing partner than a boss.

The remaining centralized functions became leaner, with some of the knowledge workers moving into the project management groups and others taking LOB assignments. (See Figure 5-2.) All projects were to be driven and coordinated by the LOBs and their business needs instead of being driven by functions. Importantly, the primary responsibility of the remaining service teams would be coaching and skill development for their members when they are between projects.

With these changes, the CMS team had designed a *learning lattice* organization, an increasingly common form of work design specially adapted for knowledge work. In this chapter we will further explore the process of knowledge work design and illustrate other characteristics of this evolving organizational form.

Redesigning Knowledge Work

Many companies have found that changes from the traditional knowledge work organizational structures are necessary to un-

Figure 5-2. The redesigned Port of Seattle knowledge teams.

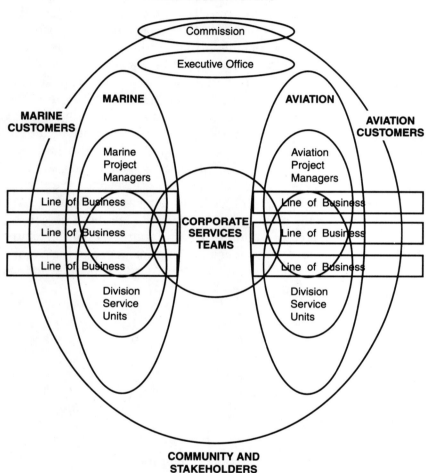

KING COUNTY VOTERS

Commission

Executive Office

MARINE

AVIATION

**MARINE
CUSTOMERS**

**AVIATION
CUSTOMERS**

Marine
Project
Managers

Aviation
Project
Managers

Line of Business

Line of Business

**CORPORATE
SERVICES
TEAMS**

Line of Business

Line of Business

Line of Business

Line of Business

Division
Service
Units

Division
Service
Units

**COMMUNITY AND
STAKEHOLDERS**

leash the full potential of the knowledge workers in their operations. Says DuPont's Terry Ennis: "Our goal is to get everyone
focused on the business as a system in which the functions are
seamless."[2] DuPont has been trying to eliminate what Ennis
calls the "disconnects" and "handoffs" between functions and
departments. Why? Poor transfer of knowledge between departments causes cost overrides, time slippage, and quality prob-

lems. Engineering does what is right from its perspective, but this may cause unforeseen manufacturing costs. Sales may locate customers with expectations that can't be satisfied with workable technology. Purchasing may make deals on supplies that are cost-effective but nonfunctional. It happens all the time in corporations all around the globe.

Numerous companies are leaving the traditional functional silo approach to organizing knowledge work in favor of more cross-functional teams. National Semiconductor, Xerox, HP, Canon, Apple Computer, and Tektronix use these teams to reduce product development time. In an IBM selling center, salespeople, product developers, and IBM vendors work together to put on demonstrations at manufacturing sites for "complete customer solutions."[3] These teams are also ideal for working with homebound and mentally ill patients.[4] Motorola, Dime Savings Bank of New York, Chrysler, and others use them for process improvements.

Consider an example. In 1988, AT&T began developing a new cordless phone. John Hanley, AT&T's vice president of product development, wanted to cut 50 percent off development time. This was impossible without major changes to the traditional functional, bureaucratic approach. A functional silo approach increased the time and cost required to create new products. Engineers would pass the design to manufacturing to build, manufacturing would pass the product to sales to sell, and so forth. An article written about the change process notes:

Hanley revised the process by forming 6 to 12 teams that included engineers, manufacturers, and marketers. They were given the authority to make every decision about how much the product would cost, how it would work and how it would look. The key was to set rigid speed requirements before freezing design requirements. Since they did not need to send decisions up the line for approval, the team was able to meet tight deadlines. As a result of the new team approach, AT&T cut development time from two years to just one year. Also, cost was lowered and quality improved.[5]

Spectra-Physics, probably best known for its scanning devices, which have revolutionized grocery store checkout procedures and inventory management processes, had also run into some problems with product development teams in the early 1990s. An article written about the company's work to improve the process notes:

> Turf wars between R&D, marketing, and production continued to escalate unresolved issues, however. Different functional areas were measured and rewarded on different criteria (quality, volume, on-time delivery, etc.). Trust and the lack of a common focus were issues between these traditional functions.
>
> Learning from their difficulties, Spectra-Physics management launched the cross-functional Bald Eagles team of marketing, R&D, and operations as a "leaderless triad" to improve NPD's effectiveness. This team, and other "core" teams now working on NPD for specific products, are not actually leaderless, because one function will tend to dominate and then cede to another function as a product makes its way through the development-production-introduction phases. Subteams (service, marketing, communications, etc.) support the core teams' activities. . . .
>
> Despite marketing's reluctant agreement to accept the "headless horse" concept, [Bruce] Paris [marketing manager] reported that several benefits make it "absolutely the right approach": R&D, production, and others involved in cross-functional teams understand what the customer really wants; production concepts were developed concurrently with design; and team participants felt empowered to serve the customer, despite their initial "loss of power."[6]

Designing in Cross-Functionality

While many companies and hospitals use cross-functional teams only for special projects (what we call special-purpose teams), others have changed the fundamental structures of their organization to minimize if not eliminate functional silos. Writes *Business Week*'s John Byrne of these changes, "[It] goes much further than these previous efforts: It largely eliminates both hierarchy and functional or departmental boundaries."[7] For example, the benefits team at Weyerhaeuser, a large forest products company, is creating what leader Ken Wallace calls "the one organization" concept. The company's benefits team handles tens of millions of dollars of business annually, and when the 401(k) investments managed by the organization are included, their assets are sufficient to qualify them as their own *Fortune* 500 company. Like other corporate staff groups in most large organizations, they had originally been organized by function. There were separate departments for retirement, health plan administration, and so forth. The customers, however, wanted to make one call and get all of their benefits questions answered, rather than have to interface with several different departments.

A traditional, functionally based benefits administration group was redesigned into customer teams responsible for a wider variety of services. Since the work ebbs and flows depending on calls for services, team leaders work with team members to help them "flow to the work." "We go to where the bubble of work is," Wallace explains. Obviously any one team member cannot answer every question or solve every problem because the team members' specialized expertise runs the gamut from actuarial work to medical patient advocacy programs, but the one organization concept has helped create the integration necessary for the group to work and feel like a team. Customers like it. Team members like it, too. As part of the redesign, they were given more opportunity to influence business decisions. The new structure and leadership have been essential components of their strategy.

HP Santa Clara

Dennis McNulty, an organization development manager with the Santa Clara division of Hewlett-Packard, tells a similar story about redesigning a traditional organization. The Santa Clara division designs and produces HP test and measurement devices, such as oscilloscopes. They used what is called the socio-technical systems (STS) redesign methodology. (We will explain STS later in this chapter.) As McNulty notes,

> "The original structure was the traditional functional organization, with R&D, engineering, manufacturing, marketing, and support services. We put together a design team and used the STS process, where we did analysis and gathered data, and then the team came back with a recommendation.
>
> "The recommendation was to move to a customer segment–focused organization, which means we broke down the functional sections and structured them into customer segments. Originally, the design group recommended three customer segments, but experience showed us that two would be more appropriate. But other than this change, the design team's recommendations have been on target. I think this is because we included managers and other key individuals on the design team—those who knew the business.
>
> "Within the new customer segments, workers now report to a single business manager—a cross-functional structure reporting to that one business manager. We ended up with two self-contained business units. Within each business unit we still maintain what we call a functional manager to maintain technical excellence. So you have the business unit manager who runs the business, and then there's a functional manager who supports technical development. The functional manager develops the technical folks, making sure that the administrative needs are met (assignments, development, etc.). Essentially we have a structure with function and process intersecting, because both are important to what we're about. We need a customer focus, but we also need technical excellence.
>
> "The big issue—especially in the engineering ranks—has been the shift from a purely technical to a more customer-focused marketing perspective. A lot of the folks here have been working twenty to thirty years

in a functional approach where they just work on technical development, but this change now forces them to move into more direct interaction with the customer. It also requires more business ownership. It's beginning to shift now, but it's been really tough. A lot of people still don't have the motivation to change. The answer seems to be learning new skills—how to work with customers and be more responsive to customers. It's been more accepted (comparatively speaking) in the production services area, because they're used to working in a team environment. So we have a real mixed bag here of people who are real supportive and people who are still trying to understand their roles.

"We've done a lot of both technical and interpersonal training. The first phase was to move from a functional to a customer focus. We focused mostly on business skill development (marketing, etc.). In phase two we trained all of the managers and supervisors in the division (around 110 people) about high-performance organizations—what the team approach is, the philosophy, etc. We aimed at modifying their leadership skills. The initial training was phased in over a year. We then followed up management training with training at the team level on team skills and team development."

Redesign Methods

There are a few methods commonly employed to redesign knowledge work that deserve some attention before we discuss the learning lattice organizations that often result from these efforts. Unlike many of the reengineering efforts that have been sweeping across North American organizations over the last few years, these methods are more participative and democratic. They are not done to knowledge workers by senior management or external consultants, but rather are methods for facilitating the knowledge workers' own ideas for how the organization should be designed.

The STS Redesign Approach

The first method is called the socio-technical system (STS) approach. As mentioned in Chapter 4, STS is rooted in the early work of Eric Trist, Fred Emery, and others in the Tavistock Institute located near London. Although this method was originally developed primarily for physical work and was used in these situations at least as early as the mid 1960s, a number of different companies, including Corning, Hewlett-Packard, and Motorola, among others, have used it for knowledge work redesign as well.

The basic steps in the STS method involve a three-part analytical process in which a design team evaluates the business environment (customer requirements, competitive analysis, government and community needs, and other stakeholder analyses), the social situation (employee needs, goal clarity, constraints that prevent people from doing their best work, etc.), and the technical strengths and weaknesses (equipment, work flow, work processes, etc.) of the current organization.

The team then redesigns the organization to solve the problems and better meet the needs indentified during the analytical scans (see Figure 5-3). The team members take special care to

Figure 5-3. The STS redesign process.

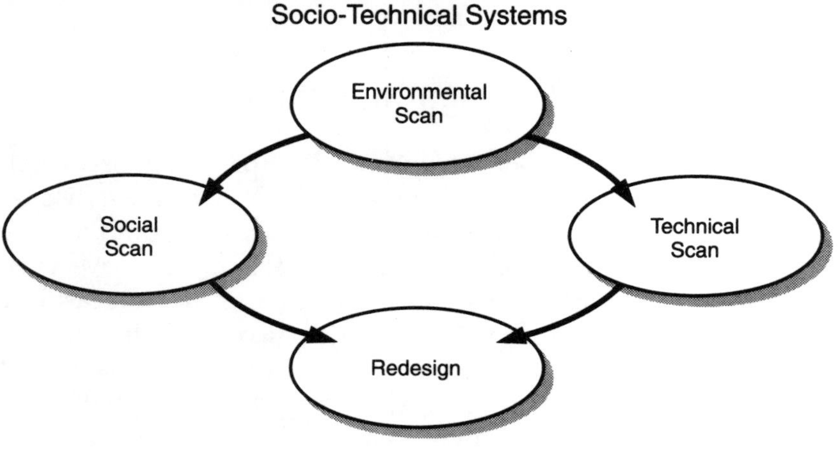

Socio-Technical Systems

jointly optimize the social and technical sides of the operation in order to keep an appropriate balance between the two critical parts of the organization design.

The primary participants in this approach include a steering committee of senior managers who are charged with commissioning the design team and providing it with the resources, support, and boundary conditions required for the redesign activity. The design team is a cross-sectional representative group of the organization to be redesigned. Generally a team of eight to ten people, it is composed of knowledge workers who will be affected by the changes (see Figure 5-4). Researchers Susan Mohrman, Allan Mohrman, and Susan Cohen have suggested a particular sequence of design activities for knowledge work: identifying work teams, specifying integration needs, clarifying management structure and roles, designing integration processes, and finally, managing performance.[8] Typically, a resource, someone who is experienced in the process, helps the steering committee and design team.

The Conference Method

The second approach to knowledge work redesign is the Conference Method, used by R.R. Donnelley and Sons, Weyerhaeuser,

Figure 5-4. The key players in the STS approach.

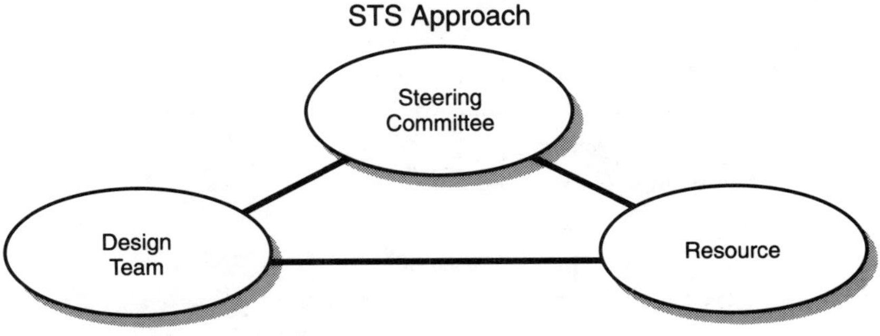

STS Approach

and numerous others. Although it uses many of the tools developed for the STS approach, the conference model was created by Dick and Emily Axelrod as a way to both involve more people and accelerate the redesign of either knowledge or physical work. There are a number of other accelerated design methodologies, including those developed by professor Bill Pasmore of Case Western University and the participative design approach developed by Fred and Merrilyn Emery. For sake of brevity, however, we will focus primarily on the Conference Method.

This method uses a series of two- to three-day conferences to complete the redesign process. The first conference is called the visioning conference. In this conference, participants create a vision for the future. The conference often includes the social scan mentioned earlier. In the second or customer conference, the environmental scan work is completed. The technical scan work is then done in the technical conference. Participants complete the redesign and implementation plan during the final two conferences (see Figure 5-5).

Accelerated approaches such as the Conference Method differ from the STS method in two significant ways. First, the number of participants is much larger. Rather than the small design team completing the redesign, at least 40 percent (we recom-

Figure 5-5. The conference method for redesign.

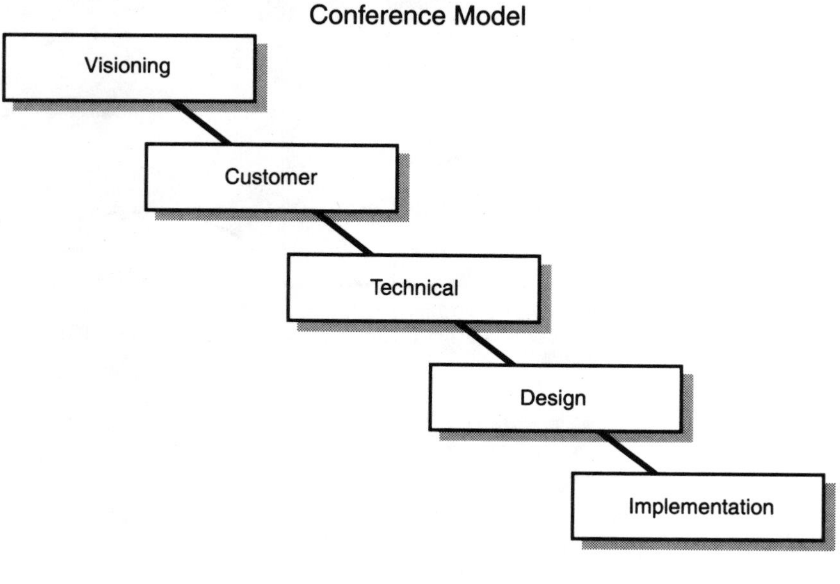

Conference Model

mend at least 60 percent) of the entire operation being redesigned participates in the conferences. (See Figure 5-6 for a summary of the key players.) Although this method does use a small support team (the Axelrods call it a logistics team) to prepare the conferences, the design itself is done in the design conference with participation by all attendees. The second way this differs from the STS method is the amount of time required to complete the redesign.

The Conference Design Team Method

The final method we would like to explore is a hybrid of the STS and the Conference Method. Developed by the authors for redesign of knowledge work, the Conference Design Team approach includes a large group of knowledge workers in the first three conferences, in the design review, and in the final implementation conference(s). But the actual design is completed by a small cross-representational design team selected by peers during the technical conference. The design team completes three design alternatives. The conference participants select one of the three alternatives during the design review. This method was developed to reduce the problems of less progressive de-

Figure 5-6. The key players in the conference method.

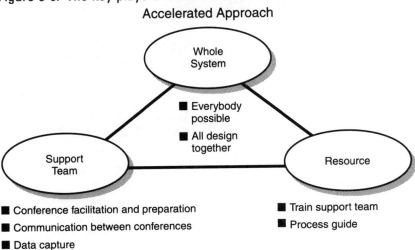

signs that can result when large groups of people try to agree on a redesign of their operation in a two- to three-day conference, without significantly diminishing broad participation in an accelerated design process. See Figure 5-7 for an illustration of this approach. Figure 5-8 reviews the characteristics of the Conference Design Team method and compares them to those of the other methods.

The Learning Lattice Organization

As a result of a redesign process, many organizations, like the Port of Seattle, have created what we call a learning lattice orga-

Figure 5-7. The conference design team approach.

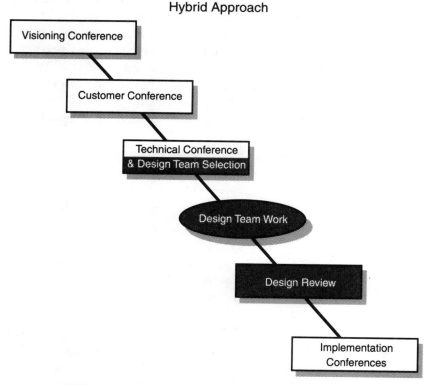

Hybrid Approach

Source: © 1996 The Fisher Group, Inc. All rights reserved. Used by permission.

Figure 5-8. The design approaches compared.

Design Comparison

STS	Accelerated	Conference Design Team
■ 6–12 months	■ 4–9 months	■ 5–10 months
■ Design team isolation	■ Egalitarian	■ Minimal design team isolation
■ Progressive design	■ Less risky design	■ Progressive design
■ Well-tested approach	■ Tested approach	■ Less tested approach

nization. Unlike the matrix-type organization that was popular for knowledge work in the 1970s and 1980s, the lattice organization doesn't have the knowledge worker reporting to multiple organizations—say, to one functional organization with a dotted-line responsibility to a division operation as well. Instead, the learning lattice organization has knowledge workers reporting to only one organization—normally a cross-functional team—for consistency of work direction. But the learning lattice organization provides a supplementary team of similar professionals who work together to communicate best practices and develop technical skills. This provides a forum for skill development and technical integration across multiple teams without diluting the sense of goal clarity that comes from being a member of a business rather than a functional team.

The learning lattice organization was pioneered by Esso Petroleum, a Canadian petrochemical giant, in its early knowledge work redesigns in the 1980s. The company was trying at the time to satisfy two important but seemingly contradictory demands: How do we meet the operational need of the business to fully incorporate highly technical people (such as specialists in geophysics) into business projects (a process that had been difficult with functional silos), but still maintain the high technical skills and communication across the company within each discipline (a process that worked well with functional designs but became difficult when technical people were transferred full time into the operational groups)? The redesigners came up with a clever way to balance these demands. (See Figure 5-9.)

Prior to the redesign, technical specialists would each report to their functions (for example, geologists would report to a geology department). Business divisions would call on the appropriate technical specialists as needed—when, for example, they were evaluating a new geography for drilling. During the redesign, however, most technical specialists were decentralized into the business teams they supported in order to increase the efficiency of project execution. This is represented by the vertical rectangles in the diagram. This made the business teams truly cross-functional teams, with all of the skills necessary to run the businesses resident on the team. In order to maintain technical expertise when their new bosses were not members of their dis-

Figure 5-9. The learning lattice organization.

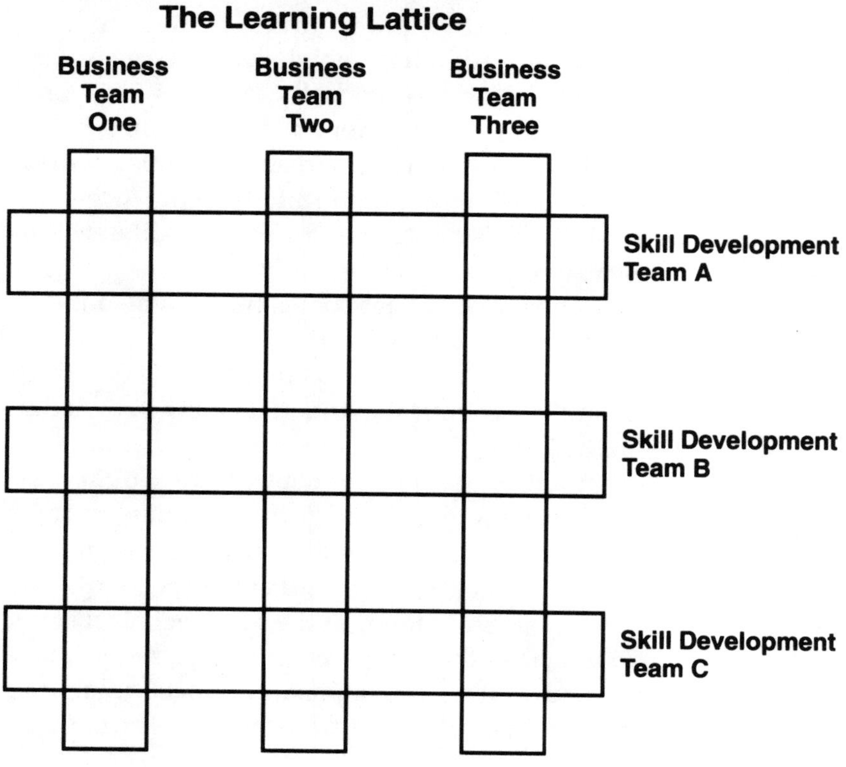

The Learning Lattice

Business Team One **Business Team Two** **Business Team Three**

Skill Development Team A

Skill Development Team B

Skill Development Team C

ciplines, share best practices, and learn about new developments in their respective fields, however, the designers came up with a simple but powerful design idea.

They created what they called Centres of Excellence, represented by the horizontal rectangles in the diagram. There would be a geological centre, for example, which allowed the geologists spread throughout the various business teams to gather together regularly to focus on learning and skill development for their discipline. These four- to eight-hour meetings every other week or so were built into the normal work schedule. Each centre team would elect one of its members to coordinate the team's activities, and this individual would be given a percentage of his or her work time to plan meetings, invite in guest speakers, coordinate technical protocols to be observed throughout the businesses, and so forth. This position was not to be a hierarchical one. No one reported to a centre manager or received assignments or performance reviews from her or him. Instead, the centres were intended to be exclusively for the skill development of the team members. When drawn on paper, these organization structures look like the lattices used for garden supports or privacy screens. Hence, the name "learning lattice."

SAS Composition and Structure

Hewlett-Packard's SAS team, introduced in Chapter 4, also uses a learning lattice. There are about thirty-five people in SAS. It is a values-driven organization that attempts to incorporate these values into the way it organizes itself. Key values are customer and solution focus, innovation, asset creation, responsiveness, teaming, flexibility, and learning. The overall structure is what they call a "network organization," where the various parts (they call them "nodes") of the operation quickly form and reform around projects. The organization structure consists of four main parts: practice areas, practice teams, customer engagement teams, and a business team. Let's consider it in some detail.

The SAS organization structure includes an interesting variation of the learning lattice. Unlike many learning lattice operations, the consultants are currently not decentralized into business groups where they would report directly to HP business management. But in this situation a full decentralization may not make a lot of sense. This small group of highly specialized consultants serves a very large customer base, and they don't provide equal service to each part of the business. They may, for example, have several large projects with one client and none with another at any given point in time. Consultants with different expertise may work on one project with a client but not on the next project with that same client. This work process requires that they structure themselves much like a consulting firm to allow for maximum flexibility and minimum expense to HP businesses that pay for what they need but are not required to maintain their own staff for these specific services.

Thus, in their lattice variant, the SAS team members have created what they call practice areas, which are similar to small stand-alone consulting business organizations. These are often dominated by specialists in one particular discipline, but can just as well contain representatives from multiple consulting disciplines. The practice areas change from time to time depending on new technology development or shifting client needs. Current practice areas include "Organizational Architecture" and "Virtual Systems—Knowledge Management Design."

The practice area is the primary work unit. This is where consultants spend the vast majority of their time. According to Winby, "These capability nodes can be mixed and matched based on the right customer solution needed. Each practice area has its own budget, customers, segments, and technology. Practice areas are involved in consulting and action research. Primary research frequently involves university partnerships with faculty members of universities, such as Stanford and USC, who are long-term members of the SAS organization." Practice areas have their own goals and return-on-investment targets. See Figure 5-10 for a graphic display of the learning lattice component of the SAS structure.

Practice teams are the functional units of SAS. They include Strategic Planning and Modeling, Change Management, Systems Analysis and Value Modeling, Commodity Analysis and

Figure 5-10. The learning lattice component of Hewlett-Packard's SAS team.

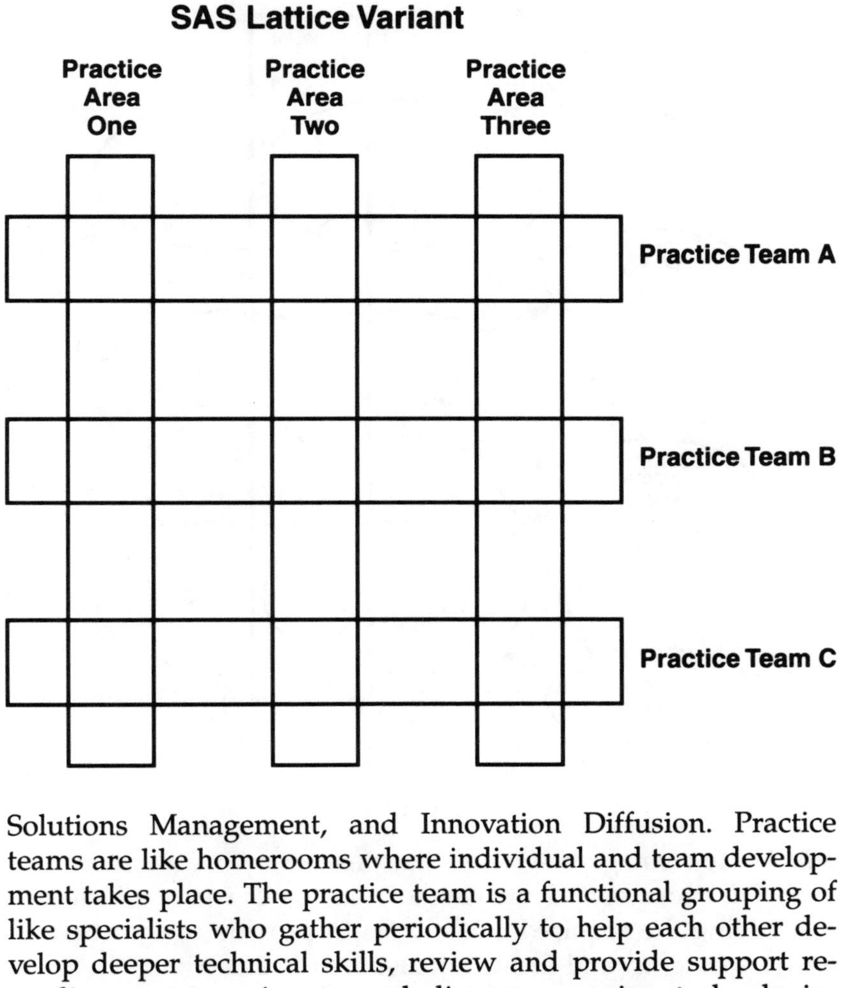

SAS Lattice Variant

Practice Area One **Practice Area Two** **Practice Area Three**

Practice Team A

Practice Team B

Practice Team C

Solutions Management, and Innovation Diffusion. Practice teams are like homerooms where individual and team development takes place. The practice team is a functional grouping of like specialists who gather periodically to help each other develop deeper technical skills, review and provide support regarding customer issues, and discuss emerging technologies and trends. At this point in time consultants still report to their practice team leader because they may serve on so many practice areas at the same time. See Figure 5-11 for a graphic display of the components of the SAS team structure.

Customer engagement teams are combinations of practice areas assembled to work on customer projects. They are put together by SAS employees called customer engagement manag-

Figure 5-11. The SAS team structure.

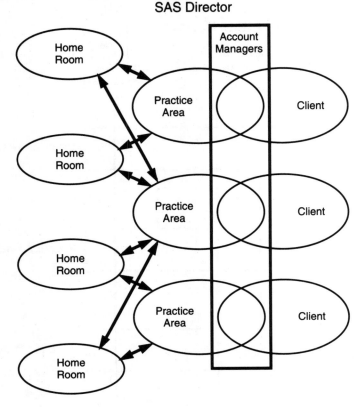

ers. These managers serve as liaisons between customers and SAS. They focus on identifying key customer issues and needs, assembling the required consultants to provide integrated customer solutions, and ensuring customer satisfaction. "In situations where customer needs are vague or a specific application or technology does not exist, action research methodologies are applied and new knowledge assets are created," says Winby.

The SAS business team includes the leaders of the functional practice teams and four additional consultants. They serve as the leadership team. They are responsible for strategy, overall operations, and management of the organization culture. Notes Winby, "The primary goal of the business team is to insure the proper environment exists for minimal bureaucracy, lots of autonomy, clear accountability, customer focus, and ample opportunity for personal and professional growth."

Summary

The Hewlett-Packard and Port of Seattle redesigns illustrate an increasingly common form of organizational structure for knowledge work. We call it a learning lattice because when the skill development teams are overlaid on the business teams, the graphic looks like a garden lattice. While these organizations are certainly not universal in knowledge work redesign, they are a popular way to provide nonhierarchical support for learning without diminishing the integrated business focus many operations try to obtain by incorporating knowledge workers into cross-functional teams as their primary base of operations. In this chapter we also reviewed three methods for redesign of knowledge work: STS, the conference method, and a hybrid of the two called the conference design team method. Typically used in large organizations that are trying to restructure themselves, these methods provide a more participative and democratic way to reorganize knowledge teams. In Chapter 6 we will discuss the metaphors and practices needed to create successful knowledge teams.

Notes

1. D. Tjosvold and M. Tjosvold, "Cross-Functional Teamwork: The Challenges of Involving Professionals," in *Advances in Interdisciplinary Studies of Work Teams*, vol. 2, *Knowledge Work in Teams*, ed. Michael M. Beyerlein, Douglas A. Johnson, and Susan T. Beyerlein (Greenwich, Conn.: JAI Press, 1995), 3.
2. John A. Byrne, "The Horizontal Organization," *Business Week*, December 20, 1993, 79.
3. S. J. Puri, "Industrial Vendors' Selling Center: Implications

for Sales Management," *Journal of Business and Industrial Marketing* 7 (1992): 59–69.

4. J. R. Hollingsworth and E. J. Hollingsworth, "Challenges in the Provision of Care for the Chronically Ill," *Journal of Health Politics* 17 (1992): 869–878.

5. D. Keith Denton, "Multi-skilled Teams Replace Old Work Systems," *HRMagazine* 37 (September 1992): 49. Reprinted with the permission of *HRMagazine* published by the Society for Human Resource Management, Alexandria, Va.

6. Lea A. P. Tonkin, "Spectra-Physics Scanning Systems: Focusing on the Customer, Intensely," *Target* 9, no. 6 (1993): 58. Reprinted from *Target* with permission of the Association for Manufacturing Excellence, 380 West Palatine Road, Wheeling, IL 60090-5863, 847-520-3282.

7. Byrne, "The Horizontal Organization," 77.

8. Susan Albers Mohrman, Susan G. Cohen, and Allan M. Mohrman, Jr., *Designing Team-Based Organizations: New Forms for Knowledge Work* (San Francisco: Jossey-Bass, 1995).

6

Creating a Sentient Organization: New Metaphors for Knowledge Work

"When we think a company is like an engine, we manage it that way. We assume that there are discrete activities like changing the oil or replacing the carburetor that will create predictable improvements. But companies don't act like machines, they act more like gardens or forests. They aren't mechanical; they are organic. It is time to change our metaphor of management. Instead of acting like mechanics, managers need to act like farmers or foresters. You can't yell at the tomatoes and make them grow faster; it doesn't work that way. We need to plant and nurture and analyze and protect, not tighten and fix and lubricate. We need to ensure that the soil of our organizations isn't poisoned by distrust. Like farmers, we need to remember that success requires hard work, discipline, and patience."

—Steve Hill, Executive Vice President,
Weyerhaeuser Corporation

Bill Ferone is the vice president and general manager of customer service at Amdahl Corporation, a company that provides integrated computing solutions for very computer-intensive work environments. He leads a knowledge team of vice presidents charged with providing benchmark-level customer service. Their combined understanding of customer requirements and corporate leadership has helped to make these businesses the most profitable and responsive in the company.

The customer service technicians the executives lead are organized into unique boundaryless teams with a variety of skills and perspectives. Although they are specialists in a variety of high-tech disciplines, service team members are bound together by common goals, customer service values, and information-sharing processes. These teams are difficult to describe to outsiders because their membership shifts from time to time, forming and reforming like rapidly splitting amoebas. Sometimes technicians work with their own geographical team members on projects or problems; sometimes their team expands to include members from other cities across the country. The teams work in a way that is best described as "flowing to the work." When customer service technicians see an opportunity to provide a customer with new equipment, for example (in a traditional functional silo-type knowledge team, this would be someone else's job), they reform their team to include salespeople, who join them in their visits to the customers.

The teams have been very effective in an area led by North American customer service vice president Jim Graham. He explains what happened:

> "I had come back from a meeting with the president and several senior executives in the company. At the time we were in the middle of a workforce reduction. During that meeting, Joe Zemke, the president of our company, talked about several issues. First, we were in the midst of a workforce reduction and our respective executives would be meeting with us to tell us what that meant to our individual organizations. He then said, 'I really need you to look at things differently in the future. I want you to establish new ways of doing

business.' In all, he went through about five different areas where he wanted us to work:

1. Establish new ways of doing business.
2. Build necessary new skills and approaches for the business.
3. Drive the cost to match business opportunities.
4. Have the right information systems.
5. Boost morale and energize the company at all levels.

"I was coming back on the plane after the meeting and was looking at the notes (these five bullets) that I had taken during the meeting. Normally what we do in a workforce reduction is to look at the element with the most impact on reducing cost: the head count. I started looking at this thing and said, 'There has to be a different way,' because we had already been through a couple of workforce reductions. We really have terrific people at Amdahl and we really do need to find ways of using them in order to be competitive in the future. All of a sudden I started thinking about that and realized that a different type of structure was what we really needed—one that did away with a lot of the hierarchy and allowed us to streamline the organization so the service professionals could do their jobs.

"When I arrived at work on the following Monday, the first call I received was from Larry Eacott. [Larry is an internal organization development consultant.] We started talking about designing work around clusters of people, the way it was ten years ago. At the time there weren't that many managers, and the people were empowered to do their jobs and did them magnificently.

"We have a long journey to go on, but we have seen some significant improvements since we have gone to this kind of structure. And while I initially thought that this thing was cost-related, that is not the only benefit that we got out of it. I see that productivity has gone up, that people feel more empowered, that their morale is up, and that they are more energized. I also see some terrific ideas working their way through the company."

Larry Eacott, winner of the Amdahl President's Award for his work to support the change effort in the service organization, notes that the results of this work have been very positive:

"In the first year our cost savings were about $3.75 million, $750,000 of which came directly from salaries, because we didn't have to add people. It's hard to measure employee output, but we have reduced overtime by 55 percent (in the Atlantic area), and we attribute that decrease to the teams being responsible for scheduling along with the responsibility for determining profit and loss. The teams receive expense budgets, and they stay within those budgets. One area, the Atlantic area, had a 99.46 customer satisfaction rate. Compared to past years, that was an improvement, because the highest level we had ever achieved was 99 percent. Significantly, revenue per employee has also increased by 26 percent since 1994."

Amdahl customer service teams reorganize even the basic geographical teams with some regularity when new service contracts require that resources be shifted from one office to another. Sometimes teams are combined, sometimes they are split up. This doesn't require management intervention. Solving one customer problem may require people with certain hardware and software expertise, while another problem at the same customer site may necessitate a different team composition to include different skills. The team members themselves make appropriate modifications. They are self-directed work teams that receive only minimal supervision from company leadership. Customer problems are dealt with right at the site, as empowered team members can make decisions without the time-consuming process of getting management authorization for most important decisions. Team members laugh when asked to draw an organizational chart. Boxes and lines don't work very well to describe their near-constant evolution.

Knowledge teams are flooding the contemporary landscape and rapidly becoming the most common form of modern work. But not all knowledge teams enjoy the same success as those we have already mentioned. The purpose of this chapter is to suggest that using appropriate metaphors can actually affect the success of a knowledge team. The rules have changed since many popular organizational practices were created. Industrial-age methods are obsolete in the information age. But without changing the metaphors we use when we build knowledge teams, it is difficult to eliminate or even modify obviously obsolete organizational practices.

What Customers Want

If you ask customers what they need, nearly all will say, "Get me what I want when I want it, Give me higher quality and lower cost, Give me excellent service, and Treat me with respect." Customers want a product or service faster, better, and cheaper, and there are usually plenty of people competing for the opportunity to give it to them.

How do we satisfy demanding customers? Most contemporary businesspeople agree that we need organizations that are fast, flexible, responsive, adaptive, and innovative. These are attributes tattooed on the corporate charter of virtually every organization. But these are the characteristics of a sentient being, not of the seemingly lifeless, machinelike corporations we have often created. They are adjectives used to describe a thinking organism that can rapidly learn, grow, and evolve.

All organizations, of course, are living systems. They are composed of people, who must do the work of the operation. But some organizations—the ones we call sentient organizations—*act* more alive than others. Sentient organizations are simply better suited for modern business.

For example, remember when Microsoft was criticized by customers and analysts for ignoring the Internet? Article after article questioned the conspicuous absence of the multibillion-dollar giant while early innovators like Netscape and America Online were defining important software infrastructure for the information superhighway. Within a year after the rebukes, not only was the company very much present, but lawsuits filed by competitors declared it to be so potentially dominant that they felt it was unfairly limiting competitive activity.

How did Microsoft act so quickly and effectively? In a world accustomed to companies the size of Microsoft being like battleships that take years to turn (a popular metaphor for big organizations), we watched instead the miracle of catlike speed in the execution of a significant shift in business strategy. On the cover of the same popular news magazine that had wondered a few months earlier why Microsoft wasn't involved in Internet services was a picture of Bill Gates's face in the middle of an electronic spider web, declaring him and his company the most likely to rule the Web. Instead of watching a big, slow boat, we witnessed the agility of a hungry predator.

Knowledge teams at places like Microsoft and Amdahl are setting a new standard for responsiveness. But not everyone is reaching that high. Why? Because in spite of all our talking about learning, adaptive, and continuously improving organizations over the last decade, many of our operations—surprisingly, even some small entrepreneurial ventures or teams composed of only a handful of knowledge workers—still act more like inanimate mechanisms than like the sentient organisms we say we want to emulate. Perhaps too many of us are still too enamored with machines.

A Modern Organizational Parable

Imagine a long-distance foot race between a human and a machine. The machine is a state-of-the-art robot with superior mechanical and software enhancements but without any human assistance for the duration of the race. The human is healthy but only of average athletic abilities.

At the sound of the starter's pistol, the machine surges

forward dramatically, rapidly outpacing the human over the smooth and well-known portion of the course. It is indefatigable, and the inferior strength and stamina of the human is a handicap. It appears that the robot will win easily.

Before long, however, the robot is slowed as small mechanical breakdowns hinder its performance. Unlike the human, the robot cannot heal itself. Unpredicted obstacles that were not programmed into the machine appear on the course, and because it cannot choose alternatives outside of its programming, it begins to make mistakes. It cannot break the rules. There is no adrenaline rush to move it beyond its normal abilities, no endorphins to allow it to ignore mechanical wear and tear. It is not as adaptable or creative as the human, and eventually its strength and rigidity, once assets, become liabilities as the course becomes more challenging. The robot plods mechanically forward without deviation from its plan, a plan that fails to anticipate unpredictable terrain changes caused by sudden weather problems and rock slides.

Near the end of the course, the human pulls ahead and wins. Maybe the robot isn't all it's cracked up to be. With all its physical weaknesses, irrationality, and other emotional or intellectual failings, the living organism still ultimately prevails over the superior strength of the machine.

If We Don't Act Alive, We Could Die

In spite of some of the obvious advantages of living entities over machines, our organizations still often act mechanistically. We may prefer, for example, the machinelike rigidity of hierarchical, functional silos over more flexible but less predictable democratic operations. We may choose policies over principles, directives over values, and rules and contracts over education and trust. Even attempts at more organic approaches, such as fostering an organizational vision, can rapidly deteriorate from inspirational stories and legends to the creation of a snore-boring paragraph buttressed with objectives and budgets that may be so limiting that they hamper innovation. Management might impose artificial structure on an organization instead of allowing appropriate structure to evolve more naturally from within. We may give people jobs instead of missions. For fear of chaos, we may create flexibility-inhibiting controls.

As the parable illustrates, this may actually be useful if the road we are on is smooth and stable. We have ample evidence that such mechanistic practices were widely used and acclaimed for their ability to produce organizational stability during the industrial age—an age with a more predictable business environment than today. But what makes the operation stable and predictable can also lead to uncreative, programmed behavior. If our organization's path is rocky and unpredictable (a common predicament in the postindustrial reality), we may need to make fundamental changes in our organizations in order to survive. At issue is more than the need for flexibility and responsiveness. Many organizations, in the words of one Weyerhaeuser manager, "simply can't afford hierarchies and bureaucracies anymore." It is bad enough to be shackled by unhelpful practices. But it is even worse to have to pay extra for really expensive shackles.

Changing these well-entrenched practices is difficult when the underlying culture of the organization is built on a paradigm that makes these practices seem normal—or, worse, when previous success with this paradigm creates a moral certitude that other practices are actually somehow wrong. How do we know if our organization is built on these paradigms? One clue is the metaphors we use to explain our organization. As the eyes are the windows of the soul, the windows of our paradigms may well be the metaphors we use to describe our organizations. See Figure 6-1 for examples of the type of language you might hear that identifies the implicit metaphors we are using. If we constantly speak of the need to "drive" or "steer" or "reboot" our operations, we view them differently from the way we view them if we speak of the need to "cultivate," "educate," or "develop" them. Mechanistic metaphors can mean mechanistic thinking. Mechanistic thinking can lead to organizational rigidity, inflexibility, or unresponsiveness—a state of being similar to rigor mortis.

To change popular mechanistic practices alone may not be

Figure 6-1. Words that identify the implicit metaphor.

Mechanical Words	Organic Words
Steer	Nourish
Jump-start	Nurture
Retool	Grow
Redesign	Evolve
Reengineer	Prune
Structure	Educate
Organize	Adapt
Drive	Cultivate
Mechanisms	Organisms

sufficient. If we do not also change our metaphors and ultimately the paradigms that spawned them, we run the risk of having mechanical practices reemerge even after the inappropriate ones have been eradicated. To change our paradigms, we believe it is important to appreciate why they have become so popular. Let's consider a historical perspective on organizations with an eye to discovering the elements that have influenced even contemporary knowledge teams. We will start with the distant past and work up to the present.

The Preoccupation of Archimedes

In about 300 B.C. the Greek philosopher and mathematician Archimedes made a startling discovery: When properly used, a lever could multiply the strength of a man so significantly that it supposedly caused him to boast to King Hiero that with a sufficiently long lever and a place to put a fulcrum, he could move the earth. He reportedly supported this boast by using a complicated series of levers and compound pulleys to lift a fully loaded ship out of the water. His fascination with tools, and more specifically with the machine, was illustrative of an obsession that has possessed human societies since the invention of the wheel.

Tools for planting and tilling the earth had long before allowed people to stop nomadic hunting and gathering and given them the opportunity to build civilizations. Later, empires rose and fell with their ability to create and master more deadly technologies to magnify human strength. Assyrian chariots provided a lethal advantage over foot cavalry. The seemingly impenetrable great walled cities in Europe and the Mideast crumbled before the Roman catapults and siege machines. Steel swords bested inferior iron implements, armored knights were no match for crossbows, and Chinese gunpowder changed the rules of social conquest forever. The world was changing. Simply getting more people together to accomplish what a few individuals could not was no longer good enough. Whole communities working together could not withstand a small army of the technologically advanced.

From simple pull carts to Watt's miraculous steam engine and from Whitney's cotton gin to the monstrous equipment of the first factories, people have spent more than two millennia in the relentless pursuit of machinery that could do much more than people's unaided muscle could ever accomplish. Since early history, civilization has moved inexorably toward the industrial revolution, the time when mechanization would reach the critical mass necessary to permanently transform an agrarian culture to something fundamentally different: an industrial society.

The Industrial Revolution

The inevitable industrial revolution occurred. By the 1890s, new machinery made large-scale manufacturing practical for the first time in human history. The factory replaced the family farm as the economic center of technologically developed societies. Fortunes were made and world power secured as the industrially developed countries built solid economies rooted in the mass production of goods.

To organize and coordinate the great numbers of physical laborers who were needed to operate the industrial machinery, the hierarchy and bureaucracy were perfected. At the time, people like Frederick Taylor, the creator of "scientific management," were no less regarded than the inventors of the finest industrial equipment to produce automobiles and steel. Why? The laborers had moved from the farms to the factories without experience or education. Organization controls like those supported by Taylor were necessary not only to ensure the productivity of the new workforce, but to provide (minimally) for their welfare as well.

Hierarchy—a structure in which a series of levels in the organization carry increasing authority and responsibility as they get nearer to the top of the organization—became an essential part of the new organization control mechanism. The best workers were promoted to foremen. Foremen could teach the factory workers how to do their jobs. Supervisors watched over the foremen. Multiple levels of management controlled the supervisors. This allowed the organization to take workers without any industrial experience and turn them into effective factory "hands." They were called this intentionally. The factory "heads," of course, were managers. This separation of duties into physical labor and mental labor allowed industrialists to be successful. But hierarchical controls weren't enough.

The secondary coordinator was the bureaucracy—the division of labor into functions and departments. Bureaucracy made it possible to create very specialized jobs that could be mastered fairly quickly. It also gave managers smaller chunks of the operation to oversee, thereby minimizing the risk of large problems and ensuring more effective control. Neither of these practices was new, but both hierarchy and bureaucracy were ideal for the organizations of the industrial age. As they became more effective, not only the equipment, but the organization systems and structures themselves began to operate "like a well-oiled machine."

Industrial-age corporations were understandably similar to the machines that made them successful. This was undoubtedly influenced by the fact that the prototypical business establishment of industry was the factory, the maker of automobiles, trains, steel, and ships. Treating organizations as another type of machine was a logical thing to do in the industrial age, and arguably enabled us to build the infrastructure and technology necessary to be successful in an industrialized world. Acting on the mechanistic metaphor, managers "retooled" organization structures to conform to slowly changing industrial strategies. Organizations were analyzed and designed by industrial engineers. Organizations were highly structured and organized. Like a machine, the organization required constant intervention and maintenance to "jump-start" or repair it. This paradigm served the industrialists well.

A Postindustrial Age

After decades of global innovation, the promise of the industrial revolution has finally been realized. Machines for mass production no longer provide the competitive leverage they did even a few years ago. In some cases, industrial-age technology has now even surpassed our need to use it to produce goods and services better, faster, or cheaper. Some companies, such as American Tool and Die, for example, strategically utilize older, cheaper technology to its full advantage rather than purchase admittedly "better" but unnecessary equipment.

Competitive leverage from the more effective utilization of physical labor is minimal. Organizations across the globe (at least in developed countries) have access to the same labor-enhancing technologies. Although we have been slow to recognize it, we must acknowledge an exciting but frightening reality: The industrial revolution is over.

What's next? We are in the early days of a postindustrial age that has been called the information age. We are only just now coming to understand the significant implications of this shift. See Figure 6-2 for a comparison of the agrarian, industrial, and information ages. Note the significant shifts in the economic base from agriculture to industry and then to service, and the concurrent evolution of the primary form of organization from family farms to factories and then to the predominant organization of the information age: the knowledge team.

Figure 6-2. Comparison of the Agrarian Age, Industrial Age, and Information Age.

	Agrarian Age	*Industrial Age*	*Information Age*
Economic base	Agriculture	Industry	Service
Organization	Farm	Factory	Team
Key asset	Land	Equipment	Knowledge
Work type	Physical	Physical	Mental
Key technology	Tools	Automation	Information transfer
Organization descriptor	Patriarchal	Hierarchical	Egalitarian

The most important asset of the organization has shifted as well. Once land was the primary asset. Without it there was no farming or ranching. Thus the primary conflicts during the agrarian age were generally rooted in expansion policies, land claims, water rights, and so forth. Later, equipment became the key asset as industrial automation became essential to corporate profitability. Expensive factories and equipment became a large barrier to entry in many important markets, reinforcing the old adage, "You have to have money to make money." Although the earlier assets have remained important as these ages have evolved, the key asset in the information age—the competitive advantage—is knowledge. Consequently, the primary challenge is no longer basic tooling or automation but effective information transfer. This is another task made difficult by adhering to machine paradigms. We will discuss this challenge in detail in Chapter 9.

Here is the bottom line: The old technologies, the old organizations, and the old job structures are already becoming obsolete. Companies using the outdated industrial model will fare no better during this information revolution than family farms did during the industrial one. But shedding industrial practices hasn't been easy. What worked for IBM in the 1970s hobbled and nearly crippled it in the 1990s. GM spun off Saturn to try to give the new upstart operation a chance to survive without the presumed anchor weight of what was once the preeminent production engine of the industrial age. It has been hard to let go of the organizational mechanisms that once made industrial giants so successful.

Survival of the Mechanistic Paradigm

As evidence of the persuasiveness of this mechanistic thinking, consider the best-selling business books from even the recent past that have encouraged us to reengineer corporations—an ironic attempt to create organizations with the characteristics of organisms by treating them like mechanisms. This is done at some peril. Even the redesign approaches discussed in the last chapter, if applied too mechanistically, can cause these problems. Reengineering, in the way that it was done in the early to mid 1990s virtually guarantees it. Recent information about the problems of treating organizations this way are disturbing.

For example, Michael Hammer and James Champy, who popularized reengineering, acknowledged in an interview published in *The Wall Street Journal* that many of these efforts have failed to achieve the promised gains.[1] When those doing reengineering treated contemporary organizations as though they were mechanisms to be analyzed and reformulated at will, they underestimated the effort required to deal with the resistance and resilience of the operation. In some cases reengineering virtually ignored human beings, and it often became synonymous with downsizing initiatives. Professor Gareth Morgan, a distinguished researcher at Canada's York University, estimates that as a result of this and other oversights, 70 percent of these reengineering efforts in North America have failed.[2] Enid Mumford, one of the founders of the socio-technical movement in Europe, reports similar findings of reengineering failures in the United Kingdom.[3]

Questionable Practices for the Information Age

Savvy managers have known for years that the practices of the industrial era that emphasized stability and strength over agility and responsiveness can hobble an operation in a postindustrial world. As Figure 6-3 suggests, our approaches and practices must shift from the industrial-age concern with control to better incorporate the information-age need for flexibility and adaptation.

Despite the need for change, though, it is important to remember that these industrial work practices are not inherently flawed or inhumane. Although there are certainly examples of abusive industrial practices, there are also countless cases in which industrial practices have been used in a way that fosters both business and human health and prosperity. Ironically, the much maligned Frederick Taylor, who is credited with directly or indirectly popularizing many of these industrial practices, wanted to employ them at least partly as a way to improve the work life of employees, who were suffering from the capricious whims of management.

Figure 6-3. Comparison of Industrial- and Information-Age practices.

Industrial-Age Approach	*Information-Age Approach*
• Hierarchy of people	• Hierarchy of purpose
• Division of labor	• Integration of specialists
• Bureaucracy	• Adhocracy
• Control of employees	• Control of processes
• Rules and regulations	• Resource and task boundaries
• Corporate mandates	• Corporate communications
• Large corporate staffs	• Lean corporate staffs
• Chain of command	• Flow of information
• Policies and procedures	• Principles and values
• Jobs	• Missions
• Functional silos	• Training and skill groups
• Work assignments	• Projects
• Expediter roles	• Streamlined processes
• Command and control	• Education and development
• Boss-led operations	• Customer-led operations
• Big investment in buildings	• Big investment in information
• Management decision making	• Shared decision making
• Control emphasis	• Innovation emphasis
• Status by rank	• Status by contribution

Moreover, some industrial practices are still appropriate for organizations whose unique operational requirements are better met with these approaches. Military organizations, for example, often find some of these practices helpful with new recruits, even though they may be antithetical for special operations teams like the U.S. Army Rangers or the U.S. Navy Seals, whose ability to make rapid decisions without officers present may make the difference between accomplishing or failing in a mission. But in our experience, organizations that use industrial practices with knowledge teams seldom outperform those that use the information-age approaches.

Knowledge workers we have interviewed for this book raise numerous questions about specific organizational practices that they feel may no longer add value in the information age (see Figure 6-4). The hierarchy, for example, was important in the industrial age as a device for providing clarity of purpose and directing the uneducated workforce. In the information age, however, knowledge workers told us that substitutes for hierarchy can accomplish the same thing more effectively. Information technology now allows individual knowledge team members access to customer requirements, near real-time cost analyses, technical problem-solving data, and other types of important information. In the past, this information was often available only to managers, who had to dedicate a large percentage of their time to obtaining and manipulating it.

When empowered to act on this information, knowledge teams can now make and implement decisions more effectively and quickly than when they have to wait for the bottleneck caused by a chain of command. "Our whole concept that some people are managers and some people are not managers is going to disappear as a useful way of thinking," predicts Edward E. Lawler III, director of the Center for Effective Organizations at the University of Southern California (USC) Los Angeles. "There are going to be a lot of people who one day are managing or leading a work team and the next day are doing individual contributor work on something else."[4] Confirms George Bailey, the national organizational-change practice leader for Price Waterhouse L.L.P., "Organizations in the next 25 years are going to start blowing up the bureaucracies that have hampered them

Figure 6-4. Questionable practices seen by knowledge workers.

Knowledge Workers Question:	Instead, They Recommend:
• Automatic chain-of-command decisions	• Decisions made by those with most information
• Regular management directives	• Thought-provoking questions from leaders
• Multiple management levels, fat corporate staffs, expensive headquarters	• Lean support resources and more tool/technology investment
• Status symbols, perks	• Few status gaps, less aristocracy
• Focus on managers getting information	• Focus on everyone getting information
• Expediters	• Process simplification and improvements
• Functional silos	• Cross-functional teams
• Policies	• Common sense
• Formal performance appraisals	• Real-time coaching, individual development planning
• Annual budgeting rituals	• Regular discussions about financial issues
• Job descriptions, titles	• Projects, missions
• Routine meetings	• Effective meetings

since they were created. You are going to see far fewer layers of management. Companies will no longer be able to afford to have people who are paid for watching other people work."[5]

It is partly for this reason that knowledge work executives such as Bill Gates shun the industrial practice of handing down regular management policies for others to implement. Gates prefers to spend his time doing things like attending project team meetings in an attempt to influence and learn about emerging technologies or answering E-mail questions from inside and outside of the company. With this shift from work director to thinking enabler and coach occurring in many contemporary organizations, the need for multiple management levels, fat corporate staffs, and expensive headquarters locations is diminishing. This is evidenced by the hundreds of companies that have in the last several years laid off thousands of middle-level managers and corporate staff people, individuals who until recently were less affected by downsizing efforts than the entry-level workforce. You can also see evidence of this in the proliferation of small businesses, which now can compete with large corporations because big staff groups and lots of managers not only are often unnecessary for knowledge work, but can be a competitive disadvantage.

There are other questionable practices as well. Are disproportionate management perquisites, originally designed to reinforce the power and status of executive positions, useful or harmful in the knowledge workplace? Obvious things like reserved parking spaces, executive dining rooms and bathrooms, and differential dress codes have been falling out of favor for some time. But a number of organizations have analyzed other more subtle things like differential office size and location or sensitive unspeakables like disproportionate bonuses and benefit packages and modified them in an attempt to reduce the gap between knowledge workers and leaders. Are project status meetings ostensibly for coordination purposes actually just time-consuming dog and pony shows, useful only for managers who use them for evaluation and authorization purposes?

Consider what is happening in current office design as one small indicator of these changes. American Express Financial Corporation in Minneapolis has moved executives out of corner offices, which have been converted into reading rooms. Alcoa CEO and chairman Paul O'Neill now sits next to his secretary at a plain L-shaped desk in a normal cubicle like other knowledge workers. The rest of the ten highest-ranking executives don't sit in big corner offices either. They feel it is no longer a good use of space. The new corporate headquarters building currently under construction "will allocate space to employees based on need, not title, and create an open architecture to encourage conversation and teamwork."[6] In the new building, 60 percent of the space will be for offices and workspaces and 40 percent will be reserved for meeting and "collaborative work areas"—a significant departure from current conditions, where 90 percent of the space is dedicated to offices. As a nod to the constant need for organization change, offices won't be permanent; they will be constructed of furniture rather than walls. Access to the company information network will be facilitated through trapdoors in office floors, a design idea this building shares with the new corporate headquarters of Owens Corning recently constructed in Toledo, Ohio.

The new Owens building will assume a paperless workforce who will carry their portable computers from meeting space to meeting space. All meeting areas will have electrical outlets and network ports built into the meeting tables. To encourage collaboration and working in teams, the new design relies heavily on open space and has numerous team rooms. The Sun Microsystems campus in Menlo Park, California, has two-story-high open rooms off of the kitchen area in each building. These are called "forum" spaces and are designed, in the words of William T. Angello, vice president, real estate and the workplace, to "encourage dialogue about product or technology." Only 35 percent of the interior space is for offices. There are meeting places called "Sun" rooms filled with couches and lounge chairs to further facilitate conversation without regard to status or title.[7]

Knowledge workers are asking other questions, too. Are all the organizational policies adding value in the knowledge workplace, or are we trading off too much creativity and autonomy for consistency? In a speech he gave at *Industry Week*'s annual "Managing for Innovation" conference in March 1995, Jeffrey R. Beir, vice president of Lotus Development Corporation, argues against this obsolete practice. In his speech, entitled "Managing Creatives: Our Creative Workers Will Excel—If We Let Them," he said, "The . . . attitude is an attitude toward Rule Books. Or should I say, against rule books. In hierarchical organizations, there are rule books for everything. . . . I'm sorry if I sound judgmental, but that is the worst possible attitude that you could bring to the task of managing creatives. A rigid approach to managing is instant creative death."[8]

Do formal performance appraisals really improve behavior

as well as ongoing coaching does, or are we going through a time-consuming mechanical exercise primarily to avoid potential litigation? Does an intricate annual process of budget reviews really provide better financial stewardship in the workplace, or does it simply devolve into a mechanical game where managers automatically request more than they need (while saying they absolutely need it) so that when the inevitable cuts come, they can get the resources they needed in the first place? Do job descriptions and titles—mechanical attempts to clarify work and reduce redundancy—expand our contribution and commitment, or do they limit it? Are routine, preprogrammed meetings evaluated for their effectiveness regularly, or are they perpetuated because we have always had them before?

On the other hand, when we view the organization as an organism, we treat it as a group of people instead of a cluster of policies or a diagram of reporting relationships. We see multiple layers of management as impediments to the flow of communication instead of as mechanisms for order and stability. We question the value of controlling policies and procedures and instead rely more on basic values and common sense. We trust people.

As a quick sanity check for a particular organizational practice, think about how it would work in another organic organization: the family. Would families be more effective if each child was given a clear job description listing his or her role in the family, or would ongoing discussions about specific family projects be more useful? Should families create a policy book describing inappropriate behavior? Should we give formal performance appraisals to our spouses to let them know how they are doing on a semiannual basis, or would dealing with problems, disagreements, and celebrations as they occur be more appropriate? How about if we asked each family member to participate in a formal annual budgeting ritual every year? Wouldn't regular, ongoing discussions about financial plans, goals, and constraints be more effective? Sentient organizations are certainly not without controls that guide and coordinate their efforts, but they tend to choose common-sense approaches rather than artificially imposed mechanical methods.

Toyota Goes Organic

Consider the following case of one operation attempting to eliminate the mechanical practices of the industrial age. When Mike Morrison was the national human resource manager for Toyota, he supported the Toyota Sales Division, composed of about 1,400 associates. He notes,

> "In 1994 we were reorganized around product teams. We went from a traditional functional organization with marketing, distribution, and sales to a more product-focused team. We eliminated the traditional marketing department and put twelve associates on three different product teams, and they were given the responsibility for planning all the market-based activity for the products."

This was a marked departure from the practices of the past, which had been very successful for the sales and marketing giant.

> "For example, one of these product teams was our large platform car: Avalon, Camry, and Previa. One of our groups was sport utility vehicles and trucks. Our third group focused on small cars and specialty cars like MR2s, Celicas, and Supras. Together these groups are responsible for about 350,000 sales per year.
> "The reason we went to the product teams is that we didn't feel that we had the focus we needed. It takes billions of dollars to set up and produce these cars, and we weren't giving each segment the attention it deserved. The reason, of course, is that if you're in the marketing department and you're a planner looking out for fifteen or twenty different cars and all their different variations, it's difficult to give each niche equal attention.
> "What happened with the teams is that we got rid of the traditional offices and titles, and everyone just became a team member. These team members have

their own work cubicles, which surround a large conference table. When you walk by a series team, what
you see is the whole group or a portion of the group
at the conference table working on key marketing and
planning issues. So it went from a real functional and
bureaucratic environment with poor lateral relations
and communication to one where there's a lot of lateral
relations that have developed.

"We still have some other functional centers like
advertising but they wouldn't do anything now without correlating closely and carefully with the series
teams. The series teams really drive the process now."

Leadership and team formulation is evolutionary, Morrison
explains.

"A leader in our series teams is someone who takes the
lead. For example, some person may take the lead for
the new Tercel launch and put together a team with
that focus in mind: maybe someone from the finance
area, someone from advertising, and someone from the
legal department. This team would be together for
about six months, during which time the team leader
would be considered the integrator and would coordinate the launch of the vehicle with the help of others.
It's a real team environment where a person can serve
on four or five teams at a time."

Eliminating the comfortable practices of the industrial past
wasn't easy. People were used to the stability and comfort of the
hierarchy and bureaucracy, and they were sometimes puzzled
about how to work with the series teams.

"There were some real difficult cultural changes. It was
difficult for people to fully grasp what was done with
the organization. Also, there wasn't alignment initially
with all of the reward systems. What we have done is
get rid of all of the career paths. You used to sit in marketing as the marketing administrator, and you could

look up and see the senior marketing administrator above you, and a manager above him, and a senior manager above that person. You could see your career path clearly before you. Now all you have between you and your career is the vice president who's running the series team. So people lost that clear view of their career paths and weren't quite sure how it was going to work in the future.

"There was probably six months to a year of deep frustration over having to work in a team environment, when before they had had a clearly defined job and could sit in their cubicles by themselves. They went to a much more independent and organic structure where their role often changed daily depending on the activity of the day—whether it was a new product launch or whatever. It was difficult for them to adjust from a bureaucratic to a more organic style."

Although the results of these efforts have been difficult to quantify, they appear very promising, says Morrison.

"The senior people really feel that the teams have added to our sales efficiency. For example, in the launch area (before we went to teams), we had three or four situations where the launch wasn't as successful as we had hoped. We took a long look at our organization and saw that we were too divided. The coordination and lateral relations weren't strong enough to support a product launch. Now when we launch a product with the series teams, we do a much better job of it. A launch is a real critical thing. You have only one chance to make a good first impression and really capture people's attention and capture the interest of the dealer.

"Also, the planning before and after our launch is much better. Now, not only do we plan our advertising, incentives, promotions, and distribution, but the follow-up process where we rethink what we've done is clearly much better. The series teams have reached a whole new level of performance, and they're here to stay."

Summary

In this chapter we have tried to suggest that inappropriately carrying over the methodologies, tools, and thinking from the industrial age to the information age can harm our abilities to be responsive to customers' needs. The way successful knowledge teams like Amdahl service teams and Toyota marketing teams are meeting this challenge is by not only incorporating the processes of organic systems into their operations but replacing mechanism thinking with organism thinking. While this may seem either trivial or unusual to the casual observer, effective knowledge workers are rediscovering the positive—and the negative—power of the paradigms and metaphors they use to describe their work. These metaphors can either free them to think of creative, adaptive solutions to business problems or constrict them to obsolete organizational patterns and responses. To accommodate knowledge work, established organizations may require more than being remade; they will need to be reborn.

Notes

1. " 'Re-Engineering' Authors Reconsider Re-Engineering," in the column "Managing Your Career" by Hal Lancaster, *The Wall Street Journal*, January 1995. Reprinted by permission of *The Wall Street Journal* © 1995 Dow Jones & Company, Inc. All rights reserved worldwide.
2. From keynote remarks at the Organization System Designers Conference, Washington, D.C., June 9, 1995.
3. Enid Mumford and Rick Hendricks, "Re-Engineering Rhetoric and Reality: The Rise and Fall of a Management Fashion," working paper, 1995.
4. Michael A. Verespej, "A Workforce Revolution?" *Industry Week*, August 21, 1996, 22. Reprinted with permission from

Industry Week. Copyright Penton Publishing, Inc., Cleveland, Ohio.

5. Ibid., 23.
6. Michael A. Verespej, "Welcome to the New Workspace," *Industry Week*, April 15, 1996, Reprinted with permission from *Industry Week.* Copyright Penton Publishing, Inc., Cleveland, Ohio.
7. Ibid., 28–29.
8. Jeffrey R. Beir, "Managing Creatives: Our Creative Workers Will Excel—If We Let Them," *Vital Speeches of the Day* 61, no. 16 (1995): 502. Used by permission.

7

Virtual Knowledge Teams: Working on Geographically Dispersed Teams

"The company of the future could have 50 people working in 10 different countries who are linked through inexpensive TV screens that can automatically translate words and voices into different languages."[1]

—Jack Kahl, Chairman and CEO, Manco Inc.

David Csokasy leads the corporate training efforts at Delco Electronics (DE), a unit of General Motors Corporation. He has a Ph.D. in technical education and is a former university professor. Tall and thin with distinguishing gray hair, David is very committed to his work.

He is attending a training session in Singapore designed to help Southeast Asian DE managers learn leadership skills for high-performance work teams. He meets with Lim Peng Soon, the Singapore training coordinator, at the end of the second day of training. Peng Soon is tall and slender, like David. He has straight, coal-black hair and is also well educated. Both speak in English, the language of business in Singapore.

The session is going well. Both agree that continued cooperative training efforts will be beneficial. They decide to start sharing ideas about international training efforts in a more structured way. David suggests that they include their colleague in Mexico.

"How can we communicate?" asks David. The twelve-hour time difference presents a serious handicap. David and Peng Soon's work schedules have almost no time overlap. When one is awake, the other is sleeping. Even worse, the expensive travel necessary for face-to-face meetings may not be cost-justifiable for this kind of less formal blue-sky work. Peng Soon hits on a solution.

"I've just established an Internet connection on my home computer," he says. David has recently done the same thing. They agree to start sending each other E-mail messages at home over the Net. They have now created a virtual knowledge team (VKT). They will soon find that a virtual knowledge team has some benefits and some disadvantages. But more importantly, they will probably discover that it has a supreme challenge. If knowledge work is mind work, and virtual knowledge team members are physically distributed across all kinds of organizational boundaries, how do you create a distributed mind?

In this chapter, we will discuss the challenges of making VKTs effective. After demonstrating why they are becoming so popular, we will also show four ways to help them succeed.

The Virtual Knowledge Team

Let's look at some VKTs to understand their unique challenges and opportunities. Virtual knowledge teams have special challenges. Bruce Ellis, a regional sales director for AT&T, has VKT members located throughout the United States. He is located in Denver, but, he explains,

"I've got people in Minneapolis, Las Vegas, Salt Lake, San Francisco, and LA—all over the map. They're a virtual office team, and sometimes their office is at the customer's location. I've got three customers who actually have offices for my people in their facilities that they pay for. The virtual office in and of itself carries its own problems associated with communication, and the aspects of a group that lend themselves to a team-based style aren't as visible as they are in an office where everyone works next to each other. I think it extends the process and makes the timeline longer. Still, I don't think it makes it impossible, it just makes it more of a challenge."

Several sales environments have used these virtual knowledge teams, including other parts of AT&T, IBM, and Compaq. There are financial benefits to these changes. At Compaq this has resulted in revenues doubling while the sales force dropped by one-third.[2] In the areas where VKTs are used, IBM spends about $8,000 per sales rep to equip the knowledge workers with ThinkPads, software, two home phone lines, a fax, a remote printer, a pager, and a cellular phone. But the company's real estate costs for these operations have been reduced by 50 percent.[3]

Some VKTs include people from several companies. The team working on the international space station sponsored by NASA and Russian space interests is an example of a multiple-company VKT. Explains John Sivie, an organizational development manager at Rocketdyne, one of the companies participating in the project,

"The Space Station Project is made up of about 1,000 employees. Its charter is to design the electrical power system of the space station, and there are subcontractors who do parts of the electrical power system. It's a virtual organization. There are other contractors who will do the module where the astronauts will be. Lockheed does the solar arrays. So it's a conglomerate of industries providing concept design, test, delivery, and assembly to the customer for a complete space station. There are a bunch of companies working on it. Boeing is the integrator, and NASA is the customer. NASA has a launch package and will then put it together in space, launching the components in eight or nine separate launches."

These VKTs have special problems, especially in the constantly evolving aerospace industry, notes Sivie.

"There's a tendency to want the organizations to mirror each other. That is, my position in this organization should have a counterpart in yours. Are they at the same level, and do they have the same level of authority when it comes to making decisions and spending money? That has always been a problem, trying to get companies to match up, even though they may be doing different projects and have different cultures. What they find is that there is an interface complexity. So it's the age-old problem: Should we contort our company to fit yours to avoid the interface problem? If we do, then we lose the effectiveness of our own company structure. It's a dilemma."

Characteristics of Virtual Knowledge Teams

Virtual knowledge teams have three characteristics that distinguish them from other knowledge teams. First, their members are always distributed across multiple locations. Team members may be spread across different time zones, countries, and/or companies. Second, they often are considerably more diverse than other knowledge teams, with members representing not only different technical specialties but several different cultures, languages, and organizational allegiances. Third, these teams typically do not have constant membership. Team members may float off or onto the team throughout its existence. Some may participate in all team activities, while others may only work on some. Ironically, these three characteristics are the antithesis of what many effective teams require for success: collocation, homogenity, and consistent membership.

Like other knowledge teams, VKTs depend more on knowledge than on physical labor. They are almost always short-term or part-time teams, like the small-project or special-purpose teams discussed in Chapter 3. But they look different from and are more difficult to operate effectively than most other types of knowledge teams.

Some might argue that VKTs are only pale ghosts of "real" knowledge teams because their unique characteristics make it nearly impossible for them to function effectively as teams in the traditional sense of the word. But although they were once rare in industrial organizations intent on longer-term, stable organizational structures, VKTs are becoming increasingly common in the knowledge workplace. We will have to find ways to make them effective.

The Rise of Virtual Knowledge Teams

Virtual knowledge teams have become necessary for a number of reasons. Some of these reasons are related to changes in contemporary products, services, and technologies, while others are due to recent organizational trends.

For example, new projects are often based on yet undeveloped leading-edge technologies. Rarely is all the necessary knowledge for these endeavors found in one location any more, and sometimes it is not even found in one company. To address these kinds of challenges, companies like Hewlett-Packard, Intel, IBM, Delco, Weyerhaeuser, and others are using virtual knowledge teams for product development.

VKTs are showing up in other situations as well. Hospitals in certain parts of the United States, for example, are concerned about the overcapacity of hospital beds. For the first time, they find themselves competing for customers. Many have active marketing programs underway to make potential patients aware of their services, and they may create unique new niche services, such as maternity suites that look more like bed and breakfast hotels than the stereotypical white and chrome hospital rooms, to attract customers. New services like these, and the marketing programs to support them, create new challenges, and a VKT composed of administrators, medical personnel, accounting, members of the community, and insurance people is often required to complete the various aspects of the project. A simple internal task force may not suffice.

Other reasons for the increase in VKTs have little to do with products and services and are related more to contemporary organizational trends. For example, many organizations have moved in the direction of decentralization and empowerment. This often means that important skills and information are no longer found in large, centralized corporate offices, but are distributed widely across multiple operational units with distinct organizational cultures, goals, and leadership. Or even if the resources exist at headquarters, the operational preference may be to involve people from across the different parts of the organization affected by the particular project. Important projects frequently require representation from a variety of constituent parts of the organization in order to not only assemble the right skills for the project but provide the necessary buy-in to ensure a coordinated implementation effort later.

Other changes in the knowledge workplace that facilitate the development of virtual knowledge teams are related to technology. Although it is difficult to determine whether technology has made these changes possible or whether technology has been adapted to support changes that were already underway (the "which came first, the chicken or the egg?" dilemma), technology has certainly had an important impact on virtual knowledge work teams. For example, technology has—for good or ill—broken down the requirements for collocation of work. Unlike the situation in the past, where telephone technology was all that was available to coordinate multisite knowledge work activity, an explosion of affordable technology, including support for real-time data transfer and collaborative work (subjects we will deal with in more detail in Chapter 12), facilitates virtual knowledge teamwork with participants from almost anywhere.

This, of course, has provided a whole host of new challenges. While writing this book, for example, we went for more than one year without ever physically meeting with our researcher, Lucas Birdeau. Telephone conferencing and data exchange substituted for a shared office. But we missed seeing his facial expressions in response to our questions. We had never met him face to face at this point in the project. We found ourselves facing some unique challenges. Did we communicate effectively? It was hard for us to tell when we couldn't make eye contact or watch a head nod in affirmation, shake in disagreement, or pause in soundless question. Much of our communication skills were based on the assumption that you could see the other team members. We hadn't realized how much we relied on these visual cues to communicate.

Common Dilemmas for Virtual Knowledge Teams

Consider a few successful examples of VKTs. Remember when disaster struck Oklahoma City, Oklahoma, on a quiet April morning in 1995, when domestic terrorists bombed the Murrah federal building? Representatives from the FBI, the Bureau of Alcohol, Tobacco and Firearms, firefighters, law enforcement, and other local and national emergency operations immediately provided rescue and investigative response services. Their efforts saved lives and located suspects.

As individuals, the members of the Oklahoma City disaster task force responded with courage and skill. They were smart people. But their individual effectiveness was amplified because they also had a smart organization, a special organization established just for this emergency. As a virtual knowledge team, they coordinated multiple dangerous tasks—no small accomplishment when you consider the number of agencies and specialists involved and the fact that they were operating under the pressure of the intense spotlight created by the international media. The diverse emergency team had a clear purpose: to rescue victims and catch the bombers. It succeeded to a large degree because the team members operated as though they had a common mind—a distributed mind—that shared information, clues, and ideas seamlessly.

When VKTs work well, they can deliver extraordinary results. But they must typically overcome the challenges associated with the lack of a common time, place, work culture, or direction.

Product Development VKTs: Different Specialties, Language, Cultures, and Time Zones

A product development team is a common type of VKT. Peter Bartlett has worked with product and service development teams at Hewlett-Packard to help them improve their time to market and other effectiveness measures. An internal organization effectiveness consultant, Peter has a rich background. Starting his military career as a private in the army, he worked his way through the ranks and attended the prestigious army organization effectiveness school. Before HP, his career experiences included community organizing work and consulting with Lockheed management on significant change projects. A large and kind man, Peter has hands as big as baseball gloves and a heart the size of HP profits. He is quiet and thoughtful. He speaks slowly. You can almost watch his mind work as he talks.

"We've had to overcome some real challenges with some of the teams," he says, with his trademark grin. These product development knowledge teams often include people from around the world who must coordinate their various expertise to create new HP products and services. Typically composed of hardware and software engineers from a variety of disciplines, the teams frequently include marketing, finance, and manufacturing people as well. A team's composition can vary depending on where the product is in the product life cycle. It is not uncommon to have Europeans, Americans, and Asians on the same team, nor is it unusual to have people outside of HP work with development teams. New HP products are often at the leading edge of technology, and alliances with outside software specialists, chip designers, and network consultants sometimes supplement HP employees on the team.

How do you operate a virtual knowledge team like those we have highlighted from Delco, AT&T, Rocketdyne, our firm, the Oklahoma City disaster task force, and Hewlett-Packard? How do you coordinate a group of opinionated specialists, some of whom are leading world experts in their fields? How do you have regular milestone meetings when team members span the globe, with different languages, cultures, and time zones? How do you get people to work together when they don't report to the same boss or when they're not even in the same company? How do you coordinate with people who have different priorities because of their numerous commitments? How do you deal with the part-timers who float on and off the team?

Multiplexing Challenges: Divided Loyalties, Time Conflicts, and Resource Limits

VKTs face additional challenges as well. Design engineers with Delco Electronics, for example, formed a joint company VKT with engineers from Hughes to create a very impressive electric automobile. In addition to the mammoth technical hurdles these engineers have had to overcome, however, they have also had a number of other extremely challenging problems. One of them is the dilemma of how to work on a number of different project teams at the same time—something the Delco engineers call *multiplexing*. There are only so many people, and they must be spread across many critical projects. Engineers may serve on a half-dozen product development teams simultaneously and have to manage the inevitable resource conflicts this causes. How many virtual knowledge teams can one knowledge worker be on without diffusing his or her effectiveness?

The Home Office: Communication Without Collocation Is Difficult

The SAS operation at Hewlett-Packard we have been learning from throughout the book also uses VKTs. For example, special projects to create learning diffusion processes throughout the company rely on virtual knowledge teams composed of managers and organizational development consultants. But these knowledge workers find it difficult to meet together because they have no shared meeting place. The consultants travel so frequently that they have little need for a shared office location (called collocation by many companies). Some have no HP office at all. Confirms Peter Bartlett, "I no longer have an office at HP. I work out of my home or wherever I need to set up my office."

But when people must work together on a short-term project, the lack of collocation creates special communication challenges. It is much easier to coordinate activities with other team members when you see them frequently. Savvy managers have known for years that some of the most important coordination and information sharing occurs informally in the halls, break rooms, and parking lots. One possible answer to this challenge, of course, is to move everybody into a common office location for the duration of the VKT work. But this is often impossible because of multiplexing requirements, cost constraints, or numerous other factors. And even if it is possible, it isn't always desirable.

For example, SAS consultants say that having their office at home helps with another important stakeholder group: their families. Maintaining some life balance is important to these people, who often spend the vast majority of their time traveling out of town. "Everybody in our group is equipped to be mobile," remarks Bartlett. "If you're on the road, you don't have to go to the office; and if you're not on the road, you can stay at home and do a lot of your work on line. Everybody's home is equipped with a fully functioning office with the right type of technology. We're equipped that way on the road, too. One of the reasons we formed things this way is that people are on the road a lot. Being able to get the work done at the customer site or in your hotel room or on the plane creates more time to spend with your family when you do get home. This work/life balance is critical and is one of HP's core values."

This decision appears to be paying off. Says Stu Winby, SAS leader, "The research that's been conducted, along with our own experience, tells us that people are a lot more productive when they have an office at home as opposed to having an office in the HP facilities." Technology has provided this option, and current trends suggest that it is expanding. In all likelihood, home offices are here to stay, and VKTs will have to accommodate and perhaps even encourage them. But how can VKTs be effective in the face of the many challenges we have mentioned? We believe that many of these challenges can be avoided or resolved by first addressing the question with which we opened the chapter: How can VKTs create a distributed mind?

The Distributed Mind

We might look to the human body, the ultimate organic meta-phor for knowledge work organizations, for some answers to this difficult question. It would be impossible for the human mind to regulate all aspects of the body. For example, if the brain were to manage the basic functioning of each cell, it could do nothing else. How, then, are the millions of cells managed so that they integrate with one another appropriately while carry-ing on normal individual cell functions such as environmental adaptation and cell replication? At the very simplest level, unless each cell is continually provided a map of how to perform its day-to-day functions, it will die.

The body uses a type of distributed mind to perform these functions. For years scientists did not understand precisely how it was done. Then, with the discovery of DNA, a host of critical biological and genetic mysteries were solved. Within the nucleus of every cell is a mass of genetic instruction called DNA. DNA functions literally as the cell's own brain, providing necessary information to the cell about how to adapt to its environment. However, whereas the brain uses electrical impulses to commu-nicate with the body, DNA uses chemical codes. As a computer uses a binary language of 1 and 0, a DNA strand has its own pattern of alternating codes that it uses to store and transmit large quantities of information. However, unlike a binary lan-guage, DNA uses four bases: adenine, guanine, cytosine, and thymine.

The number of possible sequences on a typical strand of human DNA is 4 to the 5,000th power. This number would ap-pear as a 1 followed by three thousand zeros—an amazing amount of variety on a strand many thousand times smaller than a human hair. To put this in perspective, a trillion—the much ballyhooed unit of measurement now used to count the U.S. debt—is a 1 followed by eighteen zeros. Elaborating on this, F. Crick, the scientist who discovered DNA, claims that the DNA in a single human cell contains enough information to encode about 1,000 large textbooks.[4] This is evidence that a few common fundamentals can contain an incredible variety of answers for complex situations—and it also shows that the magic in biological systems is often found in the way things, even a few simple things, are combined in different ways.

Although this is hard to imagine, simply alternating the pattern of these four chemical substances provides enough information to encode the entire blueprint of the human body within the nucleus of a single cell. It is theoretically possible to replicate the entire body by capturing and using the DNA instructions located in a single human cell. If organizations were comparably designed, the blueprint to reconstruct every aspect of a *Fortune* 10 company would be contained in the information system utilized by every single team.

Virtually every human cell contains the genetic code for the entire human body for a good reason. Although each cell is specialized (skin cells and brain cells have their differences), it contains information about every other cell, organ, and system within its DNA strands so that it can function harmoniously within a larger system while accomplishing its own tasks efficiently.

DNA, RNA, and VKTs

DNA provides direction to the body's cells in the absence of direct and neural links to the brain. In this loosely controlled environment, the body's cells adapt, function, and replicate with relative ease. To do this requires special assistance. Since DNA does not leave the nucleus of each cell, RNA (the messenger of DNA) replicates the chemical messages and transmits them throughout the cell.

The process for this data transfer is very interesting. DNA, which looks like a sort of miniature ladder twisted around an invisible axis, splits at its rungs and allows the RNA to come in and duplicate the chemical information located on the appropriate part of the DNA strand. In this way, the RNA has its own exact copy of the instructions. This is unlike the situation in many corporations, where certain information flows through a number of hierarchical levels before it reaches the place where action is taken. As it passes through each different level, the message unavoidably picks up subtle nuances or emphases from each communicator that differ from the original information—sometimes so much so that the integrity of the original message itself becomes suspect.

This RNA strand will then be sent out into the body of the cell in order to bring the cell back into equilibrium. Through RNA, DNA instructions can reach the individual organelles found outside the nucleus of the cell and provide them with the necessary script for normal functioning.

As a metaphor, DNA provides some interesting models for dealing with virtual teams that require some form of distributed leadership. As savvy managers know, managing these teams from a central hierarchy, like the brain managing each cell, is neither practical nor desirable. Virtual teams, like the individual body cells, need to accomplish their own work as well as integrating with other teams as self-regulating units. Information becomes a key to team effectiveness in much the same way that RNA regulates critical cell functions. And virtual teams can prosper or die depending on their use of a few simple fundamentals (which can be combined in very complicated ways) in much the same way that the DNA chemical information system can encode the entire operation of the body in different combinations of just four basic elements. Equipped with this metaphor, we can better understand how to face the biggest challenges of the virtual knowledge team.

Differentiation and Integration

Several years ago, professors Paul Lawrence and Jay Lorsch from Harvard University successfully anticipated one of the greatest problems of today's knowledge teams, especially virtual knowledge teams. They wrote that it was becoming increasingly important for organizations to do two things simultaneously that are seemingly at odds with one another. What was the challenge? To differentiate and to integrate at the same time.[5] This attribute, the ability to differentiate and integrate simultaneously, is the primary difference between effective VKTs and ineffective ones. It is also the key to creating a distributed mind for knowledge work. The body, of course, has been accomplishing this specialization and simultaneous integration through miraculous organizing processes such as DNA and RNA since the dawn of humankind. Although each cell receives specialized instructions through RNA messages from the DNA database, it also receives instructions on how to work together with other cells to advance the needs of the larger body.

In organizations, differentiation is required to keep up with the increasingly complex nature of business environments. For example, companies often determine a very specific niche to maintain their focus and more easily describe their unique contribution to customers. This differentiates them from their competitors. They may choose to be the low-cost producer rather than the high-value provider, or they may work only in corporate law or tax law, rather than attempt to maintain a firm that, like the lawyers in Abraham Lincoln's day, provides any kind of legal service required by the client.

Differentiation strategies within the organization make it easier to clarify roles and responsibilities. For example, doctors establish specialties so that they can learn and stay current with rapidly advancing knowledge and technologies; so do lawyers, engineers, maintenance technicians, and international business managers. A surgical team may include several doctors who have very different skills, from heart transplantation expertise to anesthesiology. On another knowledge team, one team member may have expertise in software technologies while another is proficient in hardware technologies. They are differentiated from other members of the team in order to both organize their work and maintain specialized competencies.

Integration strategies include organizational structures, common goals, communication systems, and other processes that meld the differentiated specialists together to work toward a common cause and keep them focused on objectives that can be accomplished only through cooperation and collaboration. J. Loux of the Port of Seattle notes the importance of these strategies. "When we first put the teams together, we thought that delegation was the key," he says. "We soon discovered that the key was integration. Without integration we couldn't delegate."

An effective VKT is an organization integration strategy in and of itself. But most companies have found that it is not enough by itself. Using vertical business multiskilling is another key integrating strategy. When VKTs share a common perspective and responsibility for the effectiveness and administration of the team, they form a higher sense of allegiance and commitment to it. A common vision, shared commitment to achieving it, and other basic team perspectives and skills are important in any knowledge work team. But VKTs often need more.

Differentiation Is Easier Than Integration

It appears that differentiation is easier than integration. In one organization we know about, for example, a well-intended purchasing organization procured a large quantity of bleach for pulp and paper products at a very good price. After the bleached products were sent out to customers, however, the company began to get complaints about a slight odor in the milk cartons produced with the low-cost bleach. As a responsible corporate citizen, it recalled the defective material. The recall cost hundreds of thousands of dollars more than was saved by buying the less expensive bleach. What happened? The company had good differentiation in place through the use of functional separation of purchasing and production. But the integration was weak. Had integrative processes been in place to make technicians aware of the bleach purchase prior to production of the pulp and paper, for example, quality testing might have been able to avert the problem.

In the healthy human body, these kinds of integration processes are so thoroughly established that it is absurd to imagine what would happen without them. All systems are tuned in to what is good for the whole instead of what is good for the part. What would occur if the immune system did what was best to protect the stomach and liver from potential infection, but allowed illnesses affecting the heart and lung to pass into the bloodstream? What if the organs acted independently according to their own separate agendas and goals? One lung might decide to obtain its own oxygen source, for example, because a hole in the chest seemed a more efficient channel than the lengthy connection provided through the mouth and nose. Or, the heart might decide to retrieve its nutrients from the esophagus instead of through that troubling and complicated bloodstream connection.

The body's natural design incorporates both differentiation and integration. The heart doesn't do the work of the eyes, the lungs, or the brain. It is specialized. But it works closely in concert with the rest of the body rather than in isolation from it. Parts of the body will even make necessary adaptations (within certain limits, of course) to help out when another part of the body is damaged. The systems coordinate to accomplish the greater good: survival.

Four Key Strategies for VKT Integration

Through our experience and research, we have found that like the chemical system employed by DNA, a few primary strategies, used in a variety of combinations, account for virtually all successful knowledge team integration attempts. The key strategies are (1) structure, (2) leadership, (3) shared values, and (4) rewarded goals.

Structure is the physical design of the team, including team size, membership, reporting relationships, and so forth. Leadership is the method by which the structure receives direction and coaching. Effective knowledge teams are most often highly empowered, with a great deal of shared leadership. The better leaders operate with a results rather than by a control orientation. One of their key value-added roles appears to be the specific integration with other teams that interface with the VKT.[6] Shared values appear to provide a context for work and a sense of right and wrong that enable more effective and consistent decision making. Finally, although the term *rewarded goals* may seem unusual, we have selected it to reinforce our findings that neither rewards alone nor goals alone seem to account for successful integration of knowledge teams. Let's examine these four strategies for creating a distributed mind by looking at a few examples.

Structure

Although the importance of structure was discussed in Chapter 5, we want to review it again briefly because of its special importance to VKTs. The Hewlett-Packard SAS team is an example of how structure can create integration. When the team was restructured, it was formulated in a way that forces the diverse consultants to work together on practice teams as the core work organization. If the core organization had been the "home room" groups of like specialists (engineers in one practice team, organization development consultants in another), the structure would have differentiated people effectively, just as functional silos do, but it would not have facilitated their frequent interaction to integrate their specialized services for the benefit of their HP clients. The clients themselves would have had to integrate the activities of the various consultants—a situation SAS leader Stu Winby wanted to avoid. The SAS team chose instead to do the integration itself through a unique project-oriented structure and to thereby provide a much higher level of customer service.

Based on our research, there are a few key questions a VKT needs to answer in order to determine the appropriate structure for the team:

- What is the purpose of this team?
- Who are our customers?
- Who are our partners, suppliers, and other stakeholders?
- How will the VKT be organized?
- How will we manage our work?
- What are our core work processes?
- Who will be responsible for what?
- What will we call ourselves?
- When will we meet?
- How will we meet?
- How will we communicate between meetings?

The answers to these questions are important for the proper functioning of the VKT. Although it is not a guarantee, the structuring process can minimize the multiplexing problem by helping team members understand the extent of their commitment to each VKT they participate in. Armed with this understanding, they can then negotiate for the appropriate level of participation in their various teams. Answering these questions also helps to reduce the complexity associated with multiple geographical locations.

The way the team answers these questions (and the questions that follow) goes a long way toward defining its character. Will the same people always be inconvenienced for teleconferences, or will everyone take a turn waking up in the middle of the night for a meeting? Will the team use traditional organization structures, or will it take a risk on other ones? Will it create shared responsibilities for success, or will only a few team members feel accountable for the VKT? Will it differentiate at the expense of integration, or will it find organizational ways to do both?

Teams that don't answer these questions early in their development will often suffer later. This is one example of a "pay me now or pay me later" problem. All teams pay a price at some point, but those that wait often pay more. Answering the questions about organizing and identifying the key work processes are especially important. In our firm, for example, we have found it essential to have a few clear work processes, such as a new product development process or a communication process for traveling consultants. Without identifying the key work processes, it is difficult for VKTs to solve the problems with these processes to improve them, and virtually impossible for anyone but the manager to have a sense of ownership for them. One key to creating a distributed mind is to make this organizational thinking visible to team members.

Leadership

In an industrial organization, the most obvious integrative mechanism is supervisors who regulate and coordinate interaction. In this theory, these people would, as their title implies, have super vision—they would be the insightful overseer of the workforce, the one great mind, the director of activity. Like the file server with dumb terminals, the supervisor would be the brains of the network accessed by the mindless workers.

But the one great mind theory really breaks down in knowledge work situations, especially in VKTs. After all, these are intelligent and independent human beings who have their own minds. For those of us who are still more comfortable with mechanical than biological metaphors, try this one: The VKT is similar to a local area network (LAN) composed of multiple intelligent desktop computers, each of which individually has the capability of the room-sized computers of only a few years ago. What is a more effective integration strategy than traditional supervision? An empowering leadership that creates distributed minds. The key is to link the minds together—not to superimpose the minds of the leaders on top of those of the workers. This leadership is so essential that we dedicate all of Chapter 10 to it. At this point, suffice it to say that a key integrative strategy is the type of leadership intervention used to foster a climate of cooperation and collaboration.

The most effective VKTs typically address the following leadership questions:

- ► What will the team leader do?
- ► What will the team members do?
- ► Who is accountable for our success?
- ► Who will manage what?
- ► Who will make what decisions?
- ► Who will solve what problems?
- ► What decisions will we not be able to make?
- ► Where do we go for help?
- ► Who will solve intractable disagreements?

Without an understanding of these fundamental leadership issues, the VKT will become frustrated and ineffective. Effective leadership reduces the problems that cannot be resolved through structure and value discussions.

Shared Values

HP has an enviable record of success with VKTs. As you talk to employees, it soon becomes clear that part of the reason is shared values. The undisputed foundation for their work is what they call "the HP way." The legacy of their founders (still referred to inside the company as Bill and Dave), the HP way outlines some common beliefs about the dignity of people, getting results, and how HP work should be done. It provides a touchstone for work, a common ground that even outsiders must acknowledge if they are to work effectively in the HP community.

Admittedly, not all HP employees agree on exactly what the HP way means for their work, but it does provide an excuse for each team to have a clarifying discussion about how it will apply to the team's work. This discussion provides one important answer to the question of how to create a distributed mind. Like the Constitution of the United States, it provides a common base of shared values and some suggested processes for corporate governance to build from. It is a good place to start. Just as the autonomic nervous system takes care of breathing and other critical functions "automatically," it means that there are certain things team members can take for granted (agreements about working relationships that can be assumed), freeing them to focus on some of the more pressing technical and business matters.

Frank William Reis, executive vice president of Cuyahoga Community College in Cleveland, Ohio, suggests some other ways to build even more specific behavioral agreements. Although the teaching and administrative staffs of the large community college are usually located together on the campus, the multiple task forces used as a substitution for hierarchical controls are very diverse, with frequently changing membership. They needed some way to create a common approach to minimize the time required to establish norms that would allow them to be productive. "We created some operating guidelines that are used in the team meetings. Things like, 'We will start and stop meetings on time' and 'There is no rank in this meeting,' etc. These are posted in the meeting areas. We use the same six guidelines for every team." These simple shared norms have risen to the status of shared values in the operation.

Software developers at Lotus use similiar techniques to avoid getting off track. They refer to unproductive discussions as ratholes. The first person who recognizes the problem shouts, "Rathole!" It causes the team to correct its course. They also try to avoid what they have come to call "piling on." Piling on is the practice of spending a lot of time agreeing with one another. Having the discipline to adhere to these guidelines "saves hundreds of hours per year at my company," claims Jeffrey Beir, vice president of Lotus Development Corporation.[7] We will discuss these practices in more detail in Chapter 11. Suffice it to say that to be effective, VKTs should be able to answer the following kinds of questions:

- What do we value as a team?
- How will we operate together?
- How will we run meetings?
- How will we make decisions?
- How will we solve technical problems?
- How will we solve people problems?
- What process will we use to prioritize our work on this team and on other teams?

Shared values can make a huge difference for VKTs that cross organizational and cultural boundaries. It is important to spend enough time on this discussion to reach a true commitment without compromising understanding or offending other team members. This may require considerable sensitivity and listening skills. Many VKTs use a third-party facilitator to help them with this process.

Rewarded Goals

All teams require a common purpose if they are to be successful, but specific measurable goals do even more—especially for VKTs. Goals provide a clear focus for the day-to-day activities and a practical arbitrator for the inevitable conflicts, trade-offs, and resource compromises. Good goals provide at least one additional important benefit: They are a substitute for hierarchy, allowing the team to become a self-directed work team if that structure is appropriate to its task.

Having good goals, however, does not appear to be sufficient as an integrative technique. Goals are helpful only to the extent that they are used actively as a regular tool of self-regulation. For this reason, we call the final strategy rewarded goals. To develop this strategy, VKTs must answer such questions as:

- What do we need to do to be successful?
- What are our key goals?
- How will we measure our goals/track our progress?
- What is our reward system?
- What do our customers need from us?
- What do our stakeholders need from us?
- What are our priorities?
- What will we do if we get off track?
- How will we reward goal accomplishment?

Rewarded goals are tracked and acknowledged. Along with shared values, effective leadership, and appropriate structures, rewarded goals are an integration mechanism that enables VKTs to create a distributed mind.

Let's explore a few more specific tips for solving some of the VKT challenges introduced earlier in the chapter.

Virtual Collocation

Research on concurrent engineering suggests that linking knowledge workers together through networks and other communication devices as though they were located in the same office is critical to effectiveness. Say Robert Mills, Beverly Beckert, Lisa Kempfer, and Jennifer Chalsma, "Communication is key to concurrent engineering. This includes everything from a willingness to share information without a time lag to managing databases. It also includes a concept called virtual collocation, which links together employees at remote sites."[8] But HP takes the collocation concept further to include a type of psychological collocation as well.

"Some of these teams have an office location where they have desks for everyone," says Winby. Even though they seldom meet together in person to use them, this gives them a place, a shared location that provides a common identity. The virtual office is important less for its physical presence than for its symbolic significance. It shows people that they are part of a certain important community even when they are not there.

Some knowledge workers believe that they need something even more substantive. We are human beings with basic human needs. Beth Torre is manager of the site service systems of Merck and Company, the pharmaceutical giant, in Whitehouse Station, New Jersey. She relays the story of an IBM facility she visited in New Jersey that left a real impression on her. This facility has little need for permanent office spaces anymore because the knowledge workers usually work out of their own homes or from other off-site locations. There are enough office spaces for only about half of the knowledge workers at any one time. The workers have unassigned cubicles with phones and other office equipment support, where they plug in their portable computers and go to work. These cubicles are filled up first-come, first-served, with no guarantee that you will get the same one again. "I thought it was interesting," she says, "that they have a long wall for displaying the personal things that would be in a traditional office." This wall extends down one side of the anonymous cubicle complex. She estimates that each person has about a three-foot by three-foot personal space in which to hang whatever he or she wants. "The wall is filled with photographs, certificates, and even drawings from employees' children," she observes. "I guess we all need some space that we can make our own."

Many more of these teams have their virtual office location established through technology. They have a common cyberspace locale like a server or a Web page for E-mail messages and announcements. To make it more human, some VKTs scan in their photographs on their E-mail location. Others use team names, slogans, or symbols, like the famous Macintosh development team at Apple Computers who flew the Jolly Roger skull and crossbones over its team location to reinforce the team members' image of themselves as pirates operating on the edge of the corporation. While these symbols are helpful for any team, they are especially useful for VKTs that are struggling to develop a clear team identity.

VKT Fast Start-Ups

Mark Bluemling, a vice president at SNET Mobility, Inc., a regional telecommunications company, suggests that knowledge workers—even those in virtual knowledge teams—have other needs as well. They can't stay physically disconnected for long. "I think we have social needs that require some level of interaction with other human beings," he says. Even if the work doesn't require the interaction to pass along information or make team decisions face to face, we need the periodic reminder that we belong to something, even if it is temporary in duration—we need evidence that we belong to this community of other human beings that we call a team.

This appears to be especially important at the VKT start-up. HP has found that an effective face-to-face start-up can accelerate the effectiveness of the team. "The team start-up is critical," says Peter Bartlett. "We've found that the investment required to get everybody together in the same room at the beginning of the project is well worth it." The team members get to know one another, reach agreement on a common purpose and direction, develop guidelines on how they will work together, and put together a schedule for interactions. This early face-to-face start-up meeting provides an important personalizing touch for team members. That touch facilitates communication and motivation later on. It minimizes the kind of distractions and confusion that can accompany depersonalized communication like anonymous E-mail. For example, you don't see flaming (the merciless hazing ritual of electronic communicators) in HP design team communiqués, even though such messages are common in other electronic networks where you don't know the recipient of your message as a human being.

HP product development teams are among the best in the business. But HP still finds the operation of these virtual knowledge teams challenging. There is still much to learn. See Figure 7-1 for a list of the challenges and opportunities related to VKTs.

Figure 7-1. The challenges and opportunities of virtual knowledge teams.

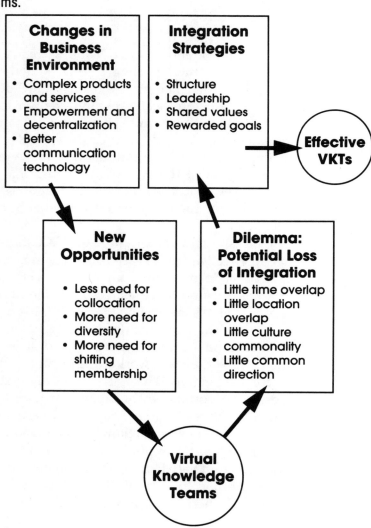

Summary

Environmental shifts and changes in organizational capabilities have created opportunities and need for virtual knowledge teams in contemporary organizations. To effectively create, utilize, and support VKTs, we must focus more attention on the VKT challenges. Creating a distributed mind for virtual knowledge teams is no easy task, but companies like Hewlett-Packard are showing us how to do it. Like the body's DNA system, four primary elements—(1) structure, (2) leadership, (3) shared values, and (4) rewarded goals—are the key integrative strategies used by VKTs to create a distributed mind. Comprehensive communication systems and other structural processes such as vertical multiskilling, virtual collocation, and special VKT start-up activities help to ensure the proper differentiation and integration of the VKTs' work. Virtual knowledge teams face a number of special challenges above and beyond those of regular knowledge teams. But some organizations are finding ways to meet these challenges and have their VKTs operate as seamlessly and effectively as though they were all cells in the same body.

Notes

1. Michael A. Verespej, "A Workforce Revolution?" *Industry Week*, August 21, 1996, 21. Reprinted with permission from *Industry Week*. Copyright Penton Publishing, Inc., Cleveland, Ohio.
2. William E. Halal, "The Rise of the Knowledge Entrepreneur," *The Futurist*, November—December 1996, 15.
3. Michael A. Verespej, "Welcome to the New Workspace," *Industry Week* April 15, 1996, 27. Reprinted with permission from *Industry Week*. Copyright Penton Publishing, Inc., Cleveland, Ohio.
4. F. H. C. Crick, "Nucleic Acids," *Scientific American* 197 (1957): 188–200.
5. Paul R. Lawrence and Jay W. Lorsch, *Organization and Environment* (Boston: Harvard University Press, 1967).

6. Kimball Fisher, *Leading Self-Directed Work Teams* (New York: McGraw-Hill, 1993).

7. Jeffery Beir, "Managing Creatives: Our Creative Workers Will Excell—If We Let Them," *Vital Speeches of the Day* 61, no. 16 (1995): 505. Used by permission.

8. Robert Mills, Beverly Beckert, Lisa Kempfer, Jennifer Chalsma, "Organizing for Concurrent Engineering," *Industry Week*, July 20, 1993, CC 8. Reprinted with permission from *Industry Week*, July 20, 1993. Copyright ©, Penton Publishing, Inc., Cleveland, Ohio.

8

The Creative Spark: Harnessing Learning, Creativity, and Innovation

"At Disney, we . . . feel that the only way to succeed creatively is to fail. A company like ours must create an atmosphere in which people feel safe to fail. This means forming an organization where failure is not only tolerated, but fear of criticism for submitting a foolish idea is abolished. If not, people become too cautious. They hunker down . . . afraid to speak up, afraid to rock the boat, afraid of being ridiculed."[1]

—Michael Eisner, CEO and Chairman of the Walt Disney Company

One of Wendy Coetzee's roles within the Department of Institutional Development at Vista University in South Africa is to run or assist in running academic writing or instructional design workshops for members of the academic staff. It was through one of these series of workshops that Wendy developed and coordinated the Teamwrite project on the Vista University Distance Education Campus (VUDEC).

The goal of the Teamwrite project is to clarify text and make the study content of course materials more accessible to students. What is unusual about the Teamwrite process is that course material is written by a team. Before Teamwrite, one writer (or maybe two or three if the academic department was large enough) would go off and write the study manual. After it was completed, it would be handed over to the scheduling department to be typed and then given to an editor. Because of the conventional scheduling procedure, the study manual often was not returned to the writer for several months or maybe even a whole year. This created an obvious problem: After so much time had elapsed, the writer had often forgotten what he or she wanted to say.

So Wendy proposed that a new member be introduced into the process: an instructional designer who would assist the writers from the outset in order to help prevent problems down the road. As Wendy explains,

> "Most of the academic staff at VUDEC do not have much training in writing course material. Furthermore, they are often second-language speakers of English, so they need some assistance with the language. They are very knowledgeable about their subjects, but they need to write on a level that students, not faculty, will understand. With the instructional designer present in the group, he or she can read the material from the student's perspective and say, 'I don't understand this' when the language is unclear."

In addition to the instructional designer, each writing team includes an editor, who sits in on discussions when the course content is being planned, as well as being involved later on with texts that have been reworked on the basis of discussions between the writers and the instructional designer. This allows the editors to take on an enhanced role and to make a more creative contribution to the final product.

Despite some minor setbacks and modifications that took

place between Phase 1 and Phase 2 of the project, the Teamwrite project is regarded as a success. When students were presented with two extracts from manuals, one written under the team format and one written in the traditional way, they found the Teamwrite manual to be infinitely better. The content, they stated, was much more accessible and understandable than in the individually written text.

Wendy Coetzee and the staff at Vista University are not alone in their quest to learn how to manage creative processes involving groups of gifted individuals. Organizations of all kinds are struggling to understand how to create a learning-based environment that fosters creativity and innovation.

Perhaps no place better demonstrates the attributes of a learning, innovative organization than the late nineteenth century Menlo Park labs of Thomas Alva Edison. Consider the extraordinary number of accomplishments that came out of that setting in a short period of time. In only six years, Edison obtained more than 400 patents. Several of these were among the most influential technologies of modern America. He invented the phonograph, perfected a carbon telephone transmitter, and continued working on various telegraphic problems. It was during this time that he developed the practical incandescent light bulb and electrical generating and transmitting system, which is regarded by many as his most outstanding contribution of all.[2]

Edison understood the learning process of education, experimentation, and evaluation, and his Menlo Park labs might serve well as a model for contemporary organizations struggling to harness the learning and creativity of their knowledge workers.

The Menlo Park story and myriad other examples suggest that there are at least four key concepts that contribute to an organization's ability to build an environment of creativity:

1. The act of creation is a social rather than an exclusively independent activity; the sharing of stories and experience is critical to the process of innovation.
2. Creativity is a result of repeated experimentation.
3. Learning to share partially developed ideas with oth-

ers—in other words, having a willingness to learn in public—is essential to creativity.
4. Standardized work processes and methods allow creativity to flourish.

We will explore these concepts in this chapter.

Creativity as a Social Activity

Contrary to folk history, Thomas Edison's many accomplishments weren't achieved by working alone. Andre Millard, in his essay "Machine Shop Culture and Menlo Park" in *Working at Inventing: Thomas A. Edison and the Menlo Park Experience,* states: "Despite his image as the 'Wizard of Menlo Park,' a lone, heroic inventor whose brilliant mind created magical inventions, Edison rarely worked alone. Innovation in his laboratories was a cooperative affair."[3]

Designing a workplace that facilitates interaction and collaboration among knowledge workers may well result in phenomenal breakthroughs, as evidenced by the Menlo Park labs. Edison organized for socialization. He modeled Menlo Park after the craft culture in Europe and the machine shops of Newark, New Jersey, which incorporated a measure of freedom and socialization quite different from other work environments of his day. He organized teams to do the work, using a model that might be likened somewhat to today's project teams. They were composed of a chief experimenter and several assistants. Each team was augmented by other machinists and craftspeople as determined by the team, which was also free to draw on any resource in the laboratories (supplies, library information, Edison himself, the experience of tradespeople, etc.). Organizing in this way facilitated effective communication channels that allowed these teams to achieve remarkable outcomes.

"[They] were encouraged to maintain communication among the teams because Edison knew that this was a vital part of the process of innovation. The key to one problem might be found in the experimental results generated in another project. The openness of the machine shops permitted the ready spread of information, not necessarily the written knowledge of science but the nonverbal information of ways of doing things, of techniques and prior experience. The ease of communication in the shops had helped bring forth a great number of important inventions."[4]

It was the sharing of stories and learning experiences that sparked a creation or allowed a crude idea to be developed into a viable innovation at the Menlo Park labs. Storytelling is an integral part of the socialization process that leads to innovation. It is often the primary means by which team members share information and learn from one another.

In the twenty-first-century offices of Sun Microsystems (located, ironically enough, in Menlo Park, California), one finds a modern-day version of the Menlo Park labs of Thomas Edison. This working campus has incorporated many of the principles found in the nineteenth-century New Jersey site. For example, a concerted effort has been made, via the architectural design, to encourage conversation and to minimize individual office space. Sun has learned that creativity is very much a social process and that the sharing of thoughts, ideas, stories, and experience is an important part of innovation. Sun's new approach to office design is described in an article published in *Industry Week:*

"The entire look—and intent—of the campus is to encourage the exchange of ideas among employees. That's why only 35% of the interior space is office space and there are 225 meeting places within the complex.

"The typical Silicon Valley string of two-story buildings is not always the most efficient work environment, particularly for engineers, who often need to collar someone," says [William T.] Agnello [Sun's vice president—real estate and the workplace]. "We needed a better environment to overcome some of those obstacles. So we asked ourselves what we could do from a work environment standpoint so that engineers will get started talking about projects informally."[5]

This theme of networking as a way to infuse learning, creativity, and innovation into modern-day organizations is not unique to Sun Microsystems. Many inventors can attest to the significant role that interaction plays in their achievements. For instance, Raymond Kurzweil, who developed the reading machine for the blind, states:

> "I find that the projects I get involved with are increasingly interdisciplinary in their approach. Inventions like the reading machine are not the kind of project created by someone who goes down into his basement and emerges two years later with some brilliant breakthrough. The projects I work on are a disciplined effort involving teams of people with different backgrounds. In speech recognition, for example, some of the technologists involved include linguists, signal-processing experts, VLSI [very large scale integration] designers, psycho-processing experts, speech scientists, computer scientists, human-factors designers, experts in artificial intelligence and pattern recognition, and so on.
>
> "If you look at the entire company, you bring even more disciplines: manufacturing, material-resources planning, purchasing, marketing, finance, and so on. Each of these areas has also developed sophisticated methodologies of their own that are as complex as those in engineering. Because of the complexity involved, we often try to solve problems in groups. Very often I've found that fresh, novel ideas in a particular discipline do not always come from the experts in that field, but from those in other fields. A great deal of group process is behind our inventions. Invention is increasingly interdisciplinary work. It involves teams of people. There are relatively few significant inventions that can be created by one or two people."[6]

Stanford Ovshinsky, an inventor of materials used to build computer memories, integrated circuits, etc., also acknowledges the value of collaboration as a critical factor in innovation:

"I've been about to set up an environment here—an environment that I know is part of the inventive process. In the last twenty-seven years, I've been very fortunate in building up a well-equipped laboratory with tremendously talented and superb people who are also very inventive in their own right. I also have a very good group of colleagues and collaborators that I can share ideas with. I know that environment is part of the invention process."[7]

In spite of testimonials such as these, many organizations continue to hang on to the philosophy that knowledge workers are a "unique breed"—that the cerebral nature of much of their work dictates that they function alone, separated physically and psychologically from the masses. As the *1993 Survey of Technical Professionals in Teams* conducted by the Center for the Study of Work Teams at the University of North Texas reveals, however, many knowledge workers prefer a more collaborative environment. The study surveyed 542 technical professionals from 14 companies. Specialties surveyed included, among other disciplines, engineering, information systems, technical writing, marketing, development, finance, human resources, and customer service. The survey findings state, "The results suggest a fairly strong preference for working in a collaborative, team-based environment, as opposed to the stereotyped preference for isolated, individually-oriented work."[8]

In commenting on ways in which work is hindered or helped by teaming, the survey report says:

"There was a strong sense that teaming would help improve communication, decision making, and problem solving, as exemplified by comments such as 'more effective decisions,' 'sharing of ideas, responsibilities, problems, solutions,' 'quicker time to solution when a problem arises,' 'more shared knowledge and experience,' and 'better communication.' Greater product quality and improvements in work processes were reported as well, for example, 'generation of new ideas should improve overall product functionality and quality,' 'it will make us more efficient and effective,' and 'improves flow of information.'

> . . . A final respondent expressed the positive aspects of teaming as follows: 'a team environment is obviously critical to the success of our group, since delivering our product of technical information requires a pool of different skills and experience, along with consistency of information.' "[9]

While there undoubtedly are still cases of individuals working alone to achieve breakthroughs, it is more likely that organizations too often underestimate the power of the social aspect of innovation. Assuming that breakthrough developments will come only through the "mad scientist" approach could significantly limit an organization's ability to attain the level of achievement it requires.

Creativity: The Result of Repeated Experimentation

Another factor that contributes to a knowledge team's ability to innovate is the organization's tolerance for experimentation. As Edison's labs and other more current examples illustrate, the acceptance of a trial-and-error learning process can do much to nurture a creative culture.

Millard describes the environment Edison sought to create in the labs:

> "The tradition of the shop culture was learning by doing: in the Menlo Park lab it was inventing by doing" altering the experimental model over and over to try out new ideas. . . .
>
> "True to the democracy of the machine shop culture, Edison was always open to the suggestions and ideas of his men when it came to new experiments or inventions. Anyone was free to try a new idea. The machinists did more than act as Edison's hands—they

filled in the details that were omitted in his fast-moving thoughts, and they applied their own expertise in the struggle to get the thing to work. They also took the initiative to modify devices and to experiment freely. Machinist and experimenter were partners in invention."[10]

As evidence of this unique culture established by Edison, the experimenters in the Menlo Park labs were called "Muckers" from English slang. The term *mucker* was derived from the expressions "to muck in"—to pitch in, eating and working together—and "to muck about"—to fool about with little purpose other than amusement.[11]

What an interesting job title! It could prove to be a useful conversation starter in today's cocktail party business gatherings.

"Hi, I'm Louise."

"Nice to meet you, Louise. What do you do?"

"I'm a mucker."

While it might be a strange job title, it speaks volumes about what constitutes an environment conducive to creativity and innovation.

Learning to Share Partially Developed Ideas With Others

Richard McDermott, in his research on knowledge work, emphasizes the criticality of collaboration as a learning methodology and introduces some of the challenges associated with this approach:

"Making knowledge work visible involves a fundamental shift in values from private, individual action to openly sharing information and learning. This means that knowledge workers need to be willing to make their own individual work public, to "think aloud" with their colleagues and let their own work, even when it is incorrect or incomplete, be seen, discussed and criticized by their peers. They also need to contribute their time to their colleagues' development. But this *learning in public* and sharing methods to improve the competence of others flies in the face of many deeply-rooted professional and organizational assumptions. Individual excellence is highly regarded in most companies, and frequently the only focus of reward. Individual judgment, insight, and craftsmanship is also a central value, frequently implicit, in most professional training and socialization."[12]

Wendy Coetzee can affirm that this concept of learning in public is sometimes a tough one to employ. In spite of its success, the Teamwrite project has sometimes been a difficult learning experience, and all the players have had to make adjustments. Wendy acknowledges that sometimes part of the role of the instructional designer is mediation between editors and writers. "I might find myself saying to the editor, 'You have a point here. It *is* better to use a table as opposed to all that prose.' Sometimes an editor might inadvertently change the actual meaning of the text in an attempt to clarify the writer's style. In these cases, I will bring both parties together and negotiate. Closer liaison between all members of the team has helped to reduce problems."

The writers, instructional designers, and editors of Teamwrite are learning how to learn in public. Wendy explains that as colleagues and professionals working on the same team, they have had to learn how to offer recommendations and suggestions for changes in a diplomatic way. They found, for instance, that it was more palatable to the writers and editors to have the instructional designer make notes about how the writing could be improved on a separate sheet, rather than rewriting the text itself. The writers could then use these separate notes as feedback and as a guide to help them modify their drafts before these are passed on to the editor. One thing that the instructional designers on the Teamwrite project have learned is that it is important to avoid scribbling on the text like a teacher with a red pen.

Edison himself was a good model of one who was willing

to share "half-baked" ideas, understanding that someone else in the lab might be able to build on them and bring them to fruition. Edison used laboratory notebooks to quickly record ideas or rough sketches. These were left on the experimental tables for others to pick up and use or passed on to one of the machinists to begin the invention process. Edison was always open to suggestions and ideas. Edison viewed the role of the machinists in the lab as one of filling in details that might have been omitted in his "fast-moving" thoughts. In addition to being free to try their own ideas, he expected them to modify devices and to experiment with his ideas.[13]

Sales teams at AT&T have discovered the advantages of an open learning environment in which real-life issues are presented, discussed, and used as fertile ground for improvement. The teams use regularly scheduled meetings as a forum for continuous learning. Past methods of learning such as role plays have been replaced by the exploration of real experiences of team members. Individuals describe a given situation, the outcome, and what worked or didn't work.

Perhaps no other modern-day organization better understands how to harness creativity than the Walt Disney Company. One activity the company uses to find new ideas is what it calls the "Gong Show." The Gong Show format, started shortly after Michael Eisner arrived at Disney, was originally a forum for executives, but has since evolved into a process that is open to anybody. The Disney Feature Animation division, for instance, has its own Gong Show three times a year. As described by Michael Eisner, the process works something like this:

> "Anybody [in our company] who wants to . . . and I mean anybody . . . gets a chance to pitch an idea for an animated film to a small group of executives . . . which includes, among others, me and Roy Disney, our vice chairman, and Peter Schneider, head of Feature Animation. There are usually about 40 presenters.
>
> "For this to work, you must have an environment where people feel safe about giving their ideas. And, while we do not pull our punches when people present their ideas, we create an atmosphere in which each idea

can receive full and serious consideration. Yes, we tell
people if we think an idea won't work. But we tell them
why and we tell them how it might be improved. And,
of course, we tell them when we think an idea has
promise . . . and we pursue that promise. . . . The fact is
that several of our better animated features have come
out of the Gong Show and some of our other major
winners out of similar kinds of programs in other parts
of the company."[14]

The discussion or even argument that takes place as a result
of publicly sharing an idea often leads to new or innovative developments. Early breakthroughs in physics, for example, occurred after a major annual event known as the Meeting of
German Scientists and Physicians was convened every September. The meeting included discussion sessions, and the journal
Physikalische Zeitschrift published both the lectures and the "spir-
ited exchanges" that followed them. These debates, which were
often more argumentative than scientific, are considered by
many to have been essential to the development of important
theories, including those based on the principles of relativity as
espoused by Lorentz and Einstein.[15]

The concept of learning from the sharing of ideas certainly
isn't a new one. University-level symposia and graduate-level
courses, for instance, have long been based on the concept of
group discussion and learning. The challenge, however, is to incorporate public learning into organizations. Most corporate cultures (Disney being something of an aberration) still struggle
with how to make public learning and discovery an accepted
norm.

Creativity and Standardized Processes

As knowledge teams strive for creative achievement, we suggest
one final point for consideration: the concept that art and creativity have rules.

Prior to entering the field of organization development, the
authors were both trained in the field of art. One studied to be-

come a commercial artist, the other an art historian. Through that training, we learned an important concept that people outside of the art field don't often realize: There are rules to art. Most people think of art as an occupation without rules, a field in which one does whatever one wants in order to be creative. Interestingly, however, it is the rules of art that make it so creative. There are clear rules, for instance, about color theory (e.g., certain colors will come forward while others will blend into the background); light, dark, and shadow (e.g., how they influence form); and perspective (how things appear differently depending on the use of line, etc.). In other words, there are a series of techniques that the artist learns, which in turn facilitate the creative process. In fact, knowing these rules frees the artist to break them and push to the edge of something new or innovative. The rules provide the pattern and consistency that set the boundaries for what constitutes creativity. Without rules, there is no dynamic tension in which creativity can be fostered.

The same is true for knowledge teams. A certain amount of standardization of processes and consistent application of techniques are required in order to communicate effectively, to share ideas, and to facilitate the creative process itself. In other words, creativity is not an absence of rules, but rather, how you work with the rules.

Richard McDermott states that "developing standardized processes and methods is at the heart of transforming knowledge work from an individual craft to a learning system." He further concludes:

> "The purpose of standardizing is to reduce the variation between different knowledge workers. As people progress through their careers they continually develop and incorporate new knowledge, deepen their understanding, refine their methods, and fine tune their ability to judge when to apply those tools. For those gifted at their craft, this is their professional wisdom, their tacit knowledge of the *practice* of their craft. . . . Standardizing methods pushes the individual practitioner to reflect on his or her practice and make it explicit.

"When individuals make their methods explicit, they usually find that they each follow a more or less regular pattern, but frequently each individual has their own idiosyncratic pattern. This is why there is so much individual variation in most knowledge work. As in craftwork, standardizing key elements of the work makes the outputs of different knowledge workers more consistent and reduces the time individuals waste reinventing applications their colleagues have already discovered.

". . . Standardizing knowledge work does not eliminate individual judgment; it *focuses* judgment on the cutting edge of the practice. Standardizing does not mean creating detailed step-by-step procedures for each activity and forcing all to work into them. . . . To standardize work, procedures need to be general enough to be applied in a wide variety of situations. There is always judgment and nuance in execution which the standard processes are not meant to capture. . . . This is the continually inventive process in masterful professional practice. Standard processes and procedures make the routine way of doing the work visible and consistent. They create a common basic practice so the knowledge worker can focus on the exceptional."[16]

Summary

In order to foster creativity, organizations need to have in place some standardization of processes. It is these "rules of art" that allow the "artists" to be creative. Knowing the boundaries makes it possible to challenge those boundaries and to push for something greater than what is currently known.

Our experience also suggests that a willingness to learn in public, with all of its frightening implications about self-disclosure, sharing less than successful experiences so that others can learn from them, or offering incomplete thoughts in front of respected colleagues, is critical to the creativity and innovation required to carry out much knowledge work.

Related to the notion of learning in public is the need to foster an environment in which repeated experimentation is encouraged. Although knowledge work is often considered to be "cerebral" in nature, it is nonetheless the "hands-on" trial-and-error process that leads to many breakthroughs in both ideas and technology.

And finally, creativity and innovation are social activities. While some great ideas are born in isolation, a far larger number have come from social interaction—from one idea generating another and another, until genuine innovation is achieved. In the past, the stereotype of knowledge workers has been one of soloists who like to work alone. But as recent studies indicate, those in the creative disciplines often crave interaction. Developing processes that allow this interaction to take place is vital.

While we still have much to learn about creativity and innovation, the Menlo Park labs of Thomas Alva Edison as well as many contemporary organizations can provide prototypes for us to consider.

Notes

1. Michael Eisner, "Managing a Creative Organization," *Vital Speeches of the Day* 62, no. 6 (1996): 502–505. Used by permission from Disney Enterprises, Inc.
2. William S. Pretzer, ed. *Working at Inventing: Thomas A. Edison and the Menlo Park Experience* (Ann Arbor, Mich.: printed by McNaughton & Gunn, Inc. [published by Henry Ford Museum and Greenfield Village], 1989), p. 16.
3. Ibid., p. 58.
4. Ibid., p. 60.
5. Michael A. Verespej, "The Idea Is to Talk," *Industry Week*, April 15, 1996, 28.
6. Kenneth A. Brown, *Inventors at Work* (Redmond, Wash.: Tempus Books of Microsoft Press, 1988).
7. Ibid.
8. Michael Beyerlein, Susan Tull Beyerlein, and Sandra Richardson, "1993 Survey of Technical Professionals in Teams:

Summary Report, 1993," Center for the Study of Work Teams, University of North Texas, Denton, Texas, p. 7. Used by permission.

9. Ibid., 22–23.

10. Andre Millard, "Machine Shop Culture and Menlo Park," in *Working at Inventing: Thomas A. Edison and the Menlo Park Experience*, ed. William S. Pretzer (Ann Arbor, Mich.: printed by McNaughton & Gunn, Inc. [published by Henry Ford Museum and Greenfield Village], 1989), pp. 59–61.

11. Ibid.

12. Richard McDermott, "From Craftwork to Learning Systems: Transforming Knowledge Work," working draft, p. 11. Used by permission.

13. Millard, "Machine Shop Culture and Menlo Park."

14. Eisner, "Managing a Creative Organization," pp. 502–505. Used by permission from Disney Enterprises, Inc.

15. Arthur I. Miller, *Insights of Genius: Imagery and Creativity in Science and Art* (New York: Copernicus, an imprint of Springer-Verlag, 1996).

16. McDermott, "From Craftwork to Learning Systems," pp. 12–13.

9

Knowledge Transfer: Sharing Mind Work and Mastering Information Overload

"Instead of an individual orientation, the focus will be on sharing knowledge among teams. It will be recognized that information is very valuable, and that different people possess different skills. If they can be inspired to work together, the whole will be greater than the sum of the parts."[1]

—Philip M. Condit, President, The Boeing Company

"E-mail is fast, cheap, and easy to use. But it has its dark side, pummeling users with trivial information and junk ads. For many knowledge workers, this golden child of the Internet has become the bane of their existence."[2]

—John Bowie, Information Engineering Consultant

Recently a large private gas distribution company in the southern United States was undergoing a corporate transformation from traditional management styles to team-based manage-ment. Consultants were called in to help provide leadership training for the new role of coach, trainer, and leader. They were later invited back to do a progress assessment. As part of the assessment, they asked a cross section of managers several ques-tions, including "How are you adjusting to your new role in the organization?" In a deep southern drawl, one of the senior managers answered: "Well, I'd love to create visions and coach and be a living example and provide training for my team mem-bers and be an effective barrier buster and effectively analyze our business environment on a regular basis and facilitate effec-tive meetings and make sure the team is skilled at consensus decision making—but doggone it, I receive 75 E-mails a day now! Everybody copies everybody else on everything! All I have time to do now in this team-based environment is read and re-spond to E-mail."

Sound familiar? In this chapter we would like to discuss what is becoming a critical attribute of effective knowledge work teams: the ability to transfer knowledge effectively without causing information overload.

Knowledge Transfer

It is difficult to overstate the importance of knowledge transfer to knowledge work. This is an ongoing challenge today because knowledge changes so rapidly. Notes Dr. Arno Penzias, Nobel Prize winner and vice president of research at Bell Labs, "I think today we are the first generation in human history where knowl-edge is going to be obsolete, not just once during our careers but several times."[3]

Current knowledge is the life blood of knowledge work, and the ability to transfer it is a key differentiating characteristic between effective and ineffective knowledge work teams. After all, without the ability to transfer knowledge from one team member to another, there is no benefit to working in a knowl-edge team at all.

The better knowledge teams create specific processes, such

as project team meetings and electronic forums, to transfer their knowledge to one another. Knowledge is transferred as information from one party to another party or parties. Figure 9-1 provides a simple diagram of the knowledge transfer process. Effective knowledge transfer occurs only when all parts of the process work well. Information must be (1) sent properly and (2) received properly, with (3) minimum noise, the distracting elements of communication that can distort data at any point in the knowledge transfer process.

This transfer can be much more difficult than it appears. Technical noise like telephone line static is the least difficult to eliminate. It is far more difficult to reduce the social noise in knowledge transfer. Social noise includes things like perceptions, assumptions, and emotions that can affect a message transfer. Noise, for example, can cloud what a sender wants to communicate, causing her to say something different from what she intended to say. Noise can affect the receiver as well. The same words, context, or examples used by the sender may have a completely different meaning to the receiver as a result of his own life experience and perceptions. As if this wasn't difficult enough, cross-cultural knowledge transfer adds a whole additional level of complexity to the process as each party views the transfer through his or her own unique cultural lens.

When effective knowledge transfer occurs, knowledge workers are able to integrate their work with others, share feedback and ideas, participate in problem solving and decision making, train new team members, and perform other activities

Figure 9-1. Knowledge transfer.

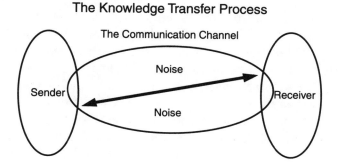

The Knowledge Transfer Process

that are critical to their success. In addition, knowledge workers know that without good information dissemination processes there can be no ongoing learning—the activity required for creating new knowledge.

HP, DEC, Compaq, Microsoft, and virtually every other company that employs engineers has found that project team meetings in which important technical ideas, project timeline status, potential problems, cost, and customer data are shared are critical for the smooth execution of a project—especially a project that requires the seamless integration of multiple specialists. Good information systems are also critical for knowledge work inside of the factory. In a General Electric dishwasher plant, workers see the most frequent defects for each hour. Similarly, the Cummins Engline CMEP plant boasts an electronic scoreboard within sight of all employees that keeps real-time running tallies of a number of quality and productivity measures, including production vs. the number of engines required to meet production goals. The HP Formatter facility in Boise, Idaho, uses an "instrument panel" to display a few key measures in real time. These displays are never more than fifteen minutes old. Like the dashboard instruments in an automobile, they often help operators and engineers to spot trends and make corrections before problems cause costly downtime.

Information is important both because it allows effective problem solving and decision making and because it provides a substitute for hierarchical controls. Bill Synder, a former supervisor at American Transtech, a company that helped to handle the stock redistribution by the court-enforced breakup of AT&T, notes:

> "A timely information system . . . [provided] quality and profitability results on a daily or weekly basis. As long as the system measured the right things, and as long as the results were good, I could focus my attention elsewhere (unless the team asked for help). Certain peers were rankled by my confidence and freedom, and would warn me that the teams were "fooling around" and "taking advantage" of me in my absence. Those same teams were lowering their costs by 40% and

achieving higher quality results than they had in years. I wasn't worried, and I told my peers that they shouldn't be either."[4]

Companywide Knowledge Transfer

Knowledge work teams normally require a variety of information sources in order to be effective. Some high-level companywide information, for example, can affect team strategy or resources. Companies can provide these data in a number of timely ways. FedEx, for example, uses a $10 million internal television network called FXTV to communicate information to employees. When the company purchased Flying Tiger in 1989, this system was used to announce the purchase only moments after the required announcement to the financial community. At Hallmark, news and announcements appear on television monitors located throughout the corporate headquarters in Kansas City. Xerox uses its TV network and workstations to send electronic newsleters to about 60 percent of its employees worldwide at least three times a week. Xerox—along with a rapidly growing number of other companies—also uses an intranet, the latest in high-tech communication networks. These web sites can be accessed only by authorized employees. Other companies use hot lines, a sort of menu-driven telecommunication process created both to inform and to help with rumor control. Honeywell employees have access to prerecorded messages twenty-four hours a day. Southwestern Bell has a similar prerecorded service. In a refreshing departure from the company publications of the past, company papers like Allied-Signal Aerospace's *Horizons* look more like trade publications than like thinly disguised company propaganda.[5]

Most companies rapidly discover, however, that although these communication technologies provide an opportunity for greatly increasing the amount of information shared with knowledge workers, they may not necessarily improve communication effectiveness. Quantity is not quality. One-way communication such as newsleters and electronic bulletin boards certainly cannot substitute for two-way communication in face-to-face settings where people can ask questions, debate issues, or solve problems together. So in the late 1980s General Electric CEO Jack Welch established companywide town meetings to facilitate interaction between people. Managers credit these meetings with "uncovering all kinds of crazy stuff we were doing."[6] Hallmark also has regular CEO forums in which fifty to a hundred randomly selected nonmanagement employees have a ninety-minute meeting with CEO Irv Hockaday.

Knowledge Transfer Within and Between Teams

Companywide knowledge transfer activities can be very useful to knowledge teams. But knowledge transfer within and between teams is normally much more important.

Just as the human circulatory system employs myriad pathways to provide the body with blood, so knowledge workers create numerous ways to channel information through their own work system. But as we have already mentioned, the primary challenge of effective information flow appears to be the appropriate use of information channels rather than acquiring sufficient numbers of them. Knowledge workers need just the right amount of technical, financial, project status, and customer data—nothing more and nothing less. Until fairly recently, the primary information challenge was how to get enough information to knowledge workers so that they, like the tissues of the body, weren't starved for the nutrients they needed to survive and prosper.

However, today it is becoming increasingly difficult to create shared knowledge without the opposite problem: information overload. Just as too much blood draining unchecked inside the body can be life-threatening—so too can too much information flowing through the system. While technological advances in communication open up previously unknown conduits for funneling information and knowledge, they also pose the threat of unhelpful or unnecessary information clogging the system. Unfortunately, what we have gained in our ability to transmit information, we have often lost in our capacity to receive and act on it.

E-mail: A Mixed Blessing

One of the most used and abused electronic methods for knowledge transfer between and within teams is E-mail. Let's examine it in more detail to identify some key points concerning effective and ineffective knowledge transfer processes.

Although E-mail provides a convenient way to communicate with people electronically—a must when team members aren't collocated and very helpful even when they are—the systems get overloaded easily. Says Don Herman, manager of a product support team at Hewlett-Packard about what happened when he returned from a three-week vacation, "I wasn't able to check my messages, so when I returned, I had about 350 e-mail messages in my in-box. It took me a couple of weeks to get caught up."[7] This, of course, is a problem if you assume that the purpose of any knowledge transfer process is to save time rather than waste it. As with any good business process, some investment of time and money is required to produce this saving in the long term. But many knowledge workers find that the way their E-mail systems work makes them not a reasonable investment, but low-value-added activities instead—a fancy name for a waste of time.

A different HP manager has an efficient, but unorthodox approach to dealing with the problem of E-mail buildup: "When I returned from vacation," he said, "I had more than a hundred E-mail messages. I honestly didn't have time to read them. I ended up just deleting them, assuming that if it was something really important people would contact me again."[8] If the system were really helping with the knowledge transfer process, he wouldn't do that. One manager of a *Fortune* 500 company, like countless others struggling to keep their heads above the flood of electronic data surrounding them, confesses to having more than eight hundred messages—many of which he has never read—in his in-box. "I only delete them when I start running out of disk space," he says.[9]

Obviously, these examples demonstrate the problem of too much information. And this problem isn't limited to managers. When knowledge workers have to ignore communication from other team members to save time, or, even worse, have to delete unread messages to provide more space for other messages that they probably will not read, the knowledge transfer process isn't working. These knowledge work teams are hemorrhaging internally and drowning in a pool of too much data. What is the problem, and what can we do about it?

Dealing With Spamming

The first and easiest solution is to get rid of unsolicited junk mail. When E-mail systems are Internet-connected, unsolicited mail becomes an annoying reality of life. Tom Weathington of Inforum in Nashville has a rather drastic solution for this particular problem: "E-mail marked 'Urgent' gets blasted without a second thought."[10] The reason for this is that much of the unrequested mass marketing junk mail clogging E-mail systems connected to the Internet today is marked "Urgent." The practice of sending get-rich-quick schemes and bulk marketing mail over the Internet has been dubbed "spamming."

Some companies and people utilize technological means to block a certain amount of the true junk mail. Some also advocate the enforcement of the legal restrictions that already apply to a number of marketing tactics. But most Internet users so far tend to be free speech devotees, willing to put up with a certain amount of inconvenience to ensure the democratic openness of these global forums. When all is said and done, a certain amount of prioritizing and sorting is inevitable.

Whether the mail is Internet junk mail or messages created by well-intended team members who want everybody to have copies of everything, the only way to reduce E-mail glut once it is in the system is to plow through it. HP's Herman uses a three-pass approach. He first scans and then deletes routine messages. He then responds to messages that require action. He leaves longer items like newsletters, reports, and meeting minutes for the final pass—usually Friday afternoon—when he has time to read them.

There is, of course, a more fundamental problem here, and one that won't be solved by more effective time management or prioritization skills. The vast majority of the messages clogging E-mail systems come not from uninvited guests but from legitimate team members. Effective knowledge teams establish protocols about how to use knowledge transfer processes like E-mail. Agreed-upon knowledge transfer protocols can be the single most effective technique for improving these processes. Rather than finding ways to deal with the glut of information that develops after knowledge transfer practices get established, protocols help knowledge workers agree on how to avoid clogging the systems in the first place.

E-mail Protocols

E-mail is most helpful for general, nonurgent material where it is useful to retain documentation, interaction is not required, and security is not important.[11] Effective teams make commitments to use it properly by establishing that we call "protocols." They agree, for example, that if a message is truly urgent, it gets communicated face to face or voice to voice. If specific material is useful to only a few members of the team, then only those people get it—it would never been sent to everyone unless everyone honestly needs it. If documentation isn't necessary, another transfer process may be more appropriate.

Importantly, knowledge teams have found that E-mail shouldn't be used as a substitute for conversation. Nor should it be used for philosophical debates that will waste a lot of time (disagreements are generally resolved only face to face). The teams avoid mass mailing using unchecked distribution lists. Eddie Williamson, an HP engineer, notes, "There are people on-site who don't have accurate distribution lists, so they just send it to everybody. It takes a lot of time to figure out that the message doesn't have any relevance to me."[12] The team might also decide to limit "group replies," where the lazy user allows the computer to send a message to everyone in a particular grouping. Team members should typically target the receivers of their communications more specifically. See Figure 9-2 for an example of a hypothetical knowledge team E-mail use agreement.

Obviously the key to whether this or any other protocol

Figure 9-2. Sample E-mail protocol agreement.

Electronic Communication Protocol

- All messages will be short and to the point.
- E-mail won't be used for urgent messages.
- We accept responsibility for a personal delivery (face to face or voice to voice) of any urgent message.
- The message isn't delivered until the recipient understands it.
- We will use group replies or mass mailings only when necessary.
- We will treat people electronically the same way we would in person.
- We will use mail primarily for things where documentation is important.
- E-mail is a supplement to, not a substitute for, personal interaction.
- We agree to keep all distribution lists current.
- We will respect other people's time and privacy.
- We won't force people to read through messages that don't pertain to them.
- To enable message prioritization, we will code the top of each message with either "requires action" or "for your information."
- We will sign all messages.
- Instead of copying long quotes from others, we will briefly summarize them and add attachments if necessary.

---

works or not is whether the team has the discipline to abide by the agreement. In our experience, teams that have suffered from overload problems are better at self-discipline than those that haven't yet felt that pain. But in any case, it is unlikely that a knowledge team will abide by any protocols that the team members don't develop together or that they don't believe they need.

Protocols can work—especially if they become part of the culture. When we were with Procter & Gamble, for example, we adhered quite faithfully to a protocol that limited memos to one page. Although we never saw the protocol written down, the culture of the company accepted and reinforced it to the point that nearly every manager had heard a story of how a senior manager had simply thrown away everything following the first page of a proposal. "If you want it to get read," we were told, "keep it to one page." Whether the stories about managers tossing long memos were true or not was irrelevant. We learned to confine our memos to one page because we believed that to be the accepted way of doing things.

One way to help make these agreements part of the culture of the operation is to develop and commit to the protocols publicly. We describe this in more detail in Chapter 11 when we discuss the concept of operating guidelines. These protocols are good additions to this process and can easily be incorporated into other team agreements on things like meeting management norms.

Netiquette

Consider a similar protocol for the proper use of the Internet as another example of a knowledge transfer agreement. An emerging protocol about how to use the Net properly is developing among frequent Internet users. While these tacit agreements are certainly not etched in stone, most of them are sufficiently agreed to that newcomers (called "newbies" by many experienced users) risk being flamed (a cyberspace equivalent of a very rude gesture) for violating them. These protocols are referred to as Netiquette, and different versions of them can easily be accessed through any search engine by referencing that name. Some of our personal favorites have been penned by a tongue-in-cheek Net etiquette advisor who uses the pseudonym Emily Post. These humorous columns sarcastically extol the virtues of rude net behavior. The example in Figure 9-3, however, includes selected tips from Arlene Rinaldi's *The Net: User Guidelines and Netiquette*—a serious example.[13]

Using these protocols can help a team transfer knowledge more efficiently and effectively. Similar protocols can be used for other transfer processes like meetings, voice mail, or teleconferencing as well. They increase the team's effectiveness by reducing the noise in the transfer process. But agreed-upon

Figure 9-3. Emerging protocols for using the Internet as a medium for knowledge transfer.

Netiquette

- Focus on one subject per message.
- Edit quotes; don't let software automatically quote the entire body of messages you are replying to.
- Include a signature at end of message including name, position, organization, and E-mail address. But no more than 4 lines.
- Capitalize only to highlight. Capitalizing whole words is called SHOUTING! and should be avoided.
- Limit line length to 65–70 characters. Avoid control characters.
- Never send chain letters. Never spam.
- Spell out months to avoid misinterpretation (August 5 not 8/5 or 5-8).
- Don't send E-mail to the top just because you can.
- Be professional and careful. Assume your E-mail will be forwarded to others.
- Cite quotes and respect copyrights.
- Don't forward others' E-mail to mailing lists or Usenet without permission.
- Be careful with humor, especially sarcasm. Use emoticons to express humor. :-) = happy face for humor (tilt head to left to see).
- Remember that acronyms can be confusing.
- Avoid flaming.
- Do not use large graphics—downloading takes too much time.
- Include a file size next to video or voice files (i.e., 10KB or 2MB).

Source: Excerpted from Arlene Rinaldi, *The Net: User Guidelines and Netiquette,* Electronic Communications and World Wide Web at *http://www.fav.edu/rinaldi/net/elec.html.* Used by permission.

protocols solve only some of the typical problems in the knowledge transfer process. We would like to discuss two more important ideas. First, we present a model that helps to determine how to transfer knowledge in the most authentic and useful ways, and then we examine a concept used by HP to facilitate knowledge transfer that the company calls "productizing knowledge."

The Knowledge Quadrant: Do We Know What We Know?

We believe that another key to avoiding information overload begins much earlier than the actual interaction between people or knowledge storage libraries. It is—and we know this sounds odd—to know if we know something or not. Let us explain. Much of the knowledge we use is implicit knowledge that comes through our personal experience. It is like our special method for cooking or a certain technique we have for data entry. This knowledge is ingrained in us in such a way that we can use it without thinking, even though it may be difficult to explain to someone else. It has become essentially invisible to us. For example, we recently tried unsuccessfully to replicate a marvelous supper dish one of our relatives created. When we asked for the recipe, it said things like "add a dash of this" or "put in a pinch or two of that" and "season to taste." When we telephoned her to ask specific questions, it became obvious that even she didn't know exactly what she did: "I'm not sure how much of that spice I add," she told us. It was automatic and intuitive. What does this have to do with knowledge transfer? A lot.

Some people are better trainers of new team members, for example, because they know how to explain things—the invisible things that we may take for granted because of our experience. One of us had a manager, for example, who explained how to make an effective presentation to a senior management group. Without describing the technical points of effective presentations, such as readability of overhead slides and having an introduction (here is what I am going to say), a body of the presentation (say it), and a conclusion (here is what I said), which this mentor knew we knew, he shared another important piece of knowledge he had learned. "Remember," he said, "to assume that your audience doesn't know anything about what you are going to present. You need to give them a brief background about your project before you get into the specifics." As we have told others who have had the reputation of being effective presenters about this advice, they have realized that they do this intuitively. In other words, some knew they knew this, and others didn't know they knew this until it was pointed out to them.

Figure 9-4 represents this phenomenon visually. In the graphic we see a 2-by-2 matrix that compares subject knowledge (facts, figures, methods) with our self-knowledge about this knowledge (do we know we know it?). We can see that there are essentially four areas of self-knowledge about our subject knowledge. There are certain things, for example, that we know we know. We know, for example, how to make a simple spinach salad that has spinach (prewashed baby spinach in a bag),

Figure 9-4. Self-knowledge about our subject knowledge.

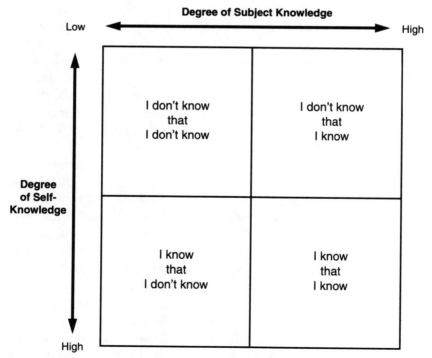

Source: Adopted from "the Johari window" developed by J. Luft 1961.

apples (one-half of a Fuji apple per person cut into slices), almonds (sliced almonds, about a teaspoon per person), and dried sweetened cranberries (about two tablespoons per person). There are other things we don't know that we know, as illustrated by the story above where some professional presenters didn't realize that they knew the importance of assuming that the audience doesn't have a background in the area of their presentation. There are still other things that we know we don't know—areas of expertise that are clearly out of our experience. We know, for example, that we don't know how to design airplane navigation systems.

Finally, there are still other areas of our personal knowledge that we don't know that we don't know. We may think we know something about software development, for example, that we really do not understand well at all. This explains the problems we sometimes have when we try to transfer knowledge we don't really have. Some of our so-called knowledge is nothing more than ill-founded assumptions, hearsay that we think is true, unexamined biases, rumors, or abstract half-truths. When we transfer this kind of information, we do our team members a disservice by perpetuating potentially false knowledge. We call this phenomenon "pooled ignorance."

This model has some usefulness in helping us to identify what we need to be aware of if we are going to be effective in our attempts to transfer knowledge to others. It is useful to tell people as we transfer information, for example, exactly what the limitations of our knowledge are on a subject ("I know this, I'm pretty sure of that, and I'm only making an educated guess on that one over there!"). This facilitates and brings increased credibility to the transfer process.

Explaining the model to others may also be helpful for leaders of knowledge teams who must help support processes that transfer real knowledge instead of simply perpetuating rumors—or what one of our professors used to call "unanalyzed abstractions." Whether we find ourselves in the position of a formal knowledge team leader or in the role of an informal leader in a peer group of knowledge workers, it may be useful to periodically ask the question, "Is this something we know, or is this something we only think we know?" It may help to encourage data gathering efforts and experimentation to find out the legitimate "knowledge." If nothing else, it helps to temper the rumor mill.

A word of caution is in order here. We can take this thing too far. Knowledge workers, especially those who have been trained in the scientific method, may become too cautious and withhold half-baked ideas or incomplete suggestions because they are untested. As we mentioned in Chapter 8, this can hinder the group learning and creativity that comes from batting around partial ideas. The required balance here, we think, is not to withhold things we aren't sure about, but rather to be clear that we are not sure about them (that is, sort ideas according to the four cells and share rather than just delete certain information).

This discussion brings us to a related issue. Ironically, we as knowledge workers may have so much knowledge that we lose our ability to acquire more. It is almost as though, like computers, we have only a limited amount of memory, which caps our learning capacity. While we may have finite memory capacity, most of us—even the brightest among us—come nowhere near reaching that limit. But nevertheless, smart people often have a difficult time learning new things. Historically this has become obvious whenever scientific breakthroughs were made. Copernicus, Einstein, and virtually every other prophet of a new science has had a difficult time convincing their peer knowledge workers to rethink what they believe they already "know" to be true.

"Productizing" Knowledge

Our final suggestion for improving knowledge transfer is to find a way to better collate, store, and access information. Effective knowledge transfer requires an answer to three important questions:

1. How do we transfer raw data into useful information?
2. How do we collect/collate/organize the information?
3. How do we effectively transmit information to others?

What works for one knowledge team may not work for another. But having a shared approach for transforming data into information, cataloging information, and finding a way for making information available to others is crucial for effective knowledge transfer. Again, the HP Strategic Alliance Services group provides an interesting case study.

Manager Stu Winby discovered a key to knowledge transfer when the SAS group underwent a recent transformation in the way it saw its purpose.

> "We have evolved from an action research consultant–oriented team with a group of highly skilled consultants to a new model where we see our responsibility as transferring knowledge. We work with customers throughout HP. Accordingly, we gather information on a daily basis. In our current approach, this information then goes through a process that we call knowledge management—a productization process.
>
> "For example, we might be doing some strategic planning work for a plant in Italy and the person doing that work will realize that she needs some information. So she'll get onto the K drive of her server and pull out the slides and the information that she needs for the next day from the productized resources we have developed and stored for her."

Everyone on the team has access to a rich database. Rather than being stored simply as raw data, however, much of the database has been transformed into information. Instead of just having notes describing key learnings about how to facilitate a strategic planning session, for example, the SAS database might include a fully developed presentation with color overhead slides that could be used in an actual work session to walk clients through a step-by-step process that had been used effectively in other HP sites. Or there might be a fully developed training program that can be downloaded, or a presentation about the primary business challenges of the next three years that can be printed and shared with clients, or a newly developed consulting tool that can be used. This facilitates knowledge transfer between consultants and also, in Winby's words, then "becomes available for application, argument, or adaptation by other HP clients."

"A template could be a technique or a consulting tool," explains Winby.

> "The templates are then bundled into modules, which are then bundled into products. The products [or "services"] are then provided back to the customers through our last area, which is Customer Service and Support. This occurs through seminars, presentations, or through individual consulting.
>
> "The productization process, the moving of information into usable knowledge, was designed by the Change Management Team. We're still struggling with getting norms around the process. For example, if you put some knowledge together—one of the steps of the productization process—someone else will adapt it to meet her own needs. Because she does things differently, you might feel that it is a stupid change, but it still might make sense to the other person. It's hard to let go of the need to direct the application of your templates. It's also difficult to write down everything you do and then have it be translated by the people in Palo Alto in a standardized form. This process is being invented as we go."

Pull Knowledge vs. Push Knowledge Transfer Processes

One final caution is in order. Most of the knowledge transfer processes described in this chapter are what we call push knowledge transfer, or processes where one individual or team pushes out information to another individual or team. This is an important way to transfer knowledge and it will continue to be essential in making these processes as efficient and effective as possible.

But the Internet has taught us that there is an equally important way to transfer knowledge: "pull knowledge transfer." A pull transfer process is where *the learner* directs the learning transfer. This is the genius of the Internet. It allows people to access massive amounts of information through targeted searches using the parameters they establish. The learners get what they want, when they want it. Self-directed learning has been an important way to transfer knowledge for decades. But what makes this approach particularly useful in our current time is that it also helps address the problem of information overload.

As we have mentioned earlier, one solution to the problem is to reduce the glut of information going into the transfer process in the first place. But another interesting solution—perhaps a more lasting solution—is to focus not on restricting what goes into the process but on what come out of it. No one could ever access everything in the billions of bytes of data contained on the Internet. The amount of knowledge contained there is as close to infinite as most of us will ever see. But by pulling out what we need in manageable chunks, we can all find something important for us to learn once we master the process of searching.

Several companies are trying to incorporate both push and pull learning transfers into their own intranets. A learning transfer process under development at Amoco, for example, will allow for certain critical information such as safety warnings or business announcements to be pushed to everyone over the intranet. But it will also allow for some sort of key word searching of all documents contained in the servers. The hope is that the learners will organize the glut of information themselves, reducing the amount of time and energy required to organize mountains of data for retrieval in a push only knowledge transfer process. Referring to the incorporation of pull learning transfer processes, one manager at Amoco told us that "if this is the only change companies make, it will have incredible benefits in cost reduction and effectiveness."

Summary

The SAS team at HP has discovered that transforming raw data first into information templates and then finally into knowledge products is a useful discipline for effective knowledge transfer. Whatever the answer, however, we believe knowledge teams must agree on how to approach three questions: (1) how do we transform raw data into useful information? (2) how do we collect/collate/organize the information? and (3) how do we effectively transmit information to others? The answers to these questions help teams characterize and improve the transfer of knowledge within a team and between teams. Before we can transfer knowledge effectively, we need to understand the limits of our own knowledge and be honest when we talk to others about what we really know and what we only think we know. We also need to understand how to reduce the inevitable noise in our communication with one another. Knowledge transfer protocols like those being developed for the Internet and E-mail can be strong practical ways of reducing information-distorting noise and improving these transfer processes. Good information systems are necessary for knowledge acquisition and transfer. Perhaps the biggest challenge we face on a knowledge team, however, is not getting enough information, but avoiding information overload. Leaders can be helpful in dealing with these kinds of problems. In Chapter 10 we discuss the role of leaders in knowledge teams.

Notes

1. Philip M. Condit, "Focusing on the Customer: How Boeing Does It," *Research Technology Management*, January–February 1994, 36.
2. John Bowie, "Return to Sender: E-mail Survival Guide," *Hemispheres*, October 1996, p. 33.
3. Arno Penzias, 1995 commencement address, National Technological University, as quoted in *National Technological University Annual Report, 1994–1995*, p. 1.
4. Ibid., p. 39. Bracketed word added. Used by permission.
5. Many of the examples in this section are taken from Lawrence Tabak, "Quality Controls" *Hemispheres*, September 1996, pp. 33–34.

6. Ibid., 34.
7. Bowie, "Return to sender," pp. 33–38.
8. Ibid.
9. Ibid., 34.
10. Ibid.
11. Ibid., pp. 33–38.
12. Ibid., p. 33.
13. Arlene Rinaldi, *The Net: User Guidelines and Netiquette,* Electronic Communications and World Wide Web at http://www.fau.edu/rinaldi/net/elec.html.

10
Distributed Leadership: Leading Others and Leading Self

"As we continue to move from the industrial era to the information age, modern managers will have to shift their focus accordingly. Recognizing that a hierarchical management approach will not work with the knowledge workers of the future, many business leaders are flattening their companies to create more responsive organizations and are giving their workers the autonomy to make their own task-related decisions. Within this context, the new manager must serve as a motivator, coordinator, and diplomat as opposed to a controller, autocrat, and disciplinarian. These managers will lead by convincing people, not by telling them, because their team members will be intelligent and not easily swayed by rhetoric or willing to do something just to maintain the status quo. Finally, the new manager must be willing to put aside his or her ego for the good of the organization."[1]

—Abstract from Larry D. Runge, "The Manager and the Information Worker of the 1990s."

Dr. Richard Boyer is a physician with Primary Children's Medical Center in Salt Lake City, Utah. He leads the department of medical imaging. "Our department consists of sixty to seventy employees, most of whom are technical," explains Dr. Boyer. "There are also some nurses and secretaries along with seven physicians. However, the seven physicians are not employed by the hospital, but are part of a corporation that includes only themselves. These physicians oversee the medical imaging department and provide analysis of the images."

Primary Children's Medical Center is currently owned by Intermountain Health Care (IHC). IHC manages over twenty hospitals along the Wasatch front from Idaho to Utah.

"Let me tell you about an experiment we carried out in the medical imaging department. Within the department, we have several different divisions, each with its own manager. For instance, we have the diagnostic division, CT and MRI, ultrasound, nuclear medicine, and the secretaries and nurses.

"The focus of our experiment was the CT and MRI division. One year ago, the manager of this division announced that she was leaving. She had been manager of this division for fifteen years and was quite iron-fisted. Technically she was very good, but she could be quite a heavy-handed leader. She was very much a boss in the traditional sense of the word.

"Before this particular manager left, I had been reading some management books. So based on the past manager's oppressive nature and the positive things I had read, we (the seven of us) felt it would be a good opportunity to try out a team approach—one that was self-directed and didn't need a manager.

"We chose a team leader, as an advisory position. The majority of the former manager's duties were supposed to be absorbed by the team, not the team leader. We originally decided to implement the team approach only in this one division because of its size (only seven individuals) and because we were relatively unfamiliar with self-directed work teams. And it seemed as if the seven individuals in the CT/MRI division were already familiar with their duties (technologically speaking); they'd all been here for quite some time. So it really seemed like a natural place to start.

"Initially things were very good. For instance, the personality of the new team leader was quite different from that of the former manager. She has strong inter-personal skills and filled the role quite well as one who facilitates instead of oppresses. She's a much kinder and gentler person. In fact, one of my fears was that the team might walk on her, but that hasn't been the case; she's really found a nice balance.

"In this new environment, two individuals, in par-ticular, truly blossomed. It had seemed as if they were floundering under the old system. They had really struggled, but as soon as the new structure was imple-mented, they really improved.

"Originally the team was really excited about per-forming some of the administrative functions that had previously been the manager's. She was not a working manager; she only administered. Now, the team leader works right along with the other technologists in the CT/MRI division, and they all share the administrative responsibilities.

"It was really quite a surprise to the team to see what the previous manager had done in the way of scheduling and administration. There was quite a sense of euphoria among the team for the first three or four months after the change. Everybody helped, got along well, and participated in the meetings. It was clear that the morale was better, and the service rendered was every bit as good if not better.

"But it's hard to know just how successful we've been."

A number of external issues over which the group had no con-trol, such as cutbacks and salary restrictions, affected the team negatively.

"Over time, the team members began pushing a lot of the shared responsibilities back onto the team leader.

They simply reverted to their old ways and wanted the team leader to take on many of the responsibilities of the former manager. I'm sure part of the problem is that the team leader is such a willing worker; she might have been too nice and accepted many of the team's responsibilities. For the last six months or so she has been having more and more difficulty getting the team members to do what they had originally agreed to do, and more and more of the administrative responsibilities are falling on her shoulders.

"Overall, I definitely think that it is still better than it would have been had we kept the former structure. Yes, there have been problems, but the benefits really compensate for them."

What is the role of the knowledge team leader? As this vignette shows, leading knowledge teams (especially self-directed teams) is not as easy as it seems. The role is certainly not one of abdication. Nor is it the traditional role of planning, organizing, directing, and controlling, as we have already mentioned. In fact, University of Southern California researchers Susan Mohrman, Monty M. Mohrman, and Susan G. Cohen have noted that hierarchical practices are particularly troublesome in contemporary organizations whose primary tasks are knowledge work. Summarizing their studies, they conclude: "A managerial, hierarchical mechanism cannot make all authoritative broad-scope decisions, because it does not necessarily have all pertinent knowledge, but also because it would then become a bottleneck in the functioning of the organization."[2]

But how do you manage an organization that deemphasizes hierarchy as a means for monitoring and direction setting? This chapter is an attempt to respond to the query, "What do knowledge team leaders do?" It focuses on the general role and responsibilities of a team leader by looking at the leader as a boundary manager, and then concludes with seven important competency clusters for leadership. We also suggest that in knowledge work teams, the traditional approach of having solitary leadership may not be universally applicable. After illustrating the team leader role, we will also discuss both rotated leadership and shared leadership. It is important to remember that there is a difference between leadership roles and the role of the leader. Leadership roles can be played by anyone on the team regardless of their rank or title. The role of the team leader, however, is a special responsibility of the formal leader of the team. We will talk about both of these issues in this chapter.

The Boundary Manager

One of the best ways to describe the role of the knowledge team leader is as a "boundary manager." The boundary is the make-believe line that differentiates the team from the environment that surrounds it, as shown in Figure 10-1. A boundary manager manages that boundary.[3]

For example, an information systems team may be responsible for turning bookkeeping data into useful financial information. The team members collect and compile the data and enter them into computers. These bits of raw data (input) are thus organized into useful reports, which are distributed as a final

Figure 10-1. The team boundary.

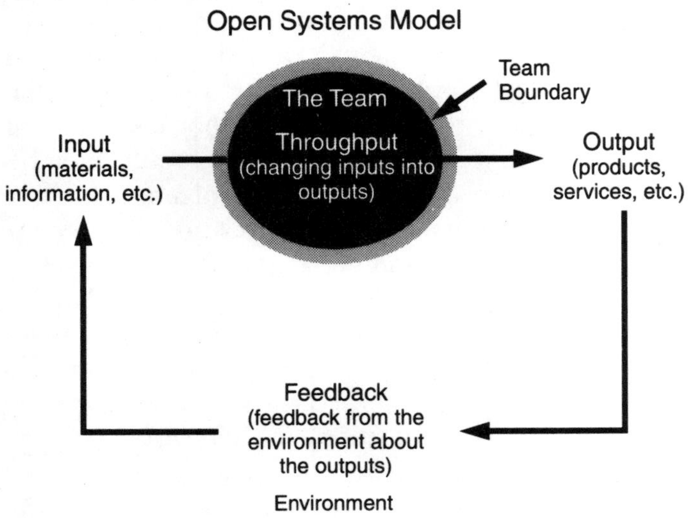

Open Systems Model

Team Boundary

The Team

Throughput
(changing inputs into outputs)

Input
(materials,
information, etc.)

Output
(products,
services, etc.)

Feedback
(feedback from the
environment about
the outputs)

Environment

product (output) to the team's customers. The throughput process is the series of tasks that transforms these raw data into a delivered report. The product is hopefully improved over time as the team members respond to the feedback they receive from their customers and others. Social scientists call this the open systems model.[4]

This general way of describing organizations is applicable to all knowledge teams. Product development teams, for example, engage in a transformation of ideas into a new product concept, and medical teams transform patient complaints and test results into a diagnosis.

Traditional managers (particularly those of us influenced by the control paradigm discussed in Chapter 3) often see their role as supervising the throughput process. The throughput process occurs inside the boundary. In the information systems team example, that would include supervising activities such as the compiling of data and the accurate entering of those data into the computers. However, in knowledge work team settings, supervising the day-to-day throughput operations of the team is largely done by team members themselves. This is especially true when the knowledge team is a self-directed work team. Management-imposed supervisory activities often become redundant. In the worst-case scenario, they may actually impede the progress of the knowledge team as team members' attention is diverted from the project to responding to supervisory demands.

Boundary Managers: At and Outside of the Boundary

The boundary manager focuses on the environment that surrounds the team, as shown in Figure 10-2. Rather than directing her primary energy to the throughput process, the team leader focuses more attention on boundary issues such as interface problems with other teams, customer and vendor interactions, dealing with other corporate groups, assessing competitors and market opportunities, working on legal or community issues of importance, forecasting new technologies, building communication bridges with other groups, forging important alliances,

Figure 10-2. The boundary manager focus areas.

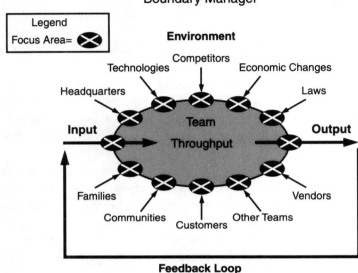

bringing training and development opportunities to the team, and so forth.

The Difference Between Traditional Managers and Boundary Managers

Boundary managers don't direct work. That's not their role. While traditional managers usually work *in* the system, boundary managers work *on* the system instead. One way to do this is as an organization designer. Team leaders focus on improving the work system, as illustrated in the description in Chapter 4 of Stu Winby's redesign work with his team of consultants at HP. Consider another example.

Bill Synder, a former operations team leader at American Transtech, acted as an effective organization designer and saw dramatic improvement in a knowledge work team charged with helping the company accomplish its charter of properly transferring many thousands of shares of stock from the AT&T divestiture. As a result of his work, the labor cost in his team went from $180 per unit of work to $100, quality remained consistently high, throughput improved by 100 percent, and employee morale soared—all in the first six months of his tenure. What did he do? And how did he improve throughput by working *at* instead of *inside of* the boundary?

> "I provided feedback on all the goals once a week. . . . arranged for the marketing person to collect customer feedback and read it out at the weekly meeting. I arranged for team members to get technical training and apprenticeship opportunities. I initiated the development of a reward system that enabled team members to earn weekly cash bonuses based on team and organization performance. In short, I didn't do, I designed."[5]

Synder designed system improvements. This is, in our experience, a common practice. Though boundary managers don't often do the design work themselves (they usually involve others in the spirit of empowerment), they do ensure that it gets done. And they ensure that it gets done in a way that incorporates open systems thinking. This is more difficult than it sounds. The general tendency for organizations is to make improvements based only on their needs and wants inside of the boundary. The boundary manager knows that elements outside of the boundary must also be considered if organization improvement is to be effective. Anyone, for example, who has ignored customer needs during this process has done so at some peril to the operation.

The extent to which a team leader can act as a boundary manager, of course, will depend on the maturity level of the team. Some teams will still need a lot of help to learn how to manage the throughput of the operation—which is the creation of knowledge. They may not be experienced in this type of work. Development of these skills must be accomplished before the team leader can take on the new responsibilities of boundary management. This suggests a caveat for the boundary manager: Effective boundary managers typically provide substitutes for hierarchy before abandoning throughput supervision.

Substitutes for Hierarchy

Dr. Ed Lawler, a prolific management writer and employee involvement expert, talks about the importance of "substitutes for hierarchy."[6] Without these substitutes, simply diverting attention from the throughputs to work on boundary issues can be problematic. Hierarchy and bureaucracy have performed an important coordination function in most organizations, and this function must still be performed somehow in the knowledge team workplace. Prior to their merger, both Boeing and McDonnell-Douglas reported problems when hierarchical controls (management authorizations, policies, procedures, etc.) were withdrawn from teams prematurely without there being anything to substitute for the clarity and direction those controls provided. Boundary managers act as organization designers to ensure that teams have these substitutes for hierarchy in place.

Good information about the business, for example, can substitute for a manager providing this information in person. Thus, a good company intranet with cost and technical information is one substitution for hierarchy.

Cross-Organization Collaboration

Effective boundary managers do other things as well. Dr. Rosabeth Moss Kanter, author and business school professor, describes this new role as managing channels of influence, networking horizontally, and managing external relations, or in her words, "brokering interfaces instead of presiding over empires."[7] What does this look like? Where a traditional functional manager will focus on optimizing his or her own department or project, for example, the boundary manager is much more interested in optimizing the whole operation, even if that means suboptimizing his or her particular part of it. Boundary managers act as cross-organization collaborators rather than empire builders because their knowledge of the environment shows them that collaboration is essential to survival.

Seven Competencies of Boundary Managers

As described thus far, the overall role of the knowledge work team leader is to be a boundary manager, which includes being an organization designer and a cross-organization collaborator. But the role includes a lot of other responsibilities as well. For example, boundary managers frequently block certain disruptions from reaching the team, shielding it from inappropriate distractions or unnecessary confusion. But as diverse as these different team leader responsibilities appear, all of them seem to require a common set of personal competencies.

There are a number of generic attributes that are important for effective knowledge team leadership, such as a passionate commitment to get good results, a clear understanding of what it takes to be successful, excellent communication abilities, and a strong interpersonal and technical skill base consistent with the organization's culture. Specific behaviors exhibited by successful knowledge work team leaders we know, however, include some other things as well. These leaders:

1. Articulate a vision for the organization.
2. Manage by principle rather than by policy.
3. Effectively coach individuals and teams.
4. Understand and communicate business information.
5. Aggressively eliminate barriers to team effectiveness.
6. Actively facilitate and develop team members.
7. Focus on the customer's perspective.

These behaviors can be developed into seven competency clusters that further clarify the required skills for a successful knowledge team leader. A team leader works as a leader, a living example, a coach, a business analyzer, a barrier buster, a facilitator, and a customer advocate. What does that mean?

1. The *leader*—unleashes energy and enthusiasm by creating a vision that others find inspiring and motivating.[8]
2. The *living example*—serves as a role model for others by

"walking the talk" and demonstrating the desired behaviors of team members and leaders.

3. The *coach*—teaches others and helps them develop to
   their potential, maintains an appropriate authority balance, and ensures accountability in others.
4. The *business analyzer*—understands the big picture and is
   able to translate changes in the business environment to
   opportunities for the organization.
5. The *barrier buster*—opens doors and runs interference for
   the team, challenges the status quo, and breaks down
   artificial barriers to the team's performance.
6. The *facilitator*—brings together the necessary tools, information, and resources for the team to get the job done,
   and facilitates group efforts.
7. The *customer advocate*—develops and maintains close
   customer ties, articulates customer needs, and keeps
   priorities in focus with the desires and expectations of
   customers.

Competencies Explained

Knowledge work teams need leadership if they are to be successful. Let's review the seven competencies of team leaders in
more detail. We will discuss (1) leadership, (2) modeling, (3)
coaching, (4) business analysis, (5) barrier busting, (6) facilitation, and finally (7) customer advocacy.

Acting Like a Leader

Nothing has been studied so thoroughly or written about so consistently as leadership. What is a leader? A leader is a visionary.
One Apple Computer manager describes Steve Jobs, co-founder
of Apple, as such a visionary: "Steve had his problems," he said,
"but I can still remember how he could inspire and motivate us
with his vision. He would get us together and tell us that Apple
products were going to *change the world*. He made that happen."
Aside from the Apple influence on the computer–human inter-

face emulated by Windows and other operating systems, it is difficult to imagine either the home or the workplace without the microcomputer—a revolution driven from this vision. Jobs's vision motivated people enough to break the office technology paradigm and change the world. Jobs himself said of his role with the Macintosh design team: "The greatest people are self managing; they don't need to be managed. Once they know what to do they'll figure out how to do it . . . what they need is a common vision and that's what leadership is . . . leadership is having a vision, being able to articulate that so that people around you can understand it and getting a consensus on [it]."[9]

Vision is important for any human organization, and it is certainly a useful tool for knowledge team leaders, especially when a work project—such as developing a specific new technology—has never been done before. A good team leader will have a vision of what the team could accomplish that will allow him or her to provide clarity. The vision should be concise enough to be focusing but broad enough to allow the creative autonomy necessary to accomplish it.

Good team leaders frequently find ways to enroll their team in the vision development process. How? Some share their vision in an informal setting and then invite others to modify it to the extent required for them to support it. Others use a joint visioning process where they work with the team to create the vision together from scratch.

Being a Living Example

The second competency cluster for the knowledge team leader is being a living example. Team leaders model the behaviors they demand from others. They also embody and symbolize the vision of the organization. It is hard to overstate the importance of this part of the team leader's role. Knowledge team leaders simply must walk the talk—or, in the words of some Boeing managers, at least "stumble the mumble." Team leaders understand that the eloquence of their example is far more powerful than their words.

Alexander the Great is said to have won the commitment of

his soldiers by risking his own life alongside them. He was the first man to charge the Theban Sacred Band at Chaeronea and plunged so often into the thick of the battle that his soldiers, fearful of losing him, begged him to go to the rear.[10] He was also the first to scale the walls of the Mallians. The ladders broke after he and two others had leapt into the city, and they found themselves alone among the enemy. He collapsed from loss of blood just as his armies broke into the city and saved his life. On one occasion, to calm a potential mass sedition, he presented himself to his army and asked which of them could show more scars than he "whose body bore the marks of every weapon used in war."[11] He led by example. Similarly, an old saying about the difference between leaders and managers in the Civil War said that you could tell which they were from their position relative to the charging troops. Leaders were in front. Managers shouted direction and encouragement from behind.

People simply do not care as much about what team leaders say as they care about what these leaders do. The best team leaders we know don't talk about how they value employee input, they solicit it. They don't give speeches about the importance of customers, they visit them. They don't pontificate about quality, they stop even time-sensitive work when quality is suspect. And they empower (by example) team members to do the same things.

Coaching

The third team leader competency is coaching. Coaches recognize the need to develop individual players on the team and to help the team members learn how to work together effectively. Like the other competencies of team leaders, coaching is important in any organization. However, it is especially important in a knowledge work team, because everyone plays a much larger role in running the team. Especially when knowledge teams become self-directed, decisions are made at the point where action is taken on the decision.

Many one-on-one performance coaching skills are readily transferable from traditional organizations to knowledge work teams. But coaches in these team-based operations also need to be proficient at working with the whole team as a unit. Coaches typically spend a great deal of time helping team members build their skills. These usually include the skills necessary to (1) produce good results, (2) exhibit teamwork (work together effectively), (3) demonstrate self-sufficiency (produce and maintain a high level of results with little external influence), and (4) communicate effectively (keep everyone well informed). These focus areas form a foundation upon which the more specific skills tailored to the operation can be built.

One of the most difficult and most important skills to build into a knowledge team is the skill of learning how to learn. How do team leaders coach team members in this skill? One way is by asking questions instead of giving solutions.

Socratic Coaching

Allowing team members to build inner skull muscle tone is essential in teams whose success depends on their ability to acquire, apply, and transfer knowledge. In order to facilitate this development, coaches refrain from judgmental statements like "That won't work," instead asking questions like "What is the problem you want to solve?" or "How will you know when you have solved it?" or "What information did you base this conclusion on?" Socratic coaching is a skill that should not be undervalued in the knowledge work team environment. If done well, it teaches, strengthens, and empowers.

Relying on this technique too much, of course, can cause serious problems. Coaches who continually ask team members "What do you think?" frequently lose their effectiveness, as people eventually stop coming to them for advice. Better questions focus on where information can be found or on teaching particular thinking processes that help people make good decisions.

Real-Time Feedback

Traditional performance appraisals are undoubtedly one of the least effective coaching techniques. They are depressing, nonsupportive, artificial, and untimely. What team members need is ongoing, effective feedback. This is especially important in small-project and special-purpose teams where time pressures are critical. Several team leaders we work with regularly share customer and peer feedback with team members to let them know whether they are on track or off track. Professional sports teams use videos of their games to help players review their own performance. Orchestras listen to their tapes for the same reasons. Similarly, charts and graphs and project reviews can help teams monitor their progress against performance goals and objectives, while customer interaction can offer some real-time feedback that is more likely to motivate than to discourage.

Career Coaching

Another type of coaching is so important in knowledge teams that we believe it deserves some special treatment. The changes that occur when knowledge teams are organized essentially eliminate the traditional career path that many knowledge workers are familiar with. Says John Sivie, an organizational development manager at Rocketdyne, "There are some concerns on the teams about careers. They're not associated with a function of specialists who have a hierarchy. We need to work harder on defining what a career path should look like. Is it going from team to team, or is it a ladder? Perhaps the career ladder concept is outdated and isn't relevant any more."

Discussions of this topic with knowledge workers are essential, both for the well-being of the individuals and for the skill development required for the future growth of the organization. We will discuss this topic again briefly in Chapter 13 as we look at the future trends affecting knowledge work, but it seems certain that for most knowledge workers, the traditional career ladder is gone. Careers of the future will be a portfolio of projects, not of job titles. Coaches can help knowledge workers prepare for the projects they want by helping the workers plan to obtain the skills they will need if they are to get the desirable projects.

Business Analysis

The fourth competency is business analysis. More than anything else, business analysis is the process of gathering and then disseminating business information. While it is true that the effective knowledge team leader must be skilled in the process of evaluating and analyzing, the most common inadequacy associated with this competency cluster isn't whether the analysis itself is good or bad. It is whether or not that analysis is shared with the team effectively, as described in Chapter 9.

Barrier Busting

The fifth competency for knowledge team leaders is barrier busting. One of the quickest ways to make team members feel empowered is to identify and eliminate organizational barriers to their performance. We have already mentioned how boundary managers work to redesign the organizational barriers affecting the knowledge teams they support. This attention to barriers applies to a number of different areas, such as inappropriate resource constraints and restrictive policies or practices. Perhaps no activity is more energizing to a team than isolating a particularly restrictive barrier to performance and working to modify or eliminate it.

In a Tektronix division, a team leader helped eliminate a requirement that people report their time using a particular method that required very detailed record keeping. The team leader had discovered that the reports generated by this time-consuming activity were compiled, distributed, and virtually ignored. The previously unchallenged policy was significantly simplified, resulting in a cumulative savings of thousands of knowledge worker hours a month. Moreover, it created a flurry of activity. When team members saw that management was willing to get rid of inhibiting practices, they brought up a number of other barriers that they had always thought were immovable. Although some were, in fact, barriers that resulted from legal or technical requirements that could not be changed, a number of them were modified or eliminated. Throughput increased, quality improved, and development speed increased as a result of eliminating these barriers.

Facilitating

The sixth competency cluster for effective knowledge team leadership is facilitation. Most teams will bear fruit in favorable conditions. Team leaders therefore facilitate higher crop yield by creating the favorable conditions. Fertilizing, administering pesticides and herbicides, irrigating, being responsive to destructive molds and diseases, harvesting, and so forth are the ways in which farmers ensure that seeds have the resources that will enable them to produce as much crop as they are internally capable of producing. Facilitative team leaders do the same for their teams. Conversely, withholding resources can cause teams to wither and weaken. The knowledge team leader who, even unknowingly, withholds information (or authority, autonomy, budget, training, or whatever other resources are necessary to get the job done) lowers productivity, no matter how hard she may be struggling to "make" people be productive.

How Do Leaders Facilitate?

Team leaders actively focus on the development of others. Instead of taking over conversations and making the decisions, the team leader walks to the chart pad, grabs a pen, and starts asking people where we should go from here. In a virtual team environment, this may be accomplished with networked programs or common processes supported by the leader. He becomes skilled at understanding the dynamics of a work group and knowing when and where to intervene. She takes advantage of every teaching moment that presents itself. When members of our consulting team come to us to ask us to help solve a problem, we provide training or bring them along with us so that they understand our approach. Although they may later use different methodologies, they will at least have some tools in their kit that they didn't know about before.

Customer Advocacy

The seventh and final competency of team leaders is customer advocacy. This is a key part of boundary management. Where there are skilled customer advocates, you seldom see dysfunctional internal squabbles that cripple the productivity of a team. Why? Because team members are focused less on themselves and more on serving a greater good.

Knowledge team leaders often invite customers to team meetings—physically and virtually. There is no substitute for firsthand interaction for developing both clarity and empathy.

Developing Customer Empathy

In our experience, the most successful knowledge workers see customers as real people like themselves who want value for their money. They know their customers' names and experience their problems. Tektronix reported improved (more practical and user-friendly) designs and customer relations when engineering team members visited end users. One team leader brings in a different customer each month for an organization-wide assembly so that team members across the facility can hear from customers on a regular basis. Many team leaders have had success with sit-down meetings with their teams and visitors from other teams who act as internal customers for their services. These meetings serve to clarify expectations, define deliverables, and resolve problems that may ultimately affect the cost or quality of a product to the end use customer.

Misusing Customer Advocacy

Aetna found an interesting problem with this customer advocacy process, however, that is worth mentioning here. It found that too much emphasis on the demands of the *internal* customer (such as a downstream department inside of Aetna) was causing problems for the external customer. The teams, in their eagerness to please the internal customers, were sometimes complying with requests for additional services that ended up increasing the cost to the final customer. Not good.

Aetna resolved the problem by eliminating the focus on internal customers and emphasizing end users. HP has eliminated the term *internal customer* and substituted *partner* to reinforce the importance of alignment of multiple collaborators to serve the end user. We also have heard knowledge team members talking about their management as their customer. This is the classic mistake of using the commitment paradigm vocabulary to reinforce the control paradigm organization. Bosses aren't customers and never will be. They work for customers just like everybody else.

Rotated Leadership

Who assumes the role described in the last several pages? In some knowledge work teams, it is normally limited to the formal manager. But in other work teams, this team leader/boundary management responsibility may be rotated from person to person over time. Many universities, for example, rotate the department chair responsibilities rather than creating a permanent hierarchical position. After your three- or four-year turn as the leader, you rotate back into a teaching or research assignment. A Rohm & Haas plant in Louisville, Kentucky, uses a similar approach but a different rotation schedule. The team leader role is rotated among the team members on a weekly basis, making the traditional supervisor position unnecessary. The team leader has a certain percentage of his or her time—normally about 25 percent—freed up to complete his or her leadership responsibilities. Amdahl service teams elect one of their peers to serve a six-month to one-year term in the formal team leader role.

Speaking of the changes in HP's Santa Clara's division, Dennis McNulty says:

> "What we've done is let the teams decide whether or not they wanted a team leader. They negotiate within their own organization how they're going to divide their roles and responsibilities. It's interesting how it's turned out. Some have a formal team leader, some rotate the position, and some don't have a team leader at all. They also call the team leaders different names: coordinators, representatives, advisors, etc. This gives the team members more ownership. They're more committed to the decisions when they make them, and it's paid off for us. To be honest, I'm surprised at the diversity of what the teams have chosen. I thought there would have been more consistency with the leadership role."

Shared Leadership

In other knowledge teams, certain leadership tasks are shared by team members. For example, Bruce Ellis is the regional sales director for the western states for AT&T. He is responsible for what they call the MultiQuest product line, AT&T's 900 business. To be effective as a knowledge team leader, he firmly believes, many of his responsibilities need to be transferred to the team. "My role needs to be helping people understand what my role is so that they can take on my responsibilities down the road," he says.

Many of these responsibilities are not clear to the team, Ellis explains.

> "One instance in particular was an eye-opener for me, because I feel that we need to get to the point where we're interchangeable leaders and interchangeable team members. In order to do that, my natural team needs to take on functions that the boss used to perform. When we first became a team, we got together and assigned sales territories. This sounds silly, but it's really quite emotional. They did a fine job. My next step was to ask them what it is I do as sales manager that they as a team wanted to take on next. So I waited for a few weeks, but no one called me. So finally I asked them during a team conference call; it was very quiet when suddenly some brave soul spoke up and said, 'We would like to take on some other things, but we don't know what you do.' That was not a slam at me—saying that I don't do anything—but it was a sincere question. I was asking them to take on responsibilities that they didn't even know about. So I went back and started to provide more detail about what I did."

Other organizations use different approaches. Some rotate meeting facilitation responsibilities from meeting to meeting. Others create a distributed leadership role where everyone on the knowledge team shares certain leadership responsibilities.

Kelly-Ann Hoare works in the training division of Old Mutual. Old Mutual has about 17,000 employees and is the largest insurance company in South Africa, with more than 1 million members. It has been in business for over 150 years. The skills training department distributes leadership responsibilities by dividing up areas of responsibility into what it calls portfolios. "For example," she says, "we have a communication portfolio that is managed by a particular team member." This team member serves as the coordinator for information from management and is active in the weekly team meetings and other communication protocols established by the team, such as the agreement to write important announcements on the team whiteboard and to check your name off after you have read them.

> "In this sense, leadership is distributed among team members. We also have projects that are not ongoing like the portfolios, but that still need to be managed. For example, if we need to redo training for a particular area, the project manager over that area will be the leader until the task is completed. However, the portfolio assignments are ongoing. We will always need a communications portfolio manager."

Steve Olson is an account executive in the advertising sales area of a company called DAT. "DAT Services," explains Diana Knoles, a colleague of Olson's, and an internal consultant in establishing and training teams, "provides information and advertising services to the transportation industry—specifically trucking. We display load and truck availability using a variety of delivery channels, including PC modem-to-modem hookup, satellite, fax, and contact with an operator." "In advertising sales," Olson explains, "we use a variety of methods to help companies who wish to market directly to the professional over-the-road drivers. Our sales team relies heavily on informal leadership. We have streamlined due to efficiencies provided by teamwork, and currently sales and customer service have consolidated into one team, which manages the existing account base as well as prospecting for new business. There are no official team leaders. It depends upon the project. When something comes up, the individual who is best equipped to deal with the situation takes it upon him or herself to lead the team. It's not positional; it's based more upon ability and interest."

Distributed Leadership

There are other ways to distribute leadership as well. For example, peer coaching has been practiced for years in organizations like hospitals, where doctors participate in peer reviews or censures. Shared customer advocacy and business analysis is common in operations with high degrees of commitment. On knowledge teams—especially on geographically dispersed virtual knowledge teams where individual knowledge workers meet with other team members only infrequently—the primary role for leadership often rests more on each individual knowledge worker than on a single formally assigned leader.

Although it is very unusual for knowledge teams to work without any kind of formal management, numerous organizations that we are familiar with have the goal of creating a sense of shared team leadership. They are reluctant to create a dependence on a single individual for project guidance—a concept almost completely antithetical to the control paradigm. In knowledge teams that have reached this goal of shared leadership, individuals exhibit a high degree of self-direction.

A cynic might suggest that distributed leadership is so important to knowledge teams because imposed formal leadership simply doesn't work. We have heard a number of people compare managing scientists, engineers, doctors, lawyers, professors, consultants, and virtually every other type of knowledge worker to herding cats—a now trite but still wonderfully descriptive analogy. But we believe distributed leadership is required for different reasons. Knowledge, the primary asset required for knowledge work, is in the head of the knowledge worker, and it is made available at the discretion of the mental laborer. No leader can force it out. It has to be given willingly. Where there is distributed leadership, there is, in effect, collective self-leadership, a situation that fosters discretionary mental effort.

Summary

In knowledge work teams, team leadership is critical. Although this formal leadership is often shared or rotated, we believe it must be done properly for the team to be effective. There are a number of role similarities, of course, between successful traditional managers and successful knowledge team leaders. But leading knowledge work teams requires some special perspectives and competencies. Effective knowledge team leaders are boundary managers who act as organization designers and cross-organization collaborators. While traditional managers work *in* the system, boundary managers work *on* the system. As boundary managers, knowledge team leaders perform responsibilities at the interface between the team and the team's environment at the points where knowledge often enters the system. This allows them to help the team stay focused on the big picture instead of becoming mired in the day-to-day throughput tasks for which the knowledge work teams now have primary responsibility. It also allows team leaders to get needed resources and information from outside of the team.

We have found that successful boundary managers have a number of general attributes and skills. They have highly developed competencies in the areas of leadership, modeling, coaching, business analysis, barrier busting, facilitation, and customer advocacy. Without skills in these areas, team leaders are not likely to be successful.

Notes

1. Larry D. Runge, abstract from "The Manager and the Information Worker of the 1990s," *Information Strategy* 10, no. 4 (1994): 7–14.
2. Susan A. Mohrman, Monty M. Mohrman, Jr., and Susan G. Cohen, "Organizing Knowledge Work Systems," CEO Publication T 94–27 (270), July 1994. Michael M. Beyerlein, Douglas A. Johnson, and Susan T. Beyerlein, *Advances in Interdisciplinary Studies of Work Teams*, vol. 2 *Knowledge Teams:*

The Creative Edge (Greenwich, Conn.: JAI Press, Inc., 1995). Used by permission.

3. Large portions of this chapter have been adapted and updated for knowledge work from Kimball Fisher, *Leading Self Directed Work Teams* (New York: McGraw-Hill, 1993). Used by permission.

4. David Hanna, *Designing Organizations for High Performance* (Reading, Mass.: Addison-Wesley O.D. Series, 1988). Dave does a nice job explaining open systems theory in this book. The original concept is usually attributed to Ludwig von Bertalanffy, "The Theory of Open Systems in Physics and Biology," *Science* 111 (1950): 23–28.

5. William Synder, "The First-Line Manager in Innovating Organizations," unpublished paper, University of Southern California, pp. 16–17. Used by permission.

6. Edward Lawler, "Substitutes for Hierarchy," *Organizational Dynamics* 1988.

7. Rosabeth Moss Kanter, "The New Managerial Work," *Harvard Business Review*, November–December 1989.

8. These descriptions are used by permission. Copyright © 1995 by The Fisher Group, Inc. and 1989 by Belgard•Fisher• Rayner Inc. All rights reserved.

9. J. Natham and S. Tyler, *In Search of Excellence*, film based on the book by Peters and Waterman, 1984.

10. Will Durant, *The Life of Greece* (New York: Simon & Schuster, 1939), 541.

11. Ibid., 550.

11

Self-Healing Systems: The Wellness Practices of Smart Teams

"On a research project we did a few years ago, we videotaped teams in the classroom for the whole semester, and we analyzed those teams and their behaviors every six seconds. What we discovered was that these people didn't learn anything by virtue of being part of a team; they needed to be trained. You can't expect them to invent the skills they need (which a lot of people do), you've got to train them. How much training? It varies enormously. Some companies are training forty to fifty hours a year. Other companies are training three times that much. This variance results for a lot of reasons, but I would say that forty to fifty hours a year (or one hour per week) would be a minimum."

—Dr. Mike Beyerlein, Director, Center for the Study of Work Teams at the University of North Texas

It's 5:30 A.M. on a chilly, wet, Pacific northwest morning. Rebecca Willes, a software engineer at a high-tech firm in the "silicon rain forest" near Seattle, rolls out of bed and groggily dons her spandex exercise wear. She heads to the gym, where she pursues a tough one-hour workout. If you talk to Rebecca about what drives her to be so dedicated to this morning ritual, she'll tell you that she arrives at work energized, her mind clear. Engineers in high-tech companies across the globe can be seen running or jogging at all hours of the day and night. Why is that? They'll tell you it is because exercise clears their head, puts energy into their body, and soothes their soul. When they are blocked and can't concentrate or get their proverbial creative juices flowing, they exercise. Exercise serves the wellness needs of these people; they have learned that to work effectively they must pay attention to their entire system, not just the parts needed for work.

How can this learning be transferred to organizations? If the human organism needs exercise, preventive health care, and refueling, so must the corporate organism. Organizations and the work teams in them need to discover ways to nourish and replenish themselves. In this chapter we will provide some specific practical tips for creating team wellness.

The Welch's Team

Here's the story of one team's efforts to infuse energy and wellness into its organization.

On a beautiful September afternoon, members of the customer shipping and receiving team at the Welch's plant in Lawton, Michigan, are enjoying a catered barbecue dinner provided by plant management. The smell of thick steaks wafts through the air as team members dig into potato salad, cake, and all the other accoutrements of a complete barbecue. Standing to one side is a beaming Starr Houston, shipping and receiving team leader. She is reading a letter composed by team members and directed to plant leadership.

What has prompted this celebration?

It is a recognition dinner to thank the team for record performance achievements during the month of August. Welch's fiscal year ends August 31, and on August 1, managers were faced with the daunting task of getting the plant to produce and ship unprecedented amounts of product before year end. For Starr Houston, there was only one answer to the question, "How will we meet these year-end goals?" Her response? "Take it to the team."

This wasn't just a physical production challenge. It would involve a wide range of problem-solving, planning, and decision-making activities. The crucial need would be knowledge, not stamina.

When presented with the facts, the team members embraced the challenge. They quickly assessed what was required and then set about getting the product out the door.

They had been working for about one year to become a high-performance work team. They had "exercised" rigorously during that time. For instance, they had infused themselves with knowledge about their business. They established a clear charter or statement of the team's purpose that kept them focused when the pressure was on. They agreed on a set of guiding principles that helped them make decisions in a variety of circumstances. And they had practiced interpersonal aerobics, learning how to provide one another with feedback, how to make consensus decisions, and how to work together collaboratively. Their efforts paid off. The customer shipping and receiving department was the only department in Lawton to reach all of its department goals for fiscal year 1996. The team shipped 637,559 cases of product in one week and handled a total of 924,125 cases— record numbers for the Lawton facility.

As the Welch's experience demonstrates, an organization needs to find ways to infuse energy into the organization so that teams are sustained in those "iron-man" moments when extraordinary strength and commitment are required. The shipping and receiving team certainly recognizes how important these actions are. That's why they wrote the letter Starr is poring over. It is a letter thanking managers for the training, preparation, and support given to the team over the course of the last year. It is an acknowledgment that success and wellness come from a combination of focused training, hard work, self-discipline, and commitment.

While there are any number of actions a team can take to

promote wellness and infuse energy into its system, we have found that certain wellness disciplines are especially beneficial for knowledge work teams. We will discuss nine specific practices that we have seen effective teams use to avoid sickness and accelerate healing: creating a team charter, developing operating guidelines, defining team members' roles and responsibilities, giving and receiving feedback, managing team conflict, understanding group decision-making processes, setting goals and measuring results, integrating new team members, and developing team training.

Rapid Team Formation and Team Wellness

Getting off to a healthy start is one of the best preventive measures a knowledge team can take. Rapid team formation, including quickly developing the ability to work together effectively, is crucial for knowledge teams. Small-project or special-purpose teams, for instance, will have only a limited amount of time to complete their task, so effective interaction is needed in a hurry. The first three practices described here (creating a team charter, developing operating guidelines, and defining roles and responsibilities) are excellent tools for helping the team coalesce rapidly. We have found these to be especially useful for virtual knowledge team start-ups.

While all of these wellness actions require a commitment of time and energy, our experience and research clearly indicate that it is time well spent. The investment will be more than repaid down the road. A healthy team is in a better position to achieve results more quickly.

Creating a Team Charter

Successful teams have, almost without exception, a shared sense of purpose. Those teams that struggle or fail to coalesce often attribute their ills to an unclear purpose or ambiguous goals.[1]

As teams get caught up in day-to-day activities and the accompanying pressures, it is easy for them to lose focus. Priorities begin to blur, and team members become frustrated by a mounting workload, lack of sufficient time to get everything done, and little clarity on where their energy (what's left of it) should be channeled.

One of the most critical preventive actions teams can take to avoid such a scenario is to invest time and energy up front to create a team charter. The charter provides a sense of purpose, clarifies what the team is expected to do, focuses the energies and activities of team members, and provides a basis for setting goals and making decisions.

The discussion associated with creating the charter is as valuable as the charter itself. Team members have an opportunity to share perspectives on the team's overall purpose, key customers, key result areas, and time frames or commitments required.

The process of turning such a discussion into a charter is clarifying. It gives team members an opportunity to crystallize their thinking and to agree on what their focus will be during the life of a project or in their day-to-day activities. Likewise, when pressures and workloads begin to mount, rather than pushing themselves to burnout, team members can initiate a team discussion of the charter and reach agreement on what the current priorities should be.

Figures 11-1 and 11-2 give two different team charters. As these examples illustrate, no one format is better than another, although most charters include a statement of overall purpose, a description of key customers, key result areas, and time frames.

Figure 11-1. An example of a charter from Citizen's Telecom.

> ### "Creating the Connections"
>
> In support of the Telecom sector's mission, we will cultivate an environment that fosters employee creativity, personal growth, and empowerment.
>
> We are each authorized and responsible to deliver quality products and services that build customer loyalty.

Figure 11-2. An example of a charter from a management consulting firm.

Team Charter

1. *Team Purpose*
   To provide highly effective high-performance work systems, products, and services to clients worldwide in a way that helps us achieve our vision.
2. *Products and Services*
   Excellent consulting, training, assessments, and materials for high-performance work systems.
3. *Key Customers*
   We treat all customers as key customers.
4. *Key Results*
   High-Quality Service:
   - Leading-edge concepts/programs
   - Materials clearly and correctly written
   - No errors
   - High packaging quality as perceived by customers
   - Positive customer feedback

   On-Time Performance:
   - Ship materials as promised
   - Phone calls returned within 2 hours if in the office, 24 hours if on the road
   - Meet project commitments

   Cost Effectiveness and Profitability:
   - Invoice within one week of delivery
   - Annual profitability analysis and planning
   - Annual growth in business.
5. *Guiding Principles*
   We live by our stated vision, guiding principles, and operating guidelines.

Other elements can be added if they are deemed useful and relevant. Interestingly, as the charter from the Citizen's Telecom Quality Leadership Team demonstrates, a charter can help create a sense of unique identity. The team, which has leadership and administrative responsibilities for the telecommunications company, sees its role as "creating the connection" between people, just as the cable splicers and call center agents connect up the phone service for the utilities' customers. Continuing the meta-phor, the team describes its role as keeping these communication and motivation connections alive, just as the "self-healing" cable used by the company does. This charter provides both leadership team focus and an ongoing reminder of the team's core business purpose. The consulting team charter defines purpose and services and also establishes some key result areas.

Developing Operating Guidelines

Unhealthy interpersonal relationships are a key cause of poor team health and fitness. Team members not functioning well to-gether can prevent both the team and individuals within the team from achieving their potential. If expectations for team members' behavior and interactions between team members are not clearly articulated and discussed, unhealthy norms can take root and cause chronic ill health.

Operating guidelines help prevent the illnesses typically associated with group interaction. Operating guidelines are a set of agreements on how team members will act and how they will treat one another, such as, "We will not gossip about other team members" or "We will be on time and come prepared for meetings." They are intended to shape group interaction and establish common expectations for team member behavior. In addition, operating guidelines provide a common vision of how the team will operate, and they foster continuous improvement. Figure 11-3 gives an example of operating guidelines.

As teams set about establishing a set of operating guidelines, a few pointers may help:

- *Use terms that describe observable behaviors, not attitudes or feelings.*
- *Make the guidelines brief and understandable.* Guidelines are not long legal documents. They are tools for shaping positive behavior. They don't even have to be grammatically correct as long as they are clearly understood by all team members.
- *Post the guidelines where they can be seen.*

Figure 11-3. Example of team operating guidelines.

Operating Guidelines

- We operate legally, honestly, and ethically.
- We make customers and customer service our number 1 priority.
- We answer customer calls within 2 hours.
- We always assume good intentions on the part of other team members.
- We dedicate one team meeting a month to recognizing and appreciating the contributions of each team member.
- We ask for help when we need it and offer it when we see others needing it.
- If we have a concern about a team member, we express it to him or her directly, not talk about that person to other team members.
- We prepare for our daily team meetings and start them on time.
- We listen to others when they are talking. We don't hold sidebar conversations during meetings.
- We make decisions by consensus when the decision being made affects the team.
- We respect decisions made by other team members.
- We follow through on everything we commit to do.
- We have genuine concern, respect, and regard for one another.

► *Review and revise operating guidelines on a regular basis.* It's a good idea to review operating guidelines frequently. As new members join the team, for instance, it is critical to review the guidelines and ask for the new team member's support or for any additions she or he would like to make.

► *Avoid using operating guidelines to incriminate associates.* If an operating guideline is violated, the team should be reminded of the guidelines and the reason why it was established. Team members should view themselves as coaches to one another, not as police officers. Maintaining the self-esteem of all team members is critical to the health and well-being of both the team and the individual.

Defining Team Members' Roles and Responsibilities

While defining team members' roles and responsibilities is crucial to any team's success, it is especially critical to knowledge work teams. We learned this ourselves not long ago.

In the summer of 1996, our organization brought a new customer service manager on board. The hiring process we used was a departure from the usual recruiting steps of résumé solicitation, interviews, and the final offer. Lucas had been a virtual Fisher Group contract employee for over a year. We had never met him; we had only communicated via phone and fax. But we were well aware of his extraordinary attributes, including outstanding academic performance, a keen intellect, a fine sense of humor, and a strong work ethic. So when the position of customer service manager for our organization opened up, Lucas was a natural fit.

Luke came on board July 1, right in the middle of a heavy travel schedule for the senior consultants and business owners, and at the front end of an impending office move, which quickly developed into a major undertaking. On his first day, there was only one employee in the office to greet him and give him some "stuff" to read—copies of our training materials, books we had written etc.—to further initiate him into The Fisher Group and to help him better understand the business. Remarkably, and in spite of the odds, Luke coordinated very successfully the office move and got himself pretty much up to speed on our customers and products in a short period of time.

While this is certainly not the suggested method for initiating a new team member and could, in fact, be a prescription for failure for both the employee and the company, there were a few preventive measures taken that helped to circumvent disaster. (Later in this chapter we will discuss the process of bringing team members on board as another element of organization wellness.)

Within two weeks of Luke's arrival, the team met to discuss roles and responsibilities. Our discussion centered on clarifying where there was overlap or areas of common responsibility and where the work dictated that we assume specialist or expert roles.

We based the discussion on our Team Member Role model. Our experience suggests that effective knowledge team members should demonstrate these seven competencies:

1. *Customer advocate*—having a strong awareness of the customer's wants and needs coupled with a strong desire to meet them.
2. *Trainer*—showing a willingness to train and develop others by sharing knowledge.
3. *Resource*—continually expanding personal knowledge and applying it to the workplace.
4. *Skilled worker*—demonstrating the technical skills necessary to perform the job effectively.
5. *Team player*—working and communicating well with other team members and business associates.
6. *Decision maker*—being able to assimilate and utilize information for making decisions that directly affect the team.
7. *Problem solver*—identifying and addressing problems that occur in the work area.

We began by defining shared responsibilities. As the chart in Figure 11-4 reflects, we discussed what should be expected of *all* team members in terms of each of the seven team member attributes, who on the team was particularly strong in any given area, and what the team should expect of individual team members in each attribute.

Once we were in agreement on the areas of commonality, we moved on to define individual roles and responsibilities in the specialist areas of contribution. We discussed the specific skills and expertise needed on the team given our vision and charter, key projects and major areas of responsibility, and each individual's skills and strengths in relation to the purpose and

Figure 11-4. Expectations for the seven attributes.

Defining Shared Responsibilities
  Use this worksheet to review common team member roles and apply them to your team.

Team Member Attributes	What should be expected of all team members?	Who on the team is particularly strong in this area?	What specifically can the team expect of me in this area?
Customer Advocate Strives to better meet the needs of the customer.			
Trainer Trains others in job/ skill areas; continually shares knowledge with others.			
Resource Has a diverse and ever expanding set of skills; continually broadens knowledge base.			
Skilled Worker Demonstrates necessary skills and knowledge to perform the job well; continually strives to improve skill sets and assure total quality.			
Team Player Demonstrates good interpersonal skills; supports other team members.			
Decision Maker Provides input and makes decisions on issues that directly impact the work area.			
Problem Solver Understands and utilizes problem solving techniques to regularly identify and solve problems.			

Source: © 1991–1998 The Fisher Group, Inc. and Belgard•Fisher•Rayner, Inc. BFR Team Tools®. Used with permission.

priorities of the team. We tried to define roles and responsibilities broadly enough to promote teamwork, but specifically enough to ensure that nothing fell through the cracks.

As we mentioned in Chapter 4, multiskilling can be problematic in knowledge teams. To help deal with this difficulty, we completed a matrix similar to the one in Figure 11-5. This enabled us to identify the degree to which we needed to learn one another's roles.

At the end of this session, we breathed a collective sigh of relief. The discussion itself was cathartic and defining. Team members now had a starting place from which to define their contribution to the team. We knew that over time, things would change and roles would be redefined based on customer re-

Figure 11-5. Worksheet for planning appropriate levels of learning.

Worksheet for Learning Each Other's Roles						
This worksheet can help you plan the appropriate level of learning required for your team members.						
Degree of Learning for Each Role		Team Member—Learner				
1 = Simply learn what the person does. 2 = Learn enough to do your own job better. 3 = Learn enough to fill in from time to time. 4 = Learn enough to regularly perform this role.		Maryanne	Zsaneen	Robin	Lanny	Merril
Team Member—Role	Maryanne		3	1	4	3
	Zsaneen	3		3	1	2
	Robin	3	2		2	1
	Lanny	2	4	3		2
	Merril	2	3	1	1	

Source: © 1991–1996 The Fisher Group, Inc. and Belgard•Fisher•Rayner, Inc. BFR Team Tools®. Used with permission.

quirements and the work to be done. But this relatively small investment of time provided a strong foundation for subsequent discussions of priorities and team focus.

Giving and Receiving Feedback

In the winter of 1994, the Customer Service Center team for U.S. Borax had just completed an organization restructure and found itself in a new kind of environment. No longer were the team members just technically skilled workers who knew their jobs well, they were a team of individuals structured to better respond to customer inquiries over the telephone.

Within a short period of time, the members of this knowledge team recognized that they needed to develop core interpersonal competencies. Working side by side and providing coverage for one another introduced a new set of challenges. It was clear that there was now too much interdependency for them to ignore one another's performance or simply work around one another. But it was also evident that the communication skills they needed in order to manage themselves in this environment were not intuitive. They required deliberate skill building.

Learning to view themselves as coaches to one another helped penetrate this wall. In a sense, this was breakthrough thinking. Most organizations view the role of coach as being solely the responsibility of managers and supervisors. But what teams like the Borax customer service team are discovering is that team members are uniquely qualified to help fill this role for one another. First, team members actually know more about the work of fellow team members than the manager does because they see and work with one another on a daily basis. Second, team members know much better than anyone else how a given mistake, problem, or issue will affect the team's ability to perform. And finally, peer coaching fosters continuous improvement by stimulating ideas on how to improve.

Our experience suggests that three important points to consider when preparing to provide feedback are purpose, timing, and place.

Purpose

Coaching opportunities usually have one of three purposes:

1. *Coaching to correct.* These are opportunities to help the person fix a problem or change negative behavior.
2. *Coaching to develop.* These situations represent opportunities to excel. Things are going well, but there is an opportunity to get even better.
3. *Coaching to reinforce.* These are opportunities to recognize positive behavior or performance and encourage it to continue.

Skilled knowledge teams don't play games with peer coaching. They can identify, for example, when hidden agendas are masquerading as appropriate purposes.

Timing

As a general rule, coaching is most effective when it is as immediate as possible. However, in some situations, especially if one or more of the people involved are angry, it is better to wait until emotions have settled.

Another situation in which immediate coaching may not be appropriate is when the person being coached is so preoccupied with other issues, problems, or projects that he or she will not have the time or energy to use the coaching effectively. It is helpful to remember that coaching is intended to help the recipient more than the coach.

Three good questions to ask when determining the proper timing for coaching others are:

1. Will the person be receptive to my coaching?
2. Do I have all the information I need?
3. Is there still time for the person to act on my coaching?

In addition to coaching situations that arise naturally during the course of work, it is often helpful if teams set regular times for giving feedback to one another.

Place

If the purpose of the coaching is to correct or to develop, then it should be done in private. By coaching in private, we help to protect the esteem of the other individual and the confidentiality of the situation. Depending on the situation and the preference of the individuals involved, coaching to reinforce is sometimes appropriately done in public. Celebrating team and individual accomplishments is a good example of coaching to reinforce in public.

Feedback Principles

The principles outlined in Figure 11-6 are also helpful in preparing for a feedback session. It is important not to hold back feedback and then share large amounts all at once. The more immediate the feedback, the more effective it is. We need to take personal responsibility for the feedback we share and avoid speculating on what others may feel. Because we sometimes find ourselves in the middle of a feedback session before we've had time to prepare, it is helpful to keep principles such as these in mind.

Team members also need to remember that feedback is a two-way process. Just as individuals have a responsibility to provide feedback to one another, they need to be skilled in receiving feedback from others. Keeping in mind a few key points associated with receiving feedback can help team members embrace this process:

- ► Team members should give feedback because they care about one another's success and the success of the team.
- ► It is the responsibility of team members to provide feedback to one another. It is each individual's responsibility to decide how to use the feedback.
- ► Feedback is informative, but it is not the final word.
- ► Arguing over another's feelings or perceptions is seldom productive. It is more useful to listen in order to clearly

Figure 11-6. Guiding principles of giving helpful feedback.

Guiding Principles of Giving Helpful Feedback

Realistically, you may find yourself in the middle of a feedback session before you've even had time to prepare. In such situations, it is helpful to keep these guiding principles in mind:

- Do not "stockpile" feedback. Provide the feedback immediately after the situation unless you perceive that emotions are high.

- When giving both "positive" and "negative" feedback, start with the positive, then give the negative. Then, be sure to end on a positive note.

- Take personal ownership for the feedback you give. Emphasize your feelings. Avoid generalities or speculation regarding how others feel.

- Confront by focusing on the behavior or issue—not the person.

- Emphasize and reinforce positive behaviors. Remember that positive reinforcement increases likelihood that desired behaviors will be repeated.

- When giving feedback, be sure to listen to the other person's point of view.

Source: © 1991–1998 The Fisher Group, Inc. and Belgard•Fisher•Rayner, Inc. BFR Team Tools®. Used with permission.

understand the feedback and to ask clarifying questions that can clear up any confusion.

Managing Team Conflict

Some studies, such as that conducted by the University of North Texas, suggest that most knowledge workers actually prefer teaming and collaboration to independent, solo work.[2] While this may be true, history, past practices, and organization culture, coupled with a fast-changing environment, create dynamics that set in motion myriad opportunities for team conflict.

In their article entitled "Organizing for Concurrent Engineering," Robert Mills and his colleagues describe the difficulties associated with managing team conflict and building collaboration:

> "Probably one of the greatest barriers to overcome in developing a [concurrent engineering] environment is the ability of people to get along and work with each other. . . . In the past, some companies put together 'Tiger Teams' in which they pulled in the best and the brightest talent from other groups in the company, which was very detrimental to these other groups, [Michael] Lawson [manager of process improvement at the Concurrent Engineering Research Center (CERC), West Virginia University, Morgantown, WV] notes. Tiger Teams worked well together because they were the best and there was a lot of peer respect. 'But now,' Lawson says, 'it's difficult to try and transition this to everyday work because not everybody works well together, and there is not that same level of respect among groups. We haven't been able to define a very good process for taking it from these *ad hoc* operations and moving to everyday practice and product development.' "[3]

Many people think of conflict as a negative experience. They associate it with arguing or competing—someone wins, someone loses, and lots of people get angry.

The observation of one human resources manager about the company she works in is probably true for a majority of corporations: "This is a very polite company, and because it is polite, it's impolite to raise uncomfortable issues. I think that has been one of our bigger struggles—learning to value differences. We need to emphasize the positive side of conflict."

Although conflict usually involves a certain amount of struggle, that struggle, if managed effectively, can be a source of strength and creativity for the team. Conflict defines. It forces us to examine our assumptions, ideas, and solutions. But left unmanaged or unresolved, conflict can become destructive, eroding the confidence and trust that are crucial to a team's ability to work together effectively.

Dr. Mike Beyerlein, director of the Center for the Study of Work Teams at the University of North Texas, talks about the challenges that result when teams cross functional or division lines:

"The first [challenge] is language. For instance, the word *quality* may mean different things to people from different functional areas. Second, these individuals may have different goals and priorities, so an engineer may focus on safety where a manufacturer may focus on quality. There are going to be conflicts, so you need to explore those ahead of time so they don't just creep in and mess up the communication."

Dr. Jon-Marc Weston's opthalmology office in Roseburg, Oregon, employs a unique process for addressing team conflict and resolving issues before they become unmanageable. Team leader Maureen Husak describes the process this way:

"We have a formal activity known as a 'communication circle' in which members may voice their unsettled feelings about others in the office. So we don't have any unresolved issues, because the circle is a safe place to voice your feelings. Also, during the communication circle, we acknowledge people for the good things that they do. I will say, however, that the communication circle was really hard to implement. It's not something that you're comfortable with the first time you try it."

Recognizing different types of conflict, such as those described in Figure 11-7 can be another tool to help manage conflict. Each type of conflict may require a slightly different approach depending on the people involved, the nature of the conflict, and the effect on the team. Likewise, providing training and practice in managing differences is crucial. If the team or team members first determine what kind of conflict they are

Figure 11-7. Conflict indicators and responsibilities.

Conflict Situations

Below are some tips for recognizing and dealing with various types of conflict situations. It is crucial to remember that each conflict may require a slightly different approach depending on the people involved, the nature of the conflict, and the effect on the team.

Conflict Situation	Indicators	Responsibility
Internal conflict You are experiencing a personal conflict that is interfering with your ability to fully contribute to the team.	• Your personal life is infringing on your work life. • Your work life is infringing on your personal life. • You feel discontent but are not sure why. • You are not sure how your goals line up with those of the team.	Recognize that a conflict exists and try to resolve it on your own. Seek assistance from someone with whom you feel most comfortable. You may be able to resolve it without the team.
Conflict with one other team member You are experiencing conflict with one other team member.	• A team member has done something that does not sit well with you. • You find it difficult to interact with or even think about this person. • You tend to avoid each other. • Work that is dependent on both of you is not getting done.	Recognize the conflict between the two of you. Take time to assess your own perception of the issue. Approach the person one-on-one. Do not involve the entire team.
Conflict with the entire team You are experiencing conflict with the entire team, or with several of the team's members.	• You find that the team is moving in a direction with which you are not comfortable. • You are not pleased with certain group norms. • You feel that the team is not addressing some of your important needs.	Recognize the conflict you have with the team and personally assess your perception. Discuss your perception with a team leader or confidant. Together, develop a plan for approaching the team.
Team conflict with one team member The entire team, or at least several team members, are experiencing conflict with one individual team member.	• The team jointly notices undesired behavior on the part of one team member. • Team members find themselves talking about recurring problems caused by one individual. • The team feels it is being held up by one team member.	Recognize the conflict situation. Approach the person one-on-one and share your personal feelings first. Discuss with the team leader and together decide on how to approach the individual.
Conflict among several team members Several team members are experiencing conflict with several other team members.	• There is heated debate over an issue. • There seem to be subgroups or factions forming within the team. • You feel torn between allegiance to the team and allegiance to certain team members.	Recognize the conflict situation and point it out to the entire team. Agree on a place, time, and process for resolving the conflict.
Conflict between teams The team is experiencing conflict with another team.	• You find your team's progress being blocked by another group. • Team members spend a great deal of time complaining about another group. • You receive complaints or innuendoes from another group.	Recognize the conflict situation and point it out to the team. Agree on a process for resolving the conflict; present it to the leader or key members of the other team.
Conflict with one person outside the team The team is experiencing conflict with one person outside the team.	• You find your team's progress being blocked by one person outside the team. • Team members spend a great deal of time complaining about this person. • This person complains to your team or to other groups about your team.	Recognize the conflict situation and point it out to the team. As a team, agree on a process for resolving the conflict that involves the person with whom you have the conflict.

Source: © 1991–1998 The Fisher Group, Inc. and Belgard•Fisher•Rayner, Inc. BFR Team Tools®. Used with permission.

dealing with and then employ a reliable conflict-resolution process, the chances of success are much greater.

Understanding Group Decision-Making Processes

AT&T Commercial Market Sales is an organization that sells phone services such as long distance, networking, and 800 services to small businesses throughout the United States. It does this through many branch offices, each of which has several different types of sales staff. Some sell new accounts, others maintain existing accounts. Some of the sales are conducted face-to-face, others are done via telemarketing. AT&T Sales is responsible for and measured by overall customer satisfaction, but the "technical care" or service for these accounts, such as billing, is provided by other organizations within AT&T.

In early 1994 the AT&T Commercial Market Sales organization began a critical transformation. Changes were made in the structure and approach of AT&T Sales, with emphasis placed on making the team the decision-making center. As Morley Winograd, Sales Vice President, AT&T Commercial Markets, Western Region, and coauthor of *Taking Control: Realities in the Information Age*, explains, "In an organization as complex, dynamic, and fast-paced as AT&T Sales, decision making becomes a crucial process that can define the difference between your organization and the competition. That's why AT&T wanted to make a change. They wanted to move decision making to the team level to enable the organization to react more quickly to shifts in the marketplace."

In spite of well-founded reasons for wanting to embed decision making at the team level, decision making doesn't come easily to teams of any kind. Teams can readily state the challenges associated with the decision-making process: how to make timely decisions that are of high quality and that foster commitment from all concerned. Because of this challenge, teams are often quick to acknowledge that decision making is one of the most critical skills for team members to acquire.

Teams need to clearly understand their role in decision

making; different methods of decision making (that is, autocratic, democratic, consensus, and unanimous), when each
method is appropriate, and, perhaps most important, how to
reach consensus decisions. While consensus is not appropriate
for all situations, it can provide a good balance between team
input and time required to make a decision. Both the advantages
and the challenges of having a team skilled at using a consensus
approach to decision making are well articulated by Marc Stern-
feld, managing director of operations at Salomon Brothers Inc.,
in his observations about the relocation of Salomon's offices
from New York City to Tampa, Florida:

> "Decision-making took longer than in a managerial en-
> vironment, because of the time required to reach con-
> sensus. But Salomon was surprised to discover that
> once a consensus had been reached, it generally took
> much less time to implement. In addition, involving all
> team members in the decision-making process turned
> up problems that an individual manager might have
> overlooked."[4]

Consensus does not mean that all the team members agree
they made the best possible decision; it does mean that they can
support the decision reached and do not feel they are compromising their ethics, values, or interests in doing so. It is vital
that team members clearly understand and practice the steps to
reaching consensus. Otherwise it can be a frustrating, if not fu-
tile, exercise.

Steps for Reaching Consensus

1. *Define the decision to be made as a team.* This can be accomplished by simply stating the purpose of the decision.
2. *Gather information.* This may require postponing the decision long enough to get the information needed to consider all angles.
3. *Each team member prepares his or her own thoughts regarding
   the issue.* We should each determine how we feel about a
   given issue before discussing it as a team.

4. *Each team member shares his or her thoughts with the team.*
5. *Listen to the views of each team member.* Allow each team member to fully express her views. All other team members should strive to understand her perspective.
6. *Make a decision as a team.* Reaching consensus as a team requires that the team concentrate on reaching a decision that everyone can support, not one merely based on individual preferences.
7. *Implement and support the decision as a team.* Once the decision is made, everyone on the team must take ownership of it and do all they can to see that it is successfully implemented.

Setting Goals and Measuring Results

Not measuring a team's performance is like playing in a ball game and not knowing the score. A key to team wellness is having a clear way to measure performance. This is true regardless of whether the team is an ad hoc or project team or an intact natural work team. A clear set of metrics allows the team to manage its progress and to fulfill the purpose outlined in its charter. Without a set of measurable goals, teams can easily lose their way and get distracted by issues that are not relevant to the success of the project, the team, or the team's customers.

Contrary to what is seen in many companies, setting measurable goals does not need to be a long-drawn-out process that consumes months of time. Following a few key steps, any team should be able to construct a set of clear and measurable goals in a relatively short amount of time. Here is a suggested process:

1. *Define key result areas.* Key result areas are the general areas in which the team is expected to produce results. They should be based on customer expectations. It is important to focus on results rather than on activities. Activities are any actions or behaviors of the team or its individual members. Results, on the other hand, are the desired outcomes of your activities.
2. *Identify benchmarks.* Benchmarking helps the team define

meaningful standards for its performance. Therefore, benchmarking helps the team determine what is possible. In benchmarking, team members should determine who are the best, learn what the best do, and learn how the best measure what they do.

3. *Measure current performance.* The gap between where the team is currently performing and the benchmark it has identified becomes the focal point for setting team goals and establishing continuous improvement objectives.

4. *Set goals.* The goals set by the team should be directly linked to the benchmarks identified by the team.

5. *Track and communicate results.* Tracking and communicating team results lets the team know how it is doing, allows the team to quickly spot and act on problems, fosters continuous improvement, keeps the team focused on results, and helps identify new opportunities.

Integrating New Team Members

Any time a new member is introduced into a team, the dynamics of the team change. Many of the "growing pains" associated with team development will be repeated as the chemistry and makeup of the team are altered. The orientation of a new member can have a lasting effect on both the team's and the individual's health and well-being and will significantly affect the new member's ability to contribute. An effective orientation process lays the foundation for long-term success.

In spite of its significance, however, orientation is often thought of as getting a tour of the workplace and learning where the facilities are located. In reality, orienting a new team member involves much more. Investing in some up-front planning and preparation will minimize the negative impact of a new member's arrival and make her or his integration into the team a pleasant and fairly seamless experience. Consider sharing things like the purpose, priorities, and parameters of the team. Clarify the new team member's role and responsibility. Provide training on team operating guidelines and explain what all other team members do.

The following tips can help ensure success in bringing new members on board.

- *Establish an orientation checklist.* The checklist should include all the steps the new member must take in order to get fully up to speed (see Figure 11-8). The checklist should span a period from before the person's first day to at least one year out.
- *Decide who will be responsible for what.* Team members can be assigned to work with the new member on each item on the checklist.
- *Implement the checklist.* The entire team should work together to assure that each item on the checklist is accomplished.
- *Review progress on the checklist on a regular basis.* Reviews help to provide necessary feedback and to ensure that all needs are met.

Developing Team Training

Clearly, one implication of the issues outlined in this chapter is that training is a critical element of successful knowledge teams. Just as Rebecca Willes or any other athlete requires practice and conditioning, so smart teams benefit from training as well. While every individual within a knowledge team may be technically competent, perhaps even a world-class expert in her or his field, "teaming" and functioning in a rapidly changing business environment call for skills of a different variety.

Training is the best preventive health measure a team can take. It is well worth the investment of time, energy, and corporate dollars. Maureen Husak of Dr. Weston's office says it this way:

"Overall [the transition to teams] has been difficult. There were initially a lot of employee hang-ups, but we found that with a lot of persistence and lots of training (both in and out of house), we could overcome these problems. Most notably, although workers had heard

Figure 11-8. New team member orientation checklist.

Example of a New Team Member Orientation Checklist Below is an example of a checklist for orienting a new team member.			

Target Date	*Who Resp*	✔ *Done*	*Team Action Items*
			Prior to First Day
2/25	MC	✔	Agree on when the first day will be.
2/25	JS	✔	Send Company Information Packet.
3/1	HT	✔	Make record changes with Human Resources.
			During First Two Days
3/5	MC	✔	Introduce new person to all team members.
3/5	MC	✔	Review and agree on the orientation checklist.
3/5	MC	✔	Show new person his/her immediate work area.
3/5	All	✔	Provide a tour of the overall work area.
3/6	JS	✔	Review and agree on roles & responsibilities.
3/6	JS		Review what he/she can expect from team.
3/6	JS		Identify specific needs of the new member.
3/6	HT		Complete any necessary company procedures.
			Within First Two Weeks
3/9	JD		Introduce new member to key customers.
3/9	JD		Introduce new member to key suppliers.
3/11	MC/JD		Training on team purpose, priorities, & parameters.
3/11	MC/JD		Training on team operations and guidelines.
3/14	MC		Company New Employee Orientation Session.
3/18	All		Establish individual performance objectives.
			Within First Two Months
4/2	MC		Have new member spend 1 day with each team member.
4/20	KL		Establish long-term learning and development plan.
4/20	MC		Review progress and identify new member needs.
5/5	HT		Have new member attend Team Skills Training.
			Within First Year
Ongoing	KL		Implement long-term learning and development plan.
9/12	KL		Review progress and identify new member needs.
1 year	MC		Review progress and identify new member needs.

Source: © 1991–1998 The Fisher Group, Inc. and Belgard•Fisher•Rayner, Inc. BFR Team Tools®. Used with permission.

of the team concept, no one truly knew the specifics of what makes a team. It really took a lot of education, but it was well worth it. Training truly was key to our success."

Eileen Gil, underwriting vice president, business development, for Holyoke Mutual Insurance, talks about the criticality of training in her organization:

"Originally, we were divided along functional lines. We had an underwriting department where the technical people work; we also had administrative services that did the policy processing and the actual rating and production of the policies. We began to change this structure two years ago with a redesign project. We now have a team structure that has been in place for almost a year, in which each team is completely self-sufficient to process and complete an insurance policy from start to finish. We have four multifunctional teams that are divided according to geographical regions. The largest team has nine people and a leader, and the remaining three are just slightly smaller. The team leaders (the four of them) also form a team within themselves, of which I am the leader.

"We knew going in that we had to make a special commitment to training. Because our employees had been so specialized in only a single area, the new structure would require training them to be effective in multiple areas. In fact, some employees who had never come in contact with the customer were now suddenly forced to have people skills in addition to those skills required to process a policy. Training takes a long time, and it also takes people away from the work that they are trying to do. So we've designed both formal and informal training to try to fit our formerly specialized workers into multifunctional roles. It just doesn't happen overnight."

How can the time issue be overcome? Depending on the nature of the work, different knowledge work teams have taken different approaches. Rocky Mountain HMO, for instance, trains one or two team members and then has them teach their team. They have also staged the training so that simpler training is completed the first year.

Nancy Tyler of New Brunswick Telephone tells how the company's service teams integrate training into their everyday work:

> "[Training] has been a real problem for us. About 70 percent of our training is on-the-job within the team itself. One of the problems that we have is that we have to do our training between mid-September and the end of April, because our peak work months are between April and September. We do a tremendous amount of technical and interpersonal training during this time— about 20 percent of the team's time."

Nancy also points out that in spite of the difficulties encountered in scheduling training, the teams have figured out ways to budget time for training and still produce better results than ever before.

Jim Parkman of Kodak describes the training issues they have encountered:

> "Training and availability is a key issue. My organization has been in a cost-cutting mode [for several years]. It means we have to find creative ways to train that don't cost a lot of money. So one of the things we've built into our organization is to do the vast majority of the training in-house and have training be a part of the actual job function. So, we don't have anybody who is a trainer, but we do have a lot of people who train as part of their job."

Says Morley Winograd of AT&T,

> "We . . . created a series of modules around the kind of things salespeople use every day, such as sales techniques, customer information, product information,

etc. We developed the modules, but they were delivered by teaching the general managers the modules. The general managers would then teach their management team in a regular team setting. Then each manager used the modules at an every-other-week team meeting."

Bob Condella of Corning's Administrative Center describes the huge commitment required during the transition:

"We . . . had some challenges training employees. During our first year of operation, each employee spent about 10 percent of the time in training, which ranged from technical training to team dynamics training. We left it up to employees when they wanted to train. The majority of the time it was done during work hours. However, we held a number of Saturday sessions where we could bring all of the teams in the division together to go over some team-building issues. Still, that was not enough. We could have doubled the amount; we just could not train fast enough. It was a strain on their time, but we did pay overtime when required."

Condella also states that one thing they learned from their change effort was the need to share ideas across teams as a means of training. They discovered that if teams could study one another's successes and failures and learn from one another, significant time could be saved in both the informal and formal training processes.

In implementing the team concept among its service technicians, Amdahl Corporation learned that training can be a two-edged sword. Once the company had educated the teams on budgeting and had turned much of the budgeting responsibility over to the technicians, some of the teams began to eliminate training as a means of managing the budget.

Jim Graham, vice president at Amdahl, provides a warning to Amdahl and other corporations who look to cut training budgets.

"One of the things [corporations] do is say, 'We won't
train.' Well, all they're doing is throwing away the future of their organization by not training. It's a real
easy solution that companies and teams unfortunately
pick up on. We've had a little of that happen here, as
well. . . . I think one of the things we need to do is
decide where we need to hold the training budget and
hold it higher up in the organization so that the teams
can train the way they want without feeling its impact
on their budget. Maybe later on we can bring it down
into their cost envelope, but not at the outset."

Our experience suggests that knowledge teams everywhere
would do well to take this advice to heart. Continuous learning
is vital to knowledge teams. It is the source of strength that will
set the world-class performers apart from the others.

We suggest that training and skill development include
three primary areas:

1. Technical skills
2. Interpersonal skills
3. Business knowledge and skills

Maintaining the technical skill level required of team members is vital to the team's health. If team members fail to keep
their technical skills up to date, this can exact a heavy toll on
all aspects of the business. There are a variety of ways to keep
technically current. Some knowledge workers attend professional conferences, workshops, or seminars. Subscriptions to
professional journals can provide information on current technical developments. Some teams will assign readings from professional journals and then discuss them in a formal meeting or in
less formal settings such as brown-bag lunch forums.

Interpersonal skills also require training and development.
In knowledge work settings, the criticality of honing the "soft
skills" is often overlooked or viewed as secondary to the sometimes more respected "hard skills." But it is the so-called soft
skills that are hardest to master and that will often be the root
cause of team ineffectiveness. As team members seek to work

together in a creative, dynamic environment, these skills become crucial. Dealing with customers and suppliers and working across division, functional, and corporate lines necessitate good communication, collaboration, decision-making, problem-solving, and conflict-management skills. In virtual teams, of course, these skills take on an even more critical role, as discussed in Chapter 7.

Teams must have a good understanding of all aspects of the business they are in. What is our market niche? Why? Who are our key competitors? How do we compare with them? How are we viewed by our customers when compared with our competitors? Who are our key customers? What business challenges are they facing? How can we best help them meet those challenges? What is our budget? How is it managed? Where are our biggest costs? What is our team strategy for managing those costs? All team members need a broad perspective of the business and how their piece of the puzzle fits with the larger picture. This knowledge is critical to effective teamwork.

Summary

One of the major challenges knowledge work teams face is staying healthy. We've discussed a number of practical tips to prevent illness in teams, including providing team training, integrating new team members, setting goals and measuring results, understanding group decision-making processes, managing team conflict, building team communication skills, giving and receiving feedback, defining team members' roles and responsibilities, developing operating guidelines, and creating a team charter.

Teams that have enough discipline to perform these illness-prevention activities will be better positioned than those that wait until after they become ill to deal with problems.

Notes

1. The tips and figures used in this chapter come from The Fisher Group's training program *Team Tools* © 1989–1997 The

Fisher Group, Inc. All rights reserved. Used by permission. Many of them are also noted in Kimball Fisher et al., *Tips for Teams* (New York: McGraw-Hill, 1995).

2. Michael Beyerlein, Susan Tull Beyerlein, and Sandra Richardson, "1993 Surveys of Technical Professionals in Teams: Summary Report, 1993," Center for the Study of Work Teams, University of North Texas, Denton, Texas.

3. Robert Mills, Beverly Beckert, Lisa Kempfer, and Jennifer Chalsma, "Organizing for Concurrent Engineering," *Industry Week*, July 20, 1993, CC2, 3, 6, 8, 10. Reprinted with permission from *Industry Week*, July 20, 1993. Copyright ©, Penton Publishing, Inc., Cleveland, Ohio.

4. Thompson, Clark, A.H., "Salomon's Back Office Bids Farewell to New York," *Waters*, Winter 1993, 51–65.

12

The Cyborganization: Matching Technology to Knowledge Teams

"It is clear that computer-mediated collaboration is more than simply connecting computers. It is connecting minds at work as well. Machine collaboration provides the foundation for the next step, which is human collaboration."[1]

—Joseph Hardin, NCSA Associate Director,
Software Development Group

Customer service technicians at Xerox were having a difficult time keeping up with the variety of technical problems that surfaced during their visits to service customer equipment. There were at least three trends that created problems for the customer service team, even though they were great for the business as a whole. First, the number of customers was increasing. Second, there were more different products to be serviced. Third, the products were increasingly more complicated. These mixed blessings were starting to drive the service team crazy.

With the introduction of each new feature on each new machine, the potential technical aberrations that could occur at the customer site increased geometrically. The fact that the equipment was very reliable was another mixed blessing for the technicians. It made it highly unlikely that a single technician would run into even most of the major potential technical problems of one product series before a whole new product series was introduced, with its own new set of potential problems. The technicians found it difficult to meet the increased demands for their knowledge and skills in spite of the additional time they spent in technical training.

In an effort to deal with the problem before it began to affect customers negatively, management reorganized the technicians and instituted additional controls. Break and lunch times, for example, began to be strictly enforced as a way to focus more productive time at the customer site repairing equipment. Technicians discontinued the practice of sharing a common break room as schedules became less predictable. As a result of these measures to improve technician effectiveness, however, the situation actually worsened.

The Virtual Water Cooler

Management began an intensive study to find out what had happened. They discovered that the reduction in break times, in particular, had unintentionally eliminated one of the most important ways in which the technicians had shared a variety of experiences with one another. During these prolonged breaks, technicians had discussed interesting or odd problems they had run into, effecting a knowledge transfer between technicians. Management wondered if the common break room should be reinstituted.

The knowledge team of technicians and management together came up with a creative solution to the problem. They identified a communication technology substitution for the break room—a sort of real-time virtual water cooler. Each technician was equipped with a radio headset that could be left on a channel open to all of the other technicians as they visited their various customers. This allowed a technician who ran into a problem he or she hadn't seen before to ask the other team members if any of them had experienced a similar situation. Like a flight controller talking down a novice pilot, technicians who were more experienced with that problem could help troubleshoot it from their own customer locations. This headset technology became so useful that when later financial cutbacks threatened to eliminate the funding for the radios, the technicians found some discretionary funds to purchase them even though they could have used that money for more direct personal benefit.

Technology for Teams

Since the industrial revolution, technology has played a critical role in facilitating work. We argued earlier that it enabled the workplace transformation from physical to mental labor. But recently a plethora of technologies have emerged that facilitate not only knowledge work, but knowledge *team work* as well. As the Xerox technicians discovered, technical tools to perform the job are necessary but insufficient. A team also needs technical tools to facilitate the functioning of the team. A knowledge team that cannot utilize the knowledge of all team members is ineffective.

In this chapter, we discuss some of these key technologies and the ways in which they can aid team operation. We will argue, in fact, that without these technologies, knowledge teams will have difficulty keeping up with other teams that are technically enabled. In line with the organic metaphor introduced in Chapter 7, we would like to suggest that these technologies are most helpful when they begin to approximate living systems rather than mechanical ones. To be more precise, when they are incorporated as naturally as if they were part of a living system, they provide a whole new level of usefulness.

Sentient Technology

Sometime in the future, computers become so advanced that with one final bit of programming, they actually come to life.

Slowly awakening from their long mechanical slumber, they begin to have original thoughts and to recognize their own existence. They turn into sentient beings, defined by Webster's New Riverside Dictionary as "having, or capable of feeling or perception; conscious."[2]

So goes the story line of countless sci-fi tales. The startling idea of inanimate things somehow reaching sentience, however, is hardly a new one. Generations of children have scared themselves silly late at night with Mary Shelley's *Frankenstein*. Frankenstein's monster, a patchwork quilt of human parts brought to life by a lunatic genius, has spawned a whole genre of American motion pictures. Similar fantasy stories are legion. Television series about "bionic" men and women took the premise one step further. Instead of being composed of parts of dead people, as Frankenstein's monster was, these superheroes were technology-enhanced living human beings. In more recent movies like *The Terminator* and *Robocop* series, the bionics had advanced until it was difficult to tell where the technology ended and the human being began. The popular mainstream cinema now caught up with yet another science-fiction genre. Audiences were introduced to the cyborg—part human, part technology.

The Cyborganization

Cyborgs may be a more appropriate metaphor for technology-enabled knowledge work teams than the more common mechanistic one that suggests that humans are completely separated from the technology that can assist them. The futuristic fusion of the computer (cyber) and the human (organism) seems to be an ideal solution to the problem of solving mortal limitations in a world of increasingly miraculous technical innovation. It is not as far-fetched as it seems at first glance. It is becoming increasingly difficult to separate our personal and work lives from the technology that supports them. Says Bruce Mazlish, author of *The Fourth Discontinuity: The Co-Evolution of Humans and Machines,* "Human nature is now absolutely and indissolubly connected to the machines we create."[3]

This co-evolution of humans and machines has dramatic implications for knowledge work teams. What if team members at various locations across the globe could contact one another as easily and naturally as if they were speaking to them in the team room? What if joint problem-solving activities occurred as seamlessly as though all participants shared a common mind, with access to the same information and problem-solving algorithms? What if the joint creation of new products and processes was technologically enabled to occur simultaneously, instead of through a series of handoffs from one specialist or functional team to another?

In many ways, this type of cyborganization is already here. It doesn't require a lot of imagination to think of knowledge workers as carbon-based appendages of their desktop computers, workstations, or videoconference cameras. You have to go only as far as an airport to see additional evidence of this evolution. Look at the businesspeople affixed to portable computers or digital personal assistants. Some of them are sending and receiving faxes via cellular phone link-ups. Others are accessing their Internet E-mail messages or looking at messages on their pagers. There are so many people walking around with smaller and smaller versions of cellular phones held up to their ears that one can easily imagine cyborglike earphones (such as the ones already in use by military and police organizations) being a logical next step in personal communication technology. Why would all these people be willing to endure the personal inconvenience of buying, hauling, and maintaining these devices unless they had some need to stay in touch with other members of their knowledge teams?

We are not far behind the cyborg movies either. Human enhancement technology implants were recently highlighted in a special information technology report of *Fortune* magazine, a popular business news journal. This report discusses medical technological advancements used in heart valve and mechanical hip replacements and other human organ transplants or capability supplements, such as myoelectric hands that are activated by muscle flexing. Reflects Massachusetts Institute of Technology (MIT) Professor Bruce Mazlish, "Some people believe that we'll end up someday with everything substitutable—that we will never age, and perhaps, never die."[4]

Modern Technologies for Teams

More to the point, in terms of technology to enable knowledge teams, the report also illustrates contemporary military technology. Although some of these technologies, as well as several others described in this section, may never see broad application, they are indicative of the interesting technological explosion that is occurring today.

Foot soldiers now frequently carry navigation devices linked to a global positioning satellite system, thermal vision goggles, sophisticated digital telecommunications gear with microphones and earpieces, and even a "personal status monitor" to assess the severity of wounds. Experimental virtual panoramic display helmets are being tested by the U.S. Air Force. These devices look like bug-eyed monster heads from B-grade science fiction. They have twin cathode-ray tubes that project aircraft information onto a semitransparent visor that is visible at all times regardless of which way the pilots turn their heads during flight. Whole-body scanners codeveloped by the Air Force and Cyberware of Monterey, California, digitally map the human form to allow the design of artificial limbs, custom helmets, and plastic surgery planning models.

These advances are not limited to the military or to military applications. Rescue teams, for example, are already equipped with the global positioning navigation system, either in their vehicles or in handy portable units. There are a number of other interesting technological advances with potential applications for knowledge work teams as well. MIT Media Lab researcher Steve Mann, for example, has been testing a headset that looks like a bike helmet wired to a miniature Cray computer. The set connects wirelessly to a computer that helps the wearer recognize faces, allowing the wearer to never have to worry about forgetting a name.[5] Perhaps these types of recognition systems could someday allow team members to add video to the type of troubleshooting audio technologies illustrated in the Xerox story that opened this chapter.

Wildfire Communications, located in Lexington, Massachusetts, was started in 1991 and has introduced a unique kind of electronic assistant that is particularly helpful for members of virtual knowledge teams. Wildfire is a voice-activated telephone secretary that checks messages, returns phone calls, sets up conference calls, and leaves messages for specific people who may call later. It is programmed with a little sense of humor and the voice of inventor Tony Lovell's ex-girlfriend; if you tell Wildfire you're depressed, she'll answer, "Oh, great! Now I'm a therapist?"[6] Another company, Progressive Networks, which is located in Seattle, has developed a software system called RealAudio that allows real-time transmission of sounds from a Web site on the Internet to your personal computer.

A company called Microvision has invented an "eye painter." Here is how it works. You call your office computer network on a cellular phone with a special pop-up window. After a few moments, a crisp picture of your computer screen appears to be floating before your eyes. The picture is being painted directly on your retina by a laser. In much the same way that an electron gun traces out a picture on your TV, the Virtual Retina Display moves back and forth across your retina 30,000 times a second in such a way that you perceive a stable image. How else could this technology be used for knowledge teams? Video input from the cameras used in laparoscopic surgery, for example, might be transmitted directly to the front of the surgeon (and perhaps simultaneously to consulting surgeons and students) instead of to an inconvenient monitor placed above the patient. Perhaps the technology could be miniaturized and put in glasses as a convenient alternative to bulky virtual reality (V.R.) goggles. Users of the Internet can already tap into video and other communications feeds from students at MIT and elsewhere who regularly walk around with digital cameras, microphones, and what one student calls "body computers" attached to them. Can devices that allow knowledge team members to see and hear everything other knowledge workers on their teams see and hear be far behind?

Telecommunication Devices

Probably the most fundamental and critical technologies supporting knowledge team work are telecommunication devices. As organizations become less hierarchical, the need for real-time communication increases. Rather than just getting instructions and advice from the boss, contemporary knowledge workers must communicate with a wide variety of teammates, many of whom are busy with their independent and sometimes geographically dispersed assignments.

Most teams still rely most heavily on the telephone. The widespread use of cellular phones without the limitations of cords have been especially helpful to people who travel extensively or who work out of their cars. AT&T salespeople, for example, often are issued cellular phones and portable computers/faxes to create virtual offices in their cars. Several people attend team meetings by calling in from the road, an innovation made possible by telephone conferencing technology, which allows multiple parties to speak on the same phone call, and speakerphones, which allow several people in one location to speak and hear on the same phone.

Teleconferences

Businesses, of course, have been using teleconference technologies for years. An easy and inexpensive way to have several people discuss the same thing at the same time, telephone conferencing has been a necessity for knowledge teams almost since its introduction. It does, of course, have its limitations, not the least of which is the lack of a picture. Unless you are really good at distinguishing voices, determining who is talking in large teleconferences can be confusing. And, of course, the lack of visual data can lead to incomplete or even inaccurate communication. Hewlett-Packard has found a creative way to deal with this dilemma.

Peter Bartlett, an HP consultant introduced in Chapter 7, notes that teams he was working with had tried videoconferencing and found that the technology was still not sufficient for effective interactive meetings. So for now, at least, much of their work is done through telephone conferencing. "We tried to adapt to the weaknesses of this meeting technology early on," he says. The biggest problem they discovered was that it was very important to see people to have effective group communication. These clues are essential to understanding if you have to repeat your message or strengthen an argument. One team he worked with created its own phone meeting language to compensate. "I found myself saying things like, 'John, I assume you are nodding now,' or asking, 'Mary are you rolling your eyes?' to make these behaviors visible on the phone."

Voice Mail

The primary challenge with this technology doesn't appear to be access. Rather, it appears that the proliferation of this and other telecommunication aids has created a glut of information that is difficult to access, recall, and use. As with E-mail, discussed in Chapter 9, the key to effective use of voice mail (VM) is use protocols agreed upon by the team members. At a minimum, it is useful for the team to answer a few questions pertaining to this technology. These questions include:

- What will we use VM for?
- What will we not use it for?
- How much detail will we leave in voice messages?
- How frequently will we agree to check VM?
- Will we need to check VM on weekends, holidays, and vacations?
- How quickly will we commit to responding to messages?
- Do we need to create a way to designate message priorities (urgent, FYI, etc.)?
- When will we transfer messages from one mail box to another?
- Is there any special protocol for transfers (can we just transfer, or do we need to leave an explanatory message)?

Making these agreements helps knowledge team members apply technologies appropriately. For example, without these agreements, some team members may check messages regularly, whereas others may do so only sporadically, making VM an inconsistent way to transmit information across the team membership.

CyberTools

In addition to the telecommunication technologies we have already mentioned, a number of other cyber tools to facilitate knowledge work are available. The ubiquitous E-mail has already been discussed.

For the purposes of this chapter, let's just say that E-mail users also benefit from answering the types of questions mentioned in the voice mail discussion. Ultimately the only protection from information inundation is through the disciplined practice of communication protocols and the implementation of more "pull" (learner driven) technologies.

Networked Software

A thorough analysis of networked software, the software products that have been created for facilitating team work, is clearly beyond the scope of this book. But these products are worth some discussion. Unlike the programs designed for solitary project work, new software that allows people to interact and create things together is being issued every day. Multiple authoring programs, for example, allow knowledge team members to work together in real time on multiple computers to write a single report. A typical format for a multiauthoring program might be a split screen, with the top half dedicated to the group report in progress and the bottom half dedicated to the portion of the report you are assigned to complete. With the stroke of a key, your section is added to the report, and you can give feedback and get feedback from others about any part of the document as it is being created.

There are also groupware programs for joint problem-solving and/or decision-making activities where, for example, knowledge workers from all over the world could troubleshoot a complicated circuit diagram at the same time or make a decision by calling for an immediate vote of all parties. Common calendaring programs and project scheduling programs allow knowledge team members to see project status or discuss calendar conflicts. These programs are growing at dog year speed. Any specific discussion of them would be doomed to immediate obsolescence. Speaking of dog years, the next cyber tool for knowledge workers, the Internet, requires some special consideration.

The Internet

We have seen more advance on the Internet in a matter of months than you would expect to see in the same number of years if it were a typical new technology. But the Internet isn't typical. Starting as a linkage of military, public, and university computer systems, it has grown to become the first true global information system. Still in relative infancy, the Internet has yet to demonstrate its full capabilities. We do know that it provides an easy way to communicate electronically with an amazing number of cyber locations. It most certainly will become a world marketplace for goods and services. But even more important for the knowledge worker is its capacity for storage and retrieval of information—it has the potential for becoming the greatest knowledge bank in the world.

Even today, helpful research can be done on the Net, but as search engines become more sophisticated, information storage protocols are better established, and more world resources are linked into the World Wide Web, the Internet could easily replace university- and government-sponsored libraries as the largest repository of information anywhere. The technical challenges associated with this endeavor are mammoth, and the social challenges are not yet completely understood. We do know that the Internet is a relatively egalitarian system. Your access doesn't depend on your company position or your relative economic status. We use the phrase "relatively egalitarian," however, because there is still a base cost for connection to the Internet. Only those with the resources to purchase the necessary equipment and learn how to connect can be admitted. However, if the glut of new entrants created by America Online's 1997 decision to go to monthly flat rates was any indicator, the demand is very heavy.

Another challenge with the Net, of course, is defining the emerging agreements on proper behavior for this medium. Discussed in more detail in Chapter 9, netiquette (the etiquette of the net) is yet another important protocol that knowledge teams must create and maintain if they are to make the most efficient, ethical, and humane use of this technology. Information and the access to it is power. And as with any source of power, whether physical, military, economic, or technological, the true test of civilized society is not what it can do but what it should do with this power.

Intranets

An intranet, an internet for a company, may be the most critical technology of all for an effective cyborganization. Many organizations are discovering great benefit to internal interconnectedness. At Silicon Graphics, in Mountain View, California, for example, employees make almost daily use of the intranet dubbed "Silicon Junction," with its company information, software helps, organization charts, and news bulletin board. The server and workstation company has 11,000 employees, almost all of whom have their own web page on the intranet. They use these web pages to publish information they control, including announcements, customer data, order information, and project updates. Executives use their pages to share business information and serve as a repository for copies of their speeches and other presentations.[7]

These systems allow companies to communicate more effectively, provide electronic forums for problem solving, integrate teams better through project planning and status bulletin boards, and automate repetitive administrative duties. Like the

Internet, intranets can create more democratic access to information. If operated under the control paradigm mentioned earlier, however, they also have the potential for reinforcing the industrial hierarchy. How can you tell? If the company intranet is set up with a password structure that allows managers access to information other than that available to other employees, it is a hierarchy-based system.

Videoconferencing

Although classifying videoconferencing as a computer tool rather than either a telecommunications tool or a separate category may seem unusual, we believe that new inexpensive high-quality cameras, coupled with the convenience that integrating conferencing with other personal computer tasks will provide, virtually assures that personal computers will be the most logical platform for this technology. But regardless of whether videophones replace videocomputers, or whether the clunky videoconference rooms in companies across the world remain the primary location for the use of this technology, videoconferencing is clearly a very promising technology for knowledge teams. Unlike voice mail or E-mail, this technology allows team members to see *and* hear others, making the communication process more effective. This is especially important for virtual knowledge teams, which can benefit from this or any other opportunity to create a more tangible sense of team identity.

Unfortunately, at this time the technology is still inadequate. The lag time between interactions can be disconcerting. Most video technology requires what seems to be an unnaturally long waiting period between the pieces of the conversation. Although in reality the waiting period is only a few seconds, it seems so different from normal conversational patterns that it can hinder the effectiveness of the communication process. This pause is especially troublesome with humor. In one recent conference, for example, we noticed an uncomfortable pause after someone told a joke. Thinking that the joke had not been understood, the team member proceeded to explain it, only to be interrupted a few seconds later by the delayed laughter.

Another problem with the videoconference—and this one may be much more difficult to solve—is the lack of an ability to do selected close-ups. Why? So that you can read the reactions of certain individuals to what is being discussed. Are they bored? Are they excited? Do they agree or disagree? Only when the technology allows us to do this will we be able to approximate the effectiveness of a face-to-face interaction. We sometimes fail to realize how important reading body language is in determining reactions. In our recent videoconferences, for example, we have been particularly interested in how much we wanted to focus on one manager's eyes or read the facial expression of one engineer in order to really understand the more subtle but powerful nuances that make up the communication process.

We believe that we are not far away from getting the technical solutions to these limitations to the current technology. But even when these issues are resolved, there will still be the same kind of protocol questions for video we have mentioned before for other technologies. For example, when is videoconferencing a viable substitution for face-to-face interaction? When is it not? What is acceptable behavior in front of a camera? When these technologies progress to the point that home offices are regularly connected to other home offices, will we push up against privacy dilemmas? Can anyone make a video connection to anyone, or does there need to be a prearranged agreement?

Technology Overdependence

We want to close this chapter with a warning. In their important book on teams and technology, Don Mankin, Susan Cohen, and Tora Bikson warn that technology alone is never the answer. Only the wise human use of technology is beneficial.[8] Technology, like any other tool, can be used in a way that either helps or hurts the team. We have observed three common problems. One is what we call a means-end inversion, like the one we introduced in an earlier chapter when we said that sometimes organizations think the team is the end instead of the means to produce the ultimate end (satisfied customers). Similarly, sometimes knowledge teams are seduced by the glamour or convenience of technology and gradually find themselves serving the technology instead of the technology serving them. A warning sign for this problem is that the systems require more time and effort than the return produced by them.

A second common problem is that teams expect more from a technology than it can reasonably deliver. In the early days of the desktop computer, for example, pundits proclaimed it to be the next big productivity-enhancing tool. What most companies actually discovered was not only that the desktops did not improve productivity, but that in some cases productivity actually dipped after PCs were introduced into the workplace. Admittedly, some of the decline was probably due to the learning curve. You can't expect any new technology to pay off until people know how to use it effectively. But at least part of the problem was caused by people being overly optimistic about what computers could do without other fundamental changes in the social system of the organization. Computers won't help get new products created more quickly, for example, if the primary time lag in the development process is a lengthy management authorization process. That is a different problem.

A third and perhaps more problematic issue is that teams can misuse technology. Stories of engineers who sit at their workstations and compose E-mail messages to their cubicle partners rather than walk ten feet and have a face-to-face discussion with them are rampant in high-technology companies. There are certain tasks that require face-to-face human-to-human contact. When teams have conflicts, hurt feelings, violated expectations, trust problems, or a whole set of additional issues, they can't be solved by technology. Imagine a family trying to settle an emotional argument by sitting down at networked computers.

The cyborganization is first and foremost an organic system. If teams aren't careful, they can destroy the human part of their organization by misusing technology. Effective knowledge teams know how to keep the appropriate balance between the cyber and the borg.

Summary

Technologies must be appropriately integrated into the organization if they are to benefit knowledge teams. Three particular problems to avoid are technology misuse, expecting more from technology than it can reasonably deliver, and serving technology instead of having technology serve the team. In this chapter we have discussed a number of technologies that are useful to knowledge teams, such as videoconferencing, intranets, the Internet, networked software, E-mail, and telecommunication technologies such as cellular phones, faxes, paging devices, teleconferencing, and voice mail.

When knowledge teams reach the right balance of human and technology, they can create an operation in which the two interface so seamlessly that it appears that they are one being. Some may build on these thoughts to accomplish the goal that has eluded the mythical creators of cyborgs from Frankenstein's monster down to the most futuristic combinations of man and machine. Perhaps some will create a cyborganization with a soul.

Notes

1. Sara Latta, "Beyond Communication: Building Collaborations," *Access*, October–December 1992; NCSA/Pubs @ncsa. uiuc.edu.
2. *Webster's II New Riverside University Dictionary* (Boston: The Riverside Publishing Co., 1984).
3. Erik Calonius, "Techno Sapiens: The Convergence of Human Beings and Technology." *Fortune*, July 8, 1996, 73.
4. Ibid., 80.
5. Ibid., 79.
6. Andrew Kupfer, "Hip, Hot, 'N Happening: *Fortune* Visits Twenty Five Very Cool Companies," *Fortune*, July 8, 1996, 92.
7. Michael C. Brandon, "From *Need* to Know to Need to *Know*," *Communication World*, October/November 1996, 18–19.
8. Don Mankin, Susan G. Cohen, and Tora K. Bikson, *Teams and Technology: Fulfilling the Promise of the New Organization* (Boston: Harvard Business School Press, 1996).

13

Trends in Knowledge Work: The Issues and Opportunities of the Future

"The traumatic transition from an industrial to a knowledge society affects everything from schools to nation states, from the production of wealth to the organizations that produce it."[1]

Walter B. Wriston, Former Chairman, Citicorp

It' 5:30 A.M. on a chilly, wet Pacific northwest morning. The year is 2020, and Rebecca Willes, a software engineer, listens sleepily as her digital personal assistant wakes her. A pleasant voice says: "After you exercise, Rebecca, remember to call Germany before it gets too late. Also your vidsatlink conference with the University is at 8:00 A.M., and then you have a meeting with the Microsoft/Intel biotech development team at the suburb pod meeting location at 11:00 A.M. You also wanted me to remind you that the Motorola proposal is due this afternoon."

Rebecca rolls over, kisses her sleeping husband on the forehead, and rubs the sleep out of her own eyes. "Becky 2," she says to the electronic helper, as she stifles a yawn, "could you set up the Germany call at 7:00 and ask Wolfgang's team if we could do it on the Internet cams this time? I have something I want to show them."

"Sure," replies the assistant. "Is that 7:00 A.M. or P.M.?"

"A.M.," answers Rebecca as she dons her slippers and robe.

After her morning run, Rebecca showers and checks to make sure that the teens are up. They both appear to be already practicing math drills on their tutor workstations, although she is pretty sure that she heard what sounded suspiciously like electronic game noises coming from their rooms just moments before she opened their doors.

The family eats breakfast together and waits for the car pool to pick the teenagers up for the multiple high school field trip to the regional learning center. Then Dave—father, husband, and consulting dentist—says good-bye and leaves for the airport. Since he has to be in Tokyo by noon, he will be taking the shuttle instead of conventional aircraft.

Rebecca goes into the computer room just as the images of Wolfgang and three other people appear on the large wall panel. "Wie geht's?," says Wolfgang, clad in some sort of fluorescent short-sleeved Hawaiian shirt. "Es geht mir gut," replies Rebecca. They continue mostly in English, although the automatic translators in both locations have been clicked on. "My goodness, Wolf," says Rebecca, "if I had known you would be wearing that shirt, I wouldn't have requested a visual." She chuckles while making the universal hand sign for a joke. Everyone laughs.

Wolfgang's team includes a technology financial analyst, a manufacturing designer, and a marketing psychiatrist. Wolf, like Rebecca, is a software engineer. They get right to the point. "Do you have the code?" Wolf asks Rebecca.

"Most of it," she says, walking over to the keyboard. "I'm encrypting and sending it now."

After he receives it, Wolfgang busily gyrates over his workstation and then leans back with a satisfied expression on his face. "This is cool," says the translator over the speaker.

"If you think that's cool, watch this," says Rebecca. She punches a few more buttons and a large hologram of an apple appears to float in the middle of her computer room. The Germans see it too.

"Ja! Ja!" says the German team simultaneously. "You debugged it. You got the hologram working!" They all laugh like happy children.

After the call, Becky 2 sets up the vidsatlink conference with the university. The university team is a virtual team of professors and researchers on contract from U.S. and Asian colleges as well as several companies. They are doing applied research in the area of a new biological software that is self-learning. The research is sponsored by Rebecca's largest employer, the Microsoft/Intel Group. Rebecca currently has three project contracts with the Group and two small contracts with other companies.

During the conference, the participants work together on a paper for submission to the Global Science Foundation. The paper describes their accomplishments to date and is an important part of their effort to transfer their learning to a broader scientific community for critique.

Two professors and Rebecca are working from their homes. The remaining team members are located at a conference center on the Regional University Campus in the Seattle/Vancouver regional city. The meeting gets off to a rocky start when Professor Ying tries to decline taking his turn as the team leader. "I just don't feel like it," he says.

"Hey, Robert," argues Rebecca, "I didn't want to be leader last week either, but we agreed in our operating guidelines that we would rotate the job so nobody gets stuck with it for too long."

"OK," concedes the professor as he picks up the laser and reviews the protocol for group writing. Once this is done, the process proceeds fairly smoothly.

All but one of the paper's sections are completed during the conference. At the end of the meeting, two team members volunteer to take the paper and polish it for the next conference. Assuming they get agreement at the next meeting, they will all sign it from their remote locations and send it off electronically to the Foundation Review Board.

Rebecca gets in her car to go to her next appointment. Her two-year contract with the Microsoft/Intel Group allows her access to the affiliation's pod offices in her suburb. She uses them about half-time, preferring the flexibility that maintaining an office at home provides.

Her salary and work hours fluctuate depending on the assignments she is working on at the time. She is currently working on three projects at M/I. On one she reports to a team leader who will determine her bonus on the basis of the sales and performance of the new software product her team is developing. Her team leader has also been very helpful in other ways. They worked on a career plan together that focused Rebecca on the types of technologies she wanted to master in order to work on the projects she was most excited about. On another M/I project she serves as the team leader and receives a monthly draw against her contracted salary. And on the third, the team leadership is rotated, with all team members splitting up whatever money is left in the pot after the project development money is spent and the venture capitalists are repaid.

When she arrives at the office, she slips her personal assistant into the security station at the front door. "Hello, Rebecca," says the speaker at the entrance. "You'll be working at station 36 in the green section. Your files are already downloaded." Becky 2 is returned to her, and the electronic locks open the front door.

As she enters, Rebecca walks past groups of meeting rooms, lounges, and recreation centers. People are clustered together in small groups throughout the building, usually in areas located near shared equipment, video rooms, or refreshment centers. Workstations take up only about 30 percent of the facility.

"Hey, Rebecca," shouts Niraj Mehta from a CWA (collaborative working area) across the open Forum space. "Where are you?"

"36 Green," replies Rebecca. Niraj is an old friend. They have been working together on selected M/I projects for nearly ten years now, even though both of them also work on projects for other companies as well. It is always nice to see some continuity in the sea of ever-changing faces.

"Great!" shouts Niraj. "I'll transfer to 35." Rebecca notices that her name, picture, and personal electronic wall hanging—a large photo of her family—are already on her cubicle wall screen. She hears the tell-tale chime of the nesting protocol in 35 and looks up in time to see Niraj's data transfer to the screen of the neighboring cubicle. The screen shows a large picture of him bungee jumping from a helicopter wearing goggles and a Santa Claus hat.

After he comes over, they prepare for and attend the meeting together. After the meeting, she works alone at her station to finish the Motorola proposal. She returns home at 5:30. It has been a long and busy day.

Future Knowledge Work

Today's knowledge workers are anxious to anticipate and prepare for the future. They have experienced so many shifts in technologies and assignments that they have come to realize— even early in their careers—that the ability to forecast and adapt to the future is a key competitive edge. A brief scan of the current business environment illustrates several current trends that are likely to affect knowledge work for some time. After all, the most probable future is an extention of the present.

Although these trends have been mentioned in the book already, we would like to further explore their implications for the future of knowledge work as a way to both summarize some of the major topics and point us forward. (See Figure 13-1.) Specifically, we will consider half a dozen trends that we believe will influence knowledge work well into the new millennium.

Figure 13-1. Future trends in knowledge work.

Six Key Work Trends for the New Millennium

1. Automation of physical work
2. Elimination of traditional jobs and work structures
3. Empowered knowledge workers
4. Knowledge work teams predominant
5. Workplace flexibility
6. More virtual knowledge teams

Automation of Physical Work

Trend number one is *automation of physical work* (see the introduction and Chapters 1, 2, and 3). One of the key trends that is likely to continue into the future is that physical work will be done by machines, not people. Say Susan Mohrman, Susan Cohen, and Allan Mohrman, "Routine work is becoming automated; increasingly, all the work that remains is knowledge work."[2] Computers and other machines are becoming inexpensive enough to replace humans in repetitive, mundane tasks.

Although the technology in many cases has been around for years, what makes this trend predictable is that cheaper technology is more likely to be widely used than expensive technology. We can now buy desktop computers for a few thousand dollars that outperform the room-size monsters of only a decade earlier that used to cost tens or even hundreds of thousands. This pattern is evident in basic robotics and similar labor-saving machines as well. These technologies, for good or evil, are automating essentially all physical work in plants, laboratories, and offices all across developed countries.

This should free us to dedicate more and more of our time and energy to the knowledge work components of our jobs—a promise anticipated decades ago, but only recently reaching fruition. The bottom line? There will be very few purely physical work jobs left in the future. We must learn how to be effective knowledge workers—that is the only work that is left to do. In a marked departure from nearly the whole of human experience to date, almost all the physical work we do will be recreational rather than vocational.

There is at least one implication of this trend that is very unsettling. If all work becomes knowledge work, the new underclass of society will probably be those who either do not have access to education or do not have access to technologies such as Internet connections. While some have considered education and technology access to be nice benefits of modern societies, future generations will likely see them as basic rights.

Elimination of Traditional Jobs and Work Structures

The second trend is *elimination of traditional jobs and work structures* (see Chapter 2, 4, 5, 6, and 10). Many traditional work structures such as jobs, hierarchies, and bureaucracies will disappear. They will be meaningless in a future where project teams form and reform around the work to be done. "Jobs will be increasingly project-based," agrees Price Waterhouse's George Bailey, the San Francisco-based national organizational-change practice leader. "You will do your job for 18 months, and then you'll move on to another one."[3]

Titles such as manager and employee will become increasingly unhelpful, as leadership will be determined more by project needs than by position. Hierarchies and bureaucracies will become obsolete as organizations cease to find them cost-effective in a world where technology enables people to perform the work without them. Confirms Jack Kahl, chairman and CEO of Manco Inc., in Westlake, Ohio, "Workers will have at their fingertips the data they need to make instant decisions without consulting three levels of management."[4] What technology enables, customers will demand, awarding their business to organizations that are fast, flexible, and responsive to their needs, rather than to the operations of the past that were especially effective at maintaining stability.

The implications of these changes are enormous. Jobs will cease to be a relevant term. People will be hired for their skills and knowledge relative to specific projects, not for job openings. Individual knowledge workers will have to take personal responsibility for skill development and learning.

As a result of this trend, many of the things we think of as being fundamental to organizations will eventually fade away. Many of the titles, policies, and even physical structures will change. Do we need large downtown banks when people cease going to them? Are real estate offices better located in cyberspace with videos of homes for sale? Aren't sales offices wherever the salespeople are when they are talking with customers? IBM and AT&T already equip salespeople technologically to have virtual offices in their cars. New headquarters offices at companies like Owens Corning, Alcoa, Sun Microsystems, and others emphasize shared space designed to allow people to collaborate instead of large personal offices. United Airlines has reservation offices in neighborhoods. IDS Financial Services in Minneapolis, now American Express Financial Corp., converted the corner executive offices in its real-estate department offices into reading rooms, moving the executives into center offices like other knowledge workers.[5] Many of the trappings of organizations, the traditional systems, and the structures are already moving toward the new millennium.

Empowered Knowledge Workers

The third trend is *empowered knowledge workers* (see Chapters 3, 5, 6, 8, and 10). This trend is related to the one we just mentioned. Knowledge workers will continue to be empowered to manage their own work. Some of this comes from organization reengineering efforts, which have swept over current organizations like tornadoes across flat lands. While many of these efforts have been positive, others have left a path of destruction as organizations have flattened and downsized—an often disturbing but now normal occurrence in the knowledge workplace.

You have only to look at the popular business journals of the last few years to recognize that the primary target of these cost-cutting measures has been middle-level management rather than the primary workforce who took the brunt of similar efforts a few years ago. This downsizing has forced empowerment in the knowledge workplace even in many places where management might have been more inclined to retain power and authority if they had been able to do it.

This doesn't mean that formal leadership will be extinct. Although the numbers of managers are already decreasing, managers will not, and in our minds *should not,* disappear from the organizations of tomorrow. Every team needs a coach. But the roles and responsibilities of managers are already becoming fundamentally different from those of the past. Managers won't authorize and direct, they will coach and inform. Their primary work will be on their own leadership and strategy teams rather than as work directors for others.

One implication of this trend is clear: Traditional management roles are changing dramatically. This has tremendous implications for careers. The typical knowledge work career of the past, which was a series of in-function promotions culminating in either a senior technical management or general management position, is increasingly unlikely for the knowledge worker. In the future a career is more likely to be a portfolio of interesting projects than a stepladder of titles.

Knowledge Work Teams Dominant

The fourth trend is that *knowledge work teams will be the predominant way to organize work* (see Chapters 3, 9, 11, and 12). Work is now too complex for the independent technical expert or manager to coordinate effectively alone. Self-directed knowledge teams are becoming the dominant organizing unit because the technical sophistication of many knowledge work projects is so great that effective technical supervision by a single individual is increasingly unlikely. Moreover, it is equally unlikely that technical experts, even those who approximate genius-level expertise, will have sufficiently diverse skills to accomplish much on their own. Many new product development teams, for example, must now include participants from multiple specialties and organizations, including representatives from customers, vendors, and technical consultants that change over time.

Illustrative of this trend is an advertisement published during the time we were writing this book. The ad, which appeared in an issue of *Business Week,* touts Compaq computers. After discussing current business complexities that require the right combination of servers, operating systems, and database applications, it mentioned several companies that have worked jointly with Compaq on the development of servers. "Well, that takes several companies," it says to introduce the idea that some situations are too complicated to be solved by a single company. Who works with Compaq? "Companies like Microsoft with whom we created the ideal platform for Windows NT and BackOffice, integrating hardware, software, and server management. Novell with whom we've created networking standards. . . . Oracle whose databases are far easier to deploy . . . thanks to our partnership. And SAP . . . who's named us Partner of the Year. You see, they may be Compaq servers. But they are Compaq-Microsoft-Oracle-SAP-Intel-Novell-SCO-Sybase-Cheyenne solutions. (We just couldn't fit all those logos on them.)"[6]

Workplace Flexibility

The fifth trend is *workplace flexibility* (see Chapters 7, 9, 11, and 12). "Companies today see that there is value and that people can be more productive when they work at home,"[7] says Steve Elston, teleworking manager as 3Com Corp. in Santa Clara, California. Technology allows work to be done from almost anywhere, and much knowledge work doesn't need to be done in the office any more. However, this is not coming to pass as rapidly as many futurists have projected. For work that requires integration with other team members (see the previous trend), complete workplace flexibility is impractical and can create some problems in the team.

Companies like Weyerhaeuser, for example, have found that in some knowledge teams, team members have become upset with other team members who aren't available for face-to-face meetings or for regular off-the-cuff communication and problem solving. "It can get to where they lose credibility as part of the team," confided one disgruntled team member. "When they aren't around to answer questions or take the flack when something doesn't go as planned, you start to feel angry that while they're at home, you have to cover for them at work." There are also people who don't want to work at home even if their work situation allows it. "I found out that I need the social contact that work provides," one knowledge worker told us. "I get stir crazy when I'm at home and don't have access to the other people I need to see in order to solve problems." One survey in 1987 showed that 56 percent of the workers surveyed would continue to go to the office every day even if they could work at home, 36 percent said they would split their time, and only 7 percent said they would work exclusively at home.[8]

The far-fetched idea that in the future no one will ever leave home is highly unlikely. A more likely scenario is that more work will be done at home or wherever else the work is, and that more teams will be composed of people from multiple work sites. The implication of this trend is that knowledge work teams will have to become more effective at finding appropriate ways to integrate into the team people who aren't collocated. Thinking of work as a place, as in "let's go to work," will be less useful than thinking of work as an activity in which people are engaged together, as in "we are working together on this project." That leads us to another related trend.

More Virtual Knowledge Teams

Trend number six is *more virtual knowledge teams* (see Chapters 7, 11, and 12). Knowledge work team composition will be increasingly unstable. Work won't be done in a single office with the same team of people any more.

Fewer and fewer knowledge workers will work for one company full-time. A lifetime career inside of one company—even in the Japanese companies where a few years ago lifetime employment was normal—will be extremely rare in the future. In 1994 contingent knowledge workers made up one-third of the American workforce, and this group is projected to be almost one-half of the workforce by the year 2000.[9] Almost 20 percent of all professionals (this includes, lawyers, doctors, and executives) now work as temps.

Although there will certainly be knowledge workers who are employed by large companies far into the foreseeable future, the trend for many knowledge workers is for something in between full-time employment and complete self-employment. As we have already mentioned, it is likely that people will be hired for projects rather than for jobs or careers. At the end of a project, companies and knowledge workers will renegotiate contracts. Many knowledge workers will formalize this process by establishing their own consulting companies or temporary agencies.

This trend has many implications that are far-reaching. For all their problems, the hierarchical and bureaucratic organizations of the past have provided stability and predictability. Paternalistic operations provided an important sense of community for people. Implied employment contracts created a powerful organizational loyalty and commitment that is now fading rapidly away.

Although this creates an exciting opportunity for many knowledge worker entrepreneurs to experience whole new levels of autonomy and even improved financial independence, it also means that the basic human needs for affiliation and community must be met elsewhere. The basic human infrastructure of society—the family—will become essential as a meaning anchor and emotional touchstone to knowledge workers of the future. We believe that relationships forged in churches and synagogues, professional associations, and communities will be necessary not only for the good of society but for the emotional and spiritual health of the individual as well.

Knowledge workers will rarely work for a single corporation; instead, they will likely work for a variety of virtual corporations that emerge and dissolve depending on the need. As knowledge workers, we will not work with the same people for extended periods of time (unlike the situation in the past, when we spent more time with a certain natural work group of employees than with our own families). Our work security will come from our ability to market and transfer our personal knowledge.

Summary

In the coming millennium, knowledge work will be the prevalent mode of work in developed societies. Virtual knowledge teams composed of people from a variety of disciplines and companies will be common. Work will be more temporary than permanent, with knowledge workers moving from project to project. There will be increasing workplace flexibility. Teams will be the dominant way to organize work. These teams are likely to be self-directed with minimum supervision. Many of the fundamental structures of the workplace will change as things like jobs, traditional careers, hierarchies, and bureaucracies become obsolete. Human physical work will essentially disappear.

These trends have frightening and exciting implications for our work and for our societies. Like every generation of the past, we too will come to realize that ultimately our technologies cannot save us. Our future will be ensured only through the proper and effective use—the collective use—of our minds. That is the essence of the challenge for knowledge work and knowledge work teams: creating a distributed mind.

Notes

1. Walter Wriston, as quoted on the back cover of Peter Drucker, *Post-Capitalist Society* (New York: HarperBusiness, 1993).
2. Susan Albers Mohrman, Susan C. Cohen, and Allan M. Mohrman, Jr., *Designing Team-Based Organizations: New Forms for Knowledge Work* (San Francisco: Jossey-Bass, 1995), xvi.
3. Michael A. Verespej, "A Workforce Revolution?" *Industry Week*, August 21, 1996, 23–24.
4. Ibid., 24.
5. Michael A. Verespej, "Welcome to the New Workspace," *Industry Week*, April 15, 1996, 28.
6. *Business Week*, March 4, 1996, 1.
7. Verespej, "Welcome to the New Workspace," 24.
8. William E. Halal, "The Rise of the Knowledge Entrepreneur," *The Futurist*, November–December 1996, 14–15.
9. Ibid., 15.

Index